# WALKING THE BACK ROADS

## A JOURNEY FROM DONEGAL TO CLONMACNOISE

First published in 2008 by
Appletree Press Ltd
The Old Potato Station
14 Howard Street South
Belfast BT7 1AP

Tel: +44 (028) 90 24 30 74
Fax: +44 (028) 90 24 67 56
Email: reception@appletree.ie
Web: www.appletree.ie

Copyright © Appletree Press, 2008
Text copyright © Michael McMonagle, 2008

All rights reserved. Printed in India. No part of this publication may be reproduced or transmitted, in any form or by any means, electronic or mechanical, photocopying, recording, or in any information and retrieval system, without permission in writing from the publisher.

**Walking the Back Roads – A Journey from Donegal to Clonmacnoise**

A catalogue record for this book is available from the British Library.

ISBN-13: 978 1 84758 083 2

Desk & Marketing Editor: Jean Brown
Copy-editing: Jim Black
Designer: Stuart Wilkinson
Production Manager: Paul McAvoy

9 8 7 6 5 4 3 2 1

AP3532

# Walking the Back Roads

## A Journey from Donegal to Clonmacnoise

Michael McMonagle

Appletree Press

*To Terry, Eoghan, Aoife and Crona*

### Acknowledgements

Thanks to the many people who took the time to stop and talk with me along the way. This book could not have been written without them.

Thanks also to my family; my wife Terry, son Eoghan and daughters Aoife and Crona for their encouragement, inspiration and support; to Winnifred Mc Nulty who wholeheartedly undertook to make observations on the manuscript; to my friends Martin Gillen, Kevin Montgomery and Siobhan Montgomery who walked part of the way with me. Their companionship enlivened the journey.

Finally, thanks to Appletree Press for publishing a first-time writer.

# Contents

Introduction     8

Chapter 1    Gartan to Letterkenny     14
Gartan the place – hope, anxiety and first steps – friendship, holy wells and the environment – cat cults – fishing, rally cars and miracles – fostering, then and now – Kilmacrennan Abbey and horses – bad-tempered fishermen – the mountains and legends of north west Donegal – encounters with traveller children – encounter with a guru in psychiatric hospital

Chapter 2    Letterkenny to Ballybofey     29
Memories and gravity – the death of my father and Killydonnell friary – lift with a mad driver – festival in Letterkenny – feelings of transience – old house in a forest – uniformity in Nature – male cuckoos on the hilltops – a dump and our waste – monuments to history – hard man from Mayo

Chapter 3    Ballybofey to Glenties     44
The mystery of signposts – frogs, crows and rams – "Go by the Croaghs!" – borders – sorting out the route in a small shop – mink and old vans – two bachelors on the road – the road where trees grow out of rocks – the Croaghs and the pied piper – the glen of Glenties

Chapter 4    Inver to Killybegs     60
A small fishing village and its relationship with the sea and weather – cycling as a means of transport – dogs in all their shapes and forms – thatched houses and visitors from America – the Riviera in the middle of a bog – definitions of madness and sanity – humming, the fairies and sand dunes – fishing port of Killybegs – changing times – encounter with a Red Setter

Chapter 5    Killybegs to Glencolmcille     75
A beautiful coastal road – a man looking for poitín – vulnerability in a miniature world – dispute over fishing rights – "why has that man got long hair?" – Sliabh League, a sick friend and the millennium – the ripples of time – the mystery of mirrors – rebellious boy and curious gardener – males communicating – the rock – demons in Glencolmcille

Chapter 6    Glencolmcille to Ardara                                      90
Donegal buses and a harrowed face – a friendly village and sustainable tourism?
– old pine forests – a contented man on top of a hill – house in the middle of a
quarry – the Gaeltacht – break time in a small school – fertiliser versus manure? –
the seeds of knowledge – Glengesh or the Granny Glen – shipwrecks, massacres
and disasters, the wrinkled waterfall and the lady of the forest – pride

Chapter 7    Mountcharles to Rossnowlagh                              102
My home place – farming, drama and nursing – the seashore – an old woman
in the village – stone quarries and Buckingham Palace – shepherd on the hill
– emigration, asylum seekers and rural life – the windmills of Diseart – power
walking – going to a Reiki master – memories – swans, movement and magic –
Rossnowlagh, the Franciscans and the Four Masters – healing – an asylum seeker
on the run

Chapter 8    Rossnowlagh to Bundoran                                  124
Starlings, hares and tractors – melancholia and the universe – pushing against the
tide – meeting with a shrew – Ballyshannon and the legacy of Colmcille – The
poor house where I was raised – the influence of teddy bears – taking a break in
Bundoran – the now moment

Chapter 9    Inishmór – The Island                                    135
The significance of islands – Colmcille on Inishmór and Tory – crossing to Inishmór
in a storm – the wedding in a church with no roof – alone in a bus with twenty
women – rain – cyclists who did not know they had a puncture! – the guardian of
Dun Aenghus – big fishing versus small fishing – the role of the Church in the
future – the black fort and the power of the sea – an argument – a race

Chapter 10    Out of Donegal: Bundoran to Sligo                       154
A little wren and a wooden donkey – postman – children at play – Mullaghmore
and the nature of violence – butterflies: their story – two men at a crossroads
lamenting the dear departed? – Ben Bulben – living and dying – Lissadell and
Constance Markievicz – a meeting with John Cleese? – evicted from Lissadell
house – networks in operation – O'Higgins and Chile – an activist on a bridge
and a drinker in the pub

Chapter 11    Sligo to Manorhamilton                                170
Yeats, Colmcille and an artist at Drumcliffe – plagiarism and a battle – wild flowers – enthusiasm about a football match – genetics and sore feet – mist and travellers beside a lake – an empty world and a languid day – a catastrophe – the silence of Nature – an escape – nowhere to stay and helpful advice in a pub!


Chapter 12    Manorhamilton to Drumshanbo                          183
Cutting the atmosphere with a knife – immigrants, past and present – the miners' walking route – shades of grey – the selfish gene – a tranquil moment – coal and collieries – casualties of hope – a unique bed and breakfast – fishermen from Yorkshire – two comrades at the bar


Chapter 13    Drumshanbo to Strokestown                            196
A queue for Nessa's breakfast – the sweet smell of success – "I knew there was something about you" – fairy hill, a guest house and a nursing home – water and cruisers – how to adopt a calf – attacked by a bullock – who the heck was Jimmy Gralton? – shadows and ghosts on the road – the town that did not exist – debate in a pub and a raft race – bees and explorers – stories from Strokestown House – the imprint of the Famine


Chapter 14    Strokestown to Kiltoom                               222
Raindrops – Percy French and 'there is an ould cow on the line' – cattle, catapults and a black hen – Seamus, Johnny Depp and politics – what is wetter than wet? – embarrassment at the high jump – generosity from grandparents and grandchildren – a room for two – a pint of Guinness from Pat Porter – a salesman, a Mercedes and anti-fatigue mats


Chapter 15    The Last Day: Kiltoom to Clonmacnoise                238
The saga of the bed and breakfast sign – a funeral and a baby – the stronghold of Athlone – developing immunity in a café – putting my foot in it with a woman from the Philippines – smiling and mental health – oaks and Colmcille – the resilience of grass – Clonmacnoise, Ciarán and warrior monks – French races – a sermon – the Shannon by moonlight – shapes in the shadows of the night – a flickering flame

# INTRODUCTION

*After a short while spent loitering at the crossroads, I spotted a man with a rolling gait, walking towards me on the road.*

*"One hundred Euro will buy you nothing these days," he vehemently exclaimed, "and a pint costs €3 10c…you can't live on the dole at those prices. One night about twenty-five years ago," he said, hitching up his trousers, "a friend of mine and I drank three bottles of poitín and a bottle of vodka."*

*He let that sink in for a moment before continuing.*

*"After that, at about three in the morning we went to a wake house to get more drink, and we stayed there until the man was taken for burial – two days later!" He laughed out loud with the memory. "Those days are gone now," he said rather mournfully.*

*It was his belief that wakes now seem to be but pale imitations of the wakes long ago. To cheer him up, I recollected the times that my wife used to get bottles of poitín, which we drank together at parties with some of our friends. A comradely look emerged into his eyes and he immediately quizzed me about where she had got the poitín and how much it cost.*

*"Nobody makes poitín around here any more," he said, rather forlornly.*

*I told him that my wife was from Tipperary and that she got the poitín from a neighbour for nothing. I really had grabbed his interest now.*

*"Is your wife still around?" he asked.*

It had been on my mind for a number of years to go on a journey along the back roads of Ireland. Even as a young child I had an obsession about where they might lead. At that time my godmother used to take me for a drive in her Volkswagen Beetle every Sunday afternoon – this was a real treat as she had one of the few cars in the locality at the time. I really looked forward to these drives and I took the opportunity to plague her with questions. It was just as well that she was a teacher, for even though others considered her to be formidable and stern, she gave me her undivided attention. My particular fascination was with all the little roads that we passed. I wanted to know where each of them led to and whether it was a big place or a small place. When she had explained everything to my satisfaction I would sometimes make a tentative suggestion.

"Could we go down that wee road, Mrs McGroarty?"

"Some time we will," was always the answer.

I now realise that the reason she always drove at 25 mph was that it took all of her energy to keep that wayward 'monster' of a car between the ditches, and really there was never a hope in hell that she would willingly drive on a small back road. I, though, would have liked to travel on all of these roads – and I built fantastic pictures in my mind of what might be at the end of them. It took many years to translate this early fascination into a decision to explore some of these back roads and to follow my curiosity.

The back road all these years later still holds the same interest for me. The scale of the back road is the human scale; it is based on tracks that people and animals walked for generations, which later developed into routes for the horse and cart. The back road follows the contour of the land, and like a river, it strives to find the easiest way to wriggle through the landscape. Its origins are based upon the shuffle of feet, the sweat of human labour, the sound of pick and shovel. In the full flush of spring or summer you can stretch out both arms and touch the vegetation on each side of the road. A person is significant in such a place and the decorum is that you should at a minimum always pass the time of day with people you meet there.

On the back road the vegetation suffuses the senses, be it grasses and briars or flowers and woodbine. You are in intimate contact with Nature. It surrounds you, it percolates into your inner being and connects you to its life force. The fragrance of whins and meadowsweet soothe and stimulate the senses, the vibrant colours of fuchsia and old abandoned roses illuminate the way. The sounds of sheep bleating, birds singing and tractors revving drift through the air and the raucous call of a rook or a magpie alerts the mind. You come upon little streams, rivers, broken bridges, crumbling parapets, croaking frogs and annoying insects. You are given shelter from the rain and the wind and a chance to pee unobserved. You can be still and take in the sounds, sights and smell of Nature far from the continuous, mechanical buzz of machines. The ruins of old houses, byres, barns and mills speak to you of the past, of people long gone from here, scattered like sycamore seeds across the globe. Stone walls and fallow potato ridges tell of the efforts to eke a living from marginal, unyielding land over generations.

The back road however, is also a place of mystery. When I see back roads I still ask myself 'Where would that road bring me?' or 'What story does it tell?' In a sense there are two ways of looking at them: they can be seen as an entry on to the main road and to the bustle of everyday life, or on the contrary they can be seen as an escape from that same bustle, providing a connection to something real and genuine that is not artificial.

If you are going on a journey one of the first things to be decided is the mode of transport. I love to cycle, and it had obvious advantages of speed and an opportunity of covering greater distances. Alternatively if I obtained an old Volkswagen Beetle to travel in, it would resonate with the past and form a connection to my godmother. However after some contemplation I decided that I should walk, as it gives time for thinking and brings you into intimate contact with the countryside. There is a great pleasure to be had from walking – you cannot walk for long and be unaware of increased sensation, not only physically but psychologically. Walking, after all, was the evolutionary step that led to the birth of human civilisation. When we stood erect and walked on two feet, our world was transformed and a whole new range of experience unfolded. Walking preceded speech and made the connection between Nature and civilisation. What better way to develop some perspective on our lives and our world than to walk and let reflections emerge from the experience?

Another component of a journey is a reason behind it. Steinbeck commented in *Travels with Charley in Search of America* that it is the 'victim' in us which seeks to justify our restlessness, with a reason for going on a journey. I had to have a reason to justify my madness to family and friends – preferably a number of them! A collection of 'reasons' crossed my mind. Should I walk the whole length of the country from Malin Head to Mizen Head or indeed walk around the coastline? Should I just walk around my own county, which has such a huge number of back roads? None of these reasons satisfied the 'victim' in me but finally the inspiration for the walk came from books I was reading, about another Donegal man who lived nearly 1,500 years ago. The fact that an aunt of mine, also a teacher, claimed that our family was from the same lineage added to the allure.

Let me introduce you to Colmcille: along with Patrick and Brigid, he is one of the patron saints of Ireland. He was born in Gartan in North

Donegal in 521 and died on the island of Iona of the coast of Scotland in 597. It could be said that he led an eventful life. He was of noble birth from the line of Cineal Conaill, one of the most powerful clans in Ireland at that time. If his life had taken a different direction he could have been High King of Ireland. He was a warrior possessed of a fiery temper in his youth and woe, betided any human or demon that stood in his path. He was the world's first convicted plagiarist and was not above cheating to get his way. He was an entrepreneur who established a network of monasteries all around the country. He was a penitent who for his sins exiled himself from the country that he loved. This led him to establishing the famous monastic settlement on Iona, from which he converted much of Scotland and Northern England to Christianity. Iona became the favoured resting-place for many Scottish kings and noblemen including Macbeth and Macduff.

Colmcille was a miracle worker and healer – he is reputed to have performed all the miracles that Christ did and a few more thrown in besides for good measure. He was also known for his prophecies and his transcriptions. More than anything else he was a leader of people who established a monastic dynasty throughout Ireland before becoming the first of the many 'holy men' who left the country to bring learning and Christianity back to Europe. This was a Europe that had been devastated during the 'Dark Ages' by wars, plague and the destruction of centres of learning. Colmcille thus set a trend, which was followed by a long line of monks such as Brendan the Navigator, Columbanus, Gall, Cathal and Fursa, all of whom headed off across the continent to spread their faith and a love of learning and books. They founded monasteries in many places such as Bobbio, Auxerre, Lyon, Würzburg, Regensburg, Salzburg and Vienna.

The Christianity that Colmcille brought with him was not the orthodoxy preached by Rome, but a religion which encompassed many features of the pagan past. This became a matter of contention in Christianity over the next hundred years or so, until as usual and regrettably orthodoxy won out. Unlike the other two patron saints Patrick and Brigid he was a definite historical figure, though some of the stories about him are undoubtedly more than far fetched. This however only adds to his mystique and stature. Adamnan a successor on Iona, wrote a book about his life, the miracles he performed and his prophecies. This was written less than seventy years after his death in the seventh century so the source is near contemporary and authentic. In the sixteenth century a Donegal chieftain called Manus O'Donnell collected all the information he could about Colmcille and published a book called *Betha Colaim Chille* – The life of Colmcille.

The idea for the walk came from a prophecy of his birth related in one of these books. In common with all other great saints there were many prophecies of his birth as this was one of the symbols of greatness. Some of these, it is certain, were written after the death of Colmcille (as all good prophecies should be). It was useful propaganda in the search for religious dominance by his followers over other Christian sects. They have to be seen as the 'spin' of those particular times and like all spin it had a political purpose. In particular his Columban dynasty was in direct competition with the 'Roman' tradition of Patrick, which was based in Armagh.

In the books whole chapters are given over to all of the prophecies, visions and portents of his birth. Fionn McCool, Ireland's most famous 'pagan' predicted his birth. Patrick and Brigid made predictions about his coming. His mother Ethne saw a cloak of wondrous colours leave her hands and spread out over all the country and the Western Isles. The vision or dream, however which became the basis for my walk came to Finnen, a holy man. Finnen said that he saw two moons arise into the sky.

*'A moon of gold and a moon of silver. And the golden moon rose up in the north of Erin; and Erin and Alba and the Western World were ablaze with its brightness and light. The silver moon rose over Clonmacnoise; and the mid parts of Erin were ablaze with its brightness and light.'*

Finnen interpreted the dream to mean that a child (Colmcille) would be born to Fedlimid (the father of Colmcille) and Ethne at Gartan in Co. Donegal, and his brightness would be like that of a golden moon that would fill the entire Western world. St Ciarán, the founder the famous monastery of Clonmacnoise, was the silver moon by virtue of his good deeds.

This dream became the inspiration for the walk. I thought that I would link the two moons together by walking along the back roads from Gartan to Clonmacnoise in order to present a snapshot of present-day Ireland, and to see for myself the sort of light that now illuminates the way.

I organised the walk into three distinct stages. The first stage was completed in March/April 2002 and this took me through Co. Donegal. The second part of the walk was a weekend visit in May to Inishmór Island in Galway Bay the largest of the Aran Islands. The final part brought me from Donegal to Clonmacnoise, which was completed in August of the same year.

# Gartan to Letterkenny

Gartan is a beautiful and remote area of mountain, trees, bog and lake situated in the midst of the countryside in north Co. Donegal. My wife Terry had dropped me off at St Colmcille's Abbey and well, the source of Finnen's dream, the place where the golden moon shone when Colmcille was born. Arriving there competing feelings were drifting around in my body.

Hope and anxiety are two feelings that entwine and weave together throughout life especially at the beginning of something new. How each of us creates our own relationship with these two demons determines to a large extent the course and direction of our lives. Hope is an expression of our potential striving to burst forth into the world and exists as a utopia in the mind; it is anxiety that makes it real in the world and lets it flow through our existence. At times one predominates over the other and it is this movement which creates the richness of human experience. It is when we get stuck in one of these feeling exclusively that we get into trouble.

The birth of Colmcille was an expression of this hope in Nature, and his birth cry was an expression of anxiety coming into an uncertain world. Colmcille was born on 7th December 521AD and his birth was heralded by many wonderful and mysterious events. One of these events was the dream of Finnen – but this was only one of many such prophecies. It is stated that St Patrick, St Brigid and Conall Gulban, as well as many other abbots and holy men, foretold his birth. Some of these had been hundreds of years before his actual birth. The portents about something wonderful about to happen increased in scale the closer to the birth one came. An example of this was when his mother received a visit from a holy man called Fergna who had been told by an angel of the imminent birth of a holy child. When Fergna blessed Colmcille in the womb, the baby put his thumb through the belly of his mother's womb in a sign of welcome.

On the night before he was born, an angel (a fair youth) came in a vision to his mother Ethne. He told her that the baby would be born the next day and that a special flagstone which would be found floating on the surface of Lough Akibbon should be moved to Rath Cno in Gartan for the birth. The next day after finding the flagstone as promised floating on the lake, Ethne organised that it should be moved to the appointed spot. On the journey Ethne rested for a little while beside a stream, and then some blood seeped from her into the soil. The clay in that spot has ever since had healing and protective properties. It protects against the perils of fire, drowning and sudden death. It also helps any woman who is in the pangs of childbirth, as well as curing a range of ailments and afflictions such as distemper. Ludar Friel, a cousin of Colmcille endeavoured to cover the spot with bracken but Ethne told him not to bother, as only he and his descendants would know where this spot was. Until this day the clay is only collected and distributed by the descendants of Ludar Friel.

Colmcille was born shortly afterwards and laid upon the flagstone assuming the shape of a cross, upon which the 'flagstone opened for him in such wise that it left a place for him therein'. The shape of the cross has remained in the stone from that day to this and had been used for cures down the generations. Ethne also brought forth a round stone of the colour of blood at the birth. This red stone had great powers of healing – it was used extensively until it disappeared in the middle of the seventeenth century. The birth of this child into the world was certainly accompanied by a lot of hope and expectation.

Standing beside me in the gentle breeze were Kevin and his wife Siobhan who had decided to accompany me until lunchtime on the first day of the journey. Kevin and I have been friends for more than twenty years. He is a big, broad shouldered Yank from Maryland who is built solid like a rock, a person who other people instinctively trust. He came to Ireland as a fresh-faced young graduate to work with young people in a peace and reconciliation hostel in Glencree, Co. Wicklow during the height of the Troubles in Northern Ireland. On finishing his volunteering assignment there he came to Donegal to work, with the intention of saving some money before continuing his round-the-world odyssey. However the best-laid plans of mice and men are often waylaid, as he is still here all these years later. The cause of this interrupted travel is of course Siobhan, a talented artist from Dublin who convinced him to tarry a while. Gartan became their home, so much so that three children decided to come along as well. Kevin's accent is now part-Donegal and part-Maryland drawl.

The three of us stood and looked out over Lough Gartan, nestling beneath us in the valley. Everything was still and quiet except for the wispy white clouds that chased each other across the blue sky, fashioning a display below, where shadows and light danced together on the lake and the rolling hillsides. Birdsong floated in the air and the sweet smell of whins wafted by on the gentle breeze. I could appreciate why Colmcille founded an Abbey here in the sixth century; it is one of those special spots which uplifts the soul.

Beginnings are always difficult, principally because you are leaving something behind. In all walks of life the first steps are always the hardest because they herald a new pattern of living. My thoughts just then went back to my children, Eoghan, Aoife and Cróna, and their first steps. This seemed particularly apt when heading off on a long walk. I was exceedingly fortunate in being present to see the first steps of all my children (unless they had been practising in secret, which is entirely possible). The look of joy and accomplishment on their faces when they managed those steps is etched in my memory. In each case a new regime was born, and glorious pandemonium was about to begin.

"Well buck, are you ready for the off?" asked Kevin grinning, and rubbing his hands as he headed off with a brisk stride down the path.

Twenty metres later we took our first rest, when we encountered St Colmcille's well. This well was blessed by Colmcille and ever since people have been coming here to pray and ask for the saint's intercession with the powers-that-be. The usual practice is to leave a symbolic offering beside the well. Siobhan pointed to the rim of the well.

"Why are those biros there?" she wondered.

No sooner was the question out than we all realised the answer. It was exam time and people were seeking the intercession of Colmcille on their behalf. As we both had children preparing for exams, we wondered whether we should leave a biro there as well. Kevin had a different entrepreneurial perspective on this.

"Should we leave a biro or take some with us?" he jokingly commented.

The upshot of this debate was that we did not leave a biro there (and we did not take any with us either!) It seems we just did not believe enough in the power of the well. This surely is one of the afflictions of our time;

unless something is rational it is not considered to be real. As a nation we have always sought divine intervention when confronted with adversity. It always seemed that there was a power greater than us out there, and that this power could be influenced to our advantage if we knew the right things to do. How long will this belief system continue into the future though is the question? Will there be a new synthesis in the future that combines rationality and faith, or will faith always continue to be beyond the realm of reason?

Along with the biros there were coins and holy medals scattered around the rim of the well. The tradition of leaving metal beside a well goes back in history to the time when metals came into use in Irish civilisation. For the early 'pagan' inhabitants of this country veneration of wells was a common practice, for there is nothing more sacred than a useful source of good drinking water which is sustainable into the future. The belief grew that these wells had a resident Spirit who had powers to heal and to sustain life. Metals transformed early civilisations and were regarded as valuable and powerful. What better offering could one make to the Spirits of the well if one wanted to obtain some favour? The early Christian saints and clergy were no fools, as they co-opted these wells by blessing them and putting crosses beside them. Colmcille during his life made a particular point of this – there are holy wells associated with his name all around the country. The public still kept on coming as before to the wells, still leaving their metal in return for cures and favours that they sought. The only thing that changed was the name of the Spirit that worked through the well. The tradition is still strong, and continues with the offerings of metal and more recently pens to the Spirits. The pen is now seen to be at least as significant as metal in accessing the magic within the water. This too is probably apt.

With my two friends we turn down a narrow road overlooking the lough. On our left there was a wooded area, comprising of hardwood trees such as ash, oak, holly, birch, and mountain ash. Along this natural habitat there were rows of notices seeking planning permission for houses. This environment of farmhouse, lake and wood which blends so well together is going to change: houses with manicured lawns will stand where the woods once grew. Of course there will be a few ornamental trees and shrubs planted in the gardens as people seek to recreate a natural environment. Continuing the environmental theme, Kevin told me that he was planning to build a new septic tank, as the one he had was not adequate. One of the builders whom he approached to do the job gave out vehemently about the standard of most septic tanks locally. He likened them to sieves through which sour milk is poured: it still tastes and smells like sour milk on the far side. Of course if you allowed him to install a septic tank for you, the emerging water would be transformed into a pure, odour free liquid!

"You are not looking for a stray cat, are you?" Siobhan asked me with a half-hopeful look in her eye.

"I have enough bother!" I ungraciously and rather quickly answered.

Siobhan is one of these people with a soft heart and a generous nature, so it seems that she had decided to feed a stray cat, and surprise surprise, it elected to stay. I thought to myself, this cat has his head screwed on in the right way, as Siobhan is one of those great cooks that one loves to visit. Seemingly this cat had not only moved into the house and was enjoying its food but, according to Siobhan, had taken on the mantle of top cat as well, driving the two resident cats into the background. That's the way to do it, not only find a new home but become boss in it as well! Unless those two cats come up quickly with an effective alliance their life will not be pleasant.

We came to a country pub at a crossroads, which had a few people sitting outside, some drinking and some treating themselves to a cooked breakfast. A couple having breakfast hailed Kevin and Siobhan.

"Are you interested in a stray cat?" was their first question to Siobhan.

'What's going on here?' I thought to myself. 'Have I landed in the middle of a cat cult?'

Seemingly this couple already had five cats and another cat had invited himself to stay. There must a good cook in that house as well, I thought. Perhaps it might be worthwhile to get to know them?" Can't people realise when they are being used? Cats, I believe are the greatest manipulators of all on God's earth. As you may realise I do not have a great affinity with cats, and I certainly cannot understand why anybody would want five or six of them.

However I am not totally immune to their charms. This is chiefly due to 'Three Legs' who was a kitten kindly donated to our house by someone who preferred to remain anonymous. 'Three Legs' got her name because a sheep stood on one of her paws and afterwards she was hobbling around on three legs for a while. (It's great to be imaginative when choosing names!) So don't get me wrong – I fully understand the wiles and charms of cats; when despite yourself you are drawn to their scheming, purring overtures, or to their fierce independence of spirit which leads them to going away for days or even weeks on end. Just when you have got over their departure they arrive back again. They even at times show a communitarian spirit, when they drag a dead rat into the house to share with you for breakfast or kill that noisy thrush which had been keeping you awake all morning. Cats get into the most unexpected places. One time I drove to a neighbour's house. When I stopped, I was perplexed on hearing meowing sounds coming from what seemed the inside of my car. I investigated everywhere and finally on opening the car bonnet I found 'Three Legs', sitting on top of the engine a bit puzzled at the turn of events.

Further on and we were in typical Donegal countryside of bog, heather, sally bushes and sheep. Two stonechats perched on top of adjacent bushes, each one seemingly trying to out chirrup the other in earnest and committed communication. We laughed as we listened to them. We could not understand the meaning of their communication but that did not stop us enjoying it. There were other worlds of meaning in that spot we could not understand, featuring the subtleties of communication between plants, worms, bacteria, animals birds etc.

We are generally totally unaware of just how much we are connected to and dependent upon these worlds, living our lives as if we are totally separate from them. These two stonechats were living out their destiny propelled by the life force that was uniquely theirs, but yet there was a connection between them and us. Only we were not just exactly sure of what it was.

Walking along a bridle way, we came to a bridge over a river. Looking over the parapet we spotted small fish in the river below. Kevin demonstrated an awareness of his relationship to all things, and a growing sense of hunger.

"We'll not starve anyway."

This seemed to strike a chord with us all, for we sat down on the bridge and brought out, not a fishing rod, but a bunch of ripe bananas.

"We should be living off the land and rivers," I said to Kevin.

However the fish were hardly quaking in fear at this statement, for even if I had a fishing rod I would be very unlikely to catch anything. In my years on this earth I have caught the grand total of one fish, which had to be returned to the lake from whence it came, as it was so small. Kevin I am sure had much more success in the fishing stakes and he is a great vegetable gardener to boot. Even when we shared a house when we were single, Kevin always took a deep pleasure in growing vegetables. Vegetables for me at that time were something that I did not have a personal relationship with! Kevin laughed knowingly when I made that suggestion; he knew my real interest in living from Nature, nice in theory but a bit too much bother in reality.

Coming across a burned out car lying in a ditch Siobhan told me that a lot of young people in the locality now buy old cars very cheaply. They then joy ride these bangers around the back roads for the thrill of it. The young people when they are finished with these cars or more likely when they crash remove all identification from the cars and burn them out. Siobhan is lucky to be alive because a few weeks earlier she had been involved in a crash with a teenager in such a car. It seems he was only after buying it and he was taking his first run in it when he lost control and crashed into Siobhan's car on the brow of a hill. They were both lucky to come out relatively unscathed. A few weeks after that another young man from the same area killed himself in his first run in one of these 'new, old cars'. Road accidents closely followed by suicide are the greatest killers of young men in Ireland. These are issues we need to address as a society.

"There's the Abbey," said Kevin pointing.

In the distance I could see an ivy-covered wall jutting into the air. The tendrils of Nature were slowly and inexorably reclaiming this spot; the building was subsiding back into Nature. The grand monuments of men are but a transient testimony to their vanity. This is the place where Colmcille grew up with his foster father Cruithnechan, which was the custom of the time for children of the nobility.

One of the first pieces of propaganda about the powers of Colmcille was contained in the following story. It was on this very walk between Gartan and Kilmacrennan that Colmcille at a very young age performed one of his first miracles. One night as his foster father and himself were returning from a wake, his foster father Cruithnechan dropped dead. Initially Colmcille did not know that Cruithnechan was dead and he started to recite the psalms to see if it would do any good. These were heard a mile away by the daughters of Cruithnechan who came to see what was happening. They knew immediately that their father was dead. In panic and knowing the special powers of Colmcille they asked him to try and awaken Cruithnechan. He approached the body and taking the hand of Cruithnechan he raised him from the dead.

In a way there is symmetry between the walk, Kevin and this place. It was here that Colmcille grew up with his foster family. Only the children of the rich and powerful were fostered. To have your child fostered was a sign of high status in society whereas children from poorer circumstances had to do mundane things like working and fighting in order to preserve the status quo of the time.

Kevin is the social worker who is now in charge of arranging foster care in Co. Donegal. In the county at the moment there are 100 children living in foster homes. However in a reversal of social circumstance it is now nearly always the poor who have their children in foster care. A child in foster care is now a public sign of failure as a parent and is associated with low status in society.

A social worker friend once told me a story of a young girl she was bringing into foster care. It was nighttime and she was driving through Barnesmore Gap, taking the child to her new foster parents. The road through Barnesmore Gap follows a narrow river valley through the Blue Stack Mountains in south Donegal. The mountains rise steeply from the road on either side. There was a full moon in a clear sky. During the journey the little girl spent time looking at the moon whenever she could through the windows of the car as it made its journey. She seemingly was fascinated by the fact that the moon seemed to be following them. She turned to Terry eventually.

"Is the moon crying too?" she asked.

I am sure that little girl – now probably a grown woman – has a connection to the moon ever since. How can a little girl make sense of a situation like this, leaving all she knows and heading into the unknown? Departures are difficult for all of us even if we really want them.

We came to the ruined Abbey. Outside of it three men were leaning on a wall looking at a horse for some reason or other. I suppose there was nothing better to look at! The fact that they hardly noticed us when we came along didn't say much for us though. They were totally absorbed in their observations. People have to get their priorities right after all! They say that each one of us should retain the ability to become totally absorbed in something, for there is nothing more relaxing and soothing.

We went into the ruins of the Abbey and there in the peace of the interior we had our lunch. I sat on the edge of a flat gravestone with indecipherable writing. I always have an urge when I see gravestones like this to read the names and dates, as if to confirm that I am still here but at the same time not totally removed from the mystery of the dust from which we spring and return to. Within these crumpled Abbey walls the echoes of people long gone still resonate. One gets the feeling that it is nearly possible to unwrap the veils of time and look again at the people who once trod here, with all the pleasures and pains of existence. What was daily life like? What did people do? What did they think about? In a place like this one can nearly grasp that reality but it remains elusive, tantalising and just out of touch. One is left with the curiosity and the questions. There was a lark singing high up in the sky. Looking up, hoping to get a glimpse, he too remained elusive. One is left with the melody and the feel of ancient footsteps.

As we left the old Abbey and head up the road to Kilmacrennan we come across more men sitting on a ditch, talking and looking at horses. What is it about men and horses in this part of the world? Is there some sort of secret communion going on? In Gartan the theme seemed to be cats – in Kilmacrennan it was definitely horses. This led Kevin and I to reminisce about a time when we rented a house together with a tall skinny redhead called Sean (a friend of ours). The house was situated in the midst of hill farms and enjoyed a lovely view over a valley. Of the three of us Sean was the tidiest. This meant that he took a notion to wash the dishes about once a week. We would sit back and listen to him sing as he worked!

One morning the last person to leave the house was in such a rush to work that he left the door open behind him, (it's great to be so enthusiastic about work). Shortly afterwards a horse that just happened to be passing thought that it looked like a friendly place to visit. When we came back from work (late at night of course!) we were astounded to find muddy hoof marks throughout the house – it was also a policy of ours never to close doors inside the house! Being quite a considerate horse he decided to leave a calling card with his personal signature attached in case we missed the fact that he had called to see us. He thoughtfully and appropriately deposited this on top of the mail in the hallway. Coincidentally most of the letters were to Sean and included a cheque from work. His efforts of salvaging the cheque afterwards gave a totally new meaning to the term 'laundering money'. Kevin and I reckoned it must have been Sean who had left the door open.

I said goodbye to Kevin and Siobhan in Kilmacrennan and I followed the Lennon River out of the town. After a while I sat down on a footbridge, which spans the river. I watched three fishermen sitting quietly on the riverbank as if in a mesmerised trance. I too stared at the river as it drifted lazily and noiselessly by. I joined with the fishermen in allowing this combination of quietness and gentle motion to percolate into my being. The tyranny of time retreated into the present moment.

Suddenly there was a bit of action. One of the fishermen started tugging at his line. 'He has caught a fish,' I thought. But no, his line had just got snagged in weeds. After some bad humoured tugging he finally cut his line and started all over again. It seemed that there was a fast flowing current in his head despite the peaceful scene. Tranquillity descended on the river again.

After the Lennon valley, the landscape became quite hilly. Views emerged of the dominant mountains in northwest Donegal – Errigal, Muckish and Sliabh Sneacht. In through these mountains, there are some of the best hiking routes in Ireland. If you stand on the top of Errigal Mountain, you can see to Scotland on a good day, and all around you are confronted by a dramatic landscape featuring quartzite mountains, which cut jagged lines in the sky. There are lakes and water everywhere set in a backdrop of heather and rocks, all tumbling together towards the sea. There are small bits of green fields sparsely littered in the lowland landscape, a testimony to generations of perseverance. Through this rugged landscape rivers wind their way to the ocean before arriving in sandy estuaries, where river and sea blend together in colours of blue, green and white. When one stands on top of these mountains and surveys with awe all this surrounding beauty, a great quietness descends; here you feel at one with all that exists. We are dragged out of the narrow world of our everyday existence and are given a small glimpse of the wonders of Creation. Here all our artificial worlds recede into the background.

The Atlantic Ocean chisels great fissures and headlands in the coastline. All the islands, including Tory, Arranmore, Rutland and Iniscearra lie scattered in the sea like errant pieces of a jigsaw. They add a sense of mystery to the surroundings. This is especially true of that ledge of rock called Tory, eight miles out over a treacherous sound. No wonder the gods of yore lived out there, at least according to the beliefs of our ancestors. Balor of the Evil Eye was one of the most infamous Gods that lived on Tory – if by chance you happened to look at his eye you were immediately consigned to the realm of ashes.

Some of his exploits live on in the place names of the area. It is said that at one time, on the island a man owned a cow called 'An Glas Gaibhleann' which gave prodigious amounts of milk. Balor wanted to own this cow so much that he decided to take the law into his own hands, as gods are wont to do. He caught the owner and with one heave threw him onto the mainland eight miles away, where he fell upon a pillar of rock. Balor then threw a large rock, which landed on top of him. To this day the rock is still perched on top of the pillar and has bloodstains on it. Cloughaneely got its name from this event. The Irish name for the area is 'Cloch Cheann Fhaolla' meaning the stone of the bloody head.

On the outer fringes of Letterkenny there was a soccer match going on in the soccer field beside the secondary college. There was an animated group of supporters standing on the sideline. I looked on for a while and contemplate going in to watch it.

"Hey mister, where are you from?"

I turned round and saw four young faces looking up at me, three girls and a boy. The three girls were aged from about six to eleven and the boy, who had curly strawberry blonde hair, was aged about five. They all had lollipops and sweets. Their spokesperson was the biggest and the plumpest girl. I think she was disappointed when I explained I was from another part of Donegal, because on seeing my rucksack she may have thought that I was from a more exotic location. She digested the information.

"Would you like a lick of my lollipop?" she asked.

"Nah, I wouldn't like your germs," I answered.

They all laughed at this.

"We live in a caravan," the oldest girl said, intent on provoking a reaction from me. I had guessed that they were from the traveller community already, from their accents.

"Where?"

"In the cathedral car park."

"We will be moving to a house soon," one of the other girls said.

"You'll like that?"

"Can I have ten cents?" the smallest girl asked (no trouble with conversion to the Euro here).

The other girl nudged her to be quiet. She was embarrassed at her asking for money.

"I don't have a cent on me," I said honestly.

"A Euro will do then," the oldest retorted, not to be outdone.

I laughed and asked their names. Two had the same name, one of whom was the main spokesperson. The young boy gave his name last. As he spoke he turned his curly red head up to look at me for the first time. His face suddenly lit up into a glorious smile at getting recognition. I asked him his age and he answered. All the other children smiled as he smiled except for the biggest.

Sensing that the focus of attention had now changed, the biggest girl pointed to the girl with the same name.

"We are twins," she said.

I replied cautiously, as they were unlikely looking twins.

"Is that right?"

As quick as a button she recognised my doubt.

"Do you not think so?" she said. "I was born ten minutes before her."

The other girl laughed.

"Why are you called the same name then?" I logically asked.

"Because we are twins," the logical answer came. "She's Ann Marie and I am Marie Ann, but we are both called Ann."

"Do you like football?" I asked, recognising that I was beat.

"Nah," they all replied.

I said goodbye to them and continued on my way. I turned round once and I saw them strolling down the road after me hands full of sweets and talking animatedly together.

After all the walking I decided that I would finish the day with a cup of coffee and a scone so I bought a newspaper and headed off towards St Conal's Hospital. St Conal's is an old psychiatric hospital, which was used as a dumping grounds for what could be classed 'deviants' in the first half of the twentieth century and indeed up to the present day. If one did not fit in to the narrow strictures of social life one was hidden away in one of these hospitals and locked within the high walls that once surrounded them. So if you were different, if you had a learning disability, or were a visionary, or challenged the mores of society, or a nuisance to family, or promiscuous, or homeless, or just *mad*, you were likely to end up in here during a certain period of our history. These people lived out their lives within the confines of the institution until the winds of change blew through here in the 1980s and 90s. The place was emptied, not through altruism, but for economic reasons. It would be cheaper to have people living in the community. This, in a strange way compounded the injustice of the incarceration in the first place, as this was the only spot that they could call a home. Leaving it forcibly after forty to fifty years was yet another trauma.

Having worked in offices in the grounds of St Conal's for five years, I recalled some of the people who lived here during that time. One man could calculate anything in numbers (a savant if one wants to put another label on him). If you told him your date of birth, he would tell you the day on which you were born. If you asked him the most difficult multiplication he would work it out in his head in no time. All the time he made these calculations he twiddled a piece of twine with both his hands in front of his eyes. He used to walk around everywhere twiddling the twine, talking to himself. This mask never came down.

Another middle-aged man used to walk around looking for someone to chat to. He was small and fat, with great big red ruddy cheeks and a broad smile. He knew everyone's name and was genuinely interested in hearing where you had been and what you had done. The only thing that ever distracted him from asking questions and listening to the answers was the sight of a pretty girl. It always pays to get priorities right! If such a being happened along he would disengage immediately and head off to try and chat to her. He was just more honest than the rest of us. If he got a snippet of information from her at all he was a happy man, because he could now say he was talking to (the name of the particular girl) and he would get us to guess what she told him. He traded on this type of fame. It was these memories that dragged me up the hill and in the gates of St Conal's hospital.

It is a sign of the changed times that one can now go to a public coffee shop in St Conal's, a place once feared and shunned by people. It was the greatest threat that could be issued on someone. Even in banter people might say to you "You should be locked up in St Conal's".

I went in the front door of the coffee shop and up to the counter to order a mug of coffee, as I definitely felt that I needed a pick me up. The woman behind the counter shook her head and said she only had cups of coffee. On seeing my disappointed face the woman said that she would fill a pot full of coffee for me, which she duly did. I doubly benefited when she only charged me for a cup of coffee despite my protestations! The bright red table that I sat down at told me that they were certainly trying to get away from the image of a drab institution. The place was full of Health Board professionals with their mobile phones, power suits, collars and ties. They were all in for a quick cup of coffee in their busy days though a few looked a tad more relaxed than that. Some of them spent their break time talking on the mobile phone; I hope there was nothing confidential, as any one could listen in. It is amazing how we have become hooked into being continuously accessible to work, friends and family. Have we become so fascinated by technology that in fact we have become a nation of compliant slaves?

With a sigh of contentment, I poured a cup of coffee, opened my newspaper and settled to a read of world news…no, I only joke; it was the sports pages. I lifted my eyes momentarily and then I became aware of a bright pair of eyes watching me closely. The life in those eyes were remarkable, more so, given the fact that they were set in a face that was deathly pale. The face and eyes were situated on a small, frail, broken body in a wheelchair. Those eyes focused on me and drew me in.

"I see you have a pot full of coffee all to yourself," he said. You knew that those eyes did not miss a beat.

"It is hard to beat a good cup of coffee," I rather lamely replied.

He rightly ignored that statement and announced to me that he was an itinerant from Dungloe. I said nothing, which seemed to be the correct response as he continued then to tell me snippets of his life story. He told me his special skill was making pandies (tin cans and containers). He used to collect all the old used and scrap tin, melt it down and then shape it into a brand new tin pandy. He went on to tell me about all the things that he used to fix, from bicycles to boat propellers. I said to him that it was a great gift to have. I then went on to say that I was useless in working with my hands. He interrupted sharply.

"You should not think like that!" he said. "It's that what beats you. That type of work is simple; all you have to do is work through it one step at a time."

People have gone to courses and spent fortunes to hear words like that. They might put more complicated words on it such as 'visualisation' or 'positive thinking' or 'lateral thinking' but the meaning is the same. How apt to hear it from a patient who is resident in a psychiatric hospital.

I did not ask him why he was a resident here now, but he did tell me that he had a number of operations in order to help stabilise his spine. Before the operation he had to be fed through a tube. With pride in his face he showed me a wooden ornament that he had made that morning in the occupational therapy department. It is great that he still has an opportunity to craft, make and shape with his hands; for him to be in a place that he could not use his hands "would be hell on earth". There is a deep satisfaction to be had from crafting something from a raw state and sculpting it with your mind. The operation has given him a quality of life again and an opportunity to use his talent. He moved easily from one topic to the next, leaving little space for interruption. He was hungry for contact and I was the new face on the block. In a room full of people who talked with their friends over coffee he was alone. The fact that they were health professionals was slightly ironic.

I too was moving on but I will never forget those bright, perceptive and calculating eyes.

## Letterkenny to Ballybofey

Some gurus reckon that memories and attachments are traps and entanglements that we have to avoid. I have never believed this, because one of the main forces on which the universe is based is gravity: all objects are drawn to each other to varying degrees. This binds us all together in a web that not only spans a moment but spans the ages, past and future. We may think of ourselves as individuals, but we are all part of the life force that bubbles up like a wellspring, all attached, one drop to another.

After my father died twenty years ago I went out to an old ruined Franciscan Friary outside Letterkenny called Killydonnell to make sense of things. It was there that I wrote a final letter of goodbye to him. I decided that before going to Ballybofey on the next stage of the walk that I would revisit the spot and the memory. Killydonnell is situated on a back road above the banks of the Swilly Estuary, three miles off the main Letterkenny to Ramelton road. A friend dropped me to the top of this road and from there I headed off, walking towards Killydonnell. I was immediately struck by the change in the size and quality of houses. The last time I was here, there had been but a few small houses; now the area was completely built up. The small dwellings were gone, replaced by huge mansions, one bigger than the next, symbols of a new and ostentatious country. They were marks of affluence upon the land. One hoped that people had not sold their souls in order to acquire them. Obviously in the intervening years this had become one of the 'sought after' and 'desirable' areas to live around Letterkenny. Similar housing sprawls have developed around every large and indeed not so large town in the country.

Early on this Sunday morning all was quiet, curtains were pulled and cars were parked at doorways. A black cat crossed the road in front of me, gave me a quick furtive glance and noiselessly disappeared into the hedge. As I got closer to Killydonnell Friary the houses thinned out and I became aware of the birdsong in the hedges and trees as I passed. My thoughts turned to my father.

I always knew my father loved me, even though he never told me that. Of course I never told him that I loved him either so we were even on that score. 'Love' is a word that means so many different things in various contexts, but I think the common denominator in all definitions of love is a strong connection. My father had lived all his life in Mountcharles on a small farm. He was a very sociable and gentle person and was intensely curious about the world. He travelled through the books he read and the people he met and had the capacity to talk about anything to anybody. He lived perfectly healthily for seventy-nine years and then out of the blue he had a heart attack, from which he died two days later.

I remember the knock on the door. It was a cousin who arrived to tell me that my father was ill and I had better go home. In a bewildered haze I arrived home at the same time as the doctor. I remember my father wheezing his way to the bathroom holding his chest, his face thin with worry. When I asked how he was feeling he replied "My chest is very tight". I can still hear the gasping sound as his body searched for a breath. My mother had been a nurse: she was trying to keep both herself and my father calm as she talked to him at the bedside. Neighbours came in and a short time afterwards the ambulance arrived. There was a flurry of activity. My father was made to sit in a wheelchair and he was wheeled out the door. There was an intensity in the way he looked at everything as he left. There is a knowing in people when their time is up. I knew he was saying goodbye to this place where he had been born and had lived all his life, a spot where he knew every inch and contour of the ground and every sound of the countryside. He was saying goodbye to the people who had made this place a home and a community. One part of him knew that he would never be here again. Through that look he absorbed as much as he could of this world into his being, so that he could take it with him to face the uncertainty of that night.

On my way home from the hospital on that first night I ran over a black cat in Donegal town. I stopped the car; the cat was still alive but died a few moments later. I knew then for certain that my father was going to die.

The next day at the hospital a young doctor came out to speak to my mother and I. He told us that we "should hope for the best but prepare for the worst". I thought afterwards that it was a good way of expressing a difficult message. I struggled with those words.

My father died that night.

I will always remember sitting beside him as he died. I was helpless.

Suddenly I was in a changed world. I will particularly remember the kindness and genuine sympathy emanating from the young nurse who was on duty. Afterwards I was all alone in the waiting room, full of confusion and grief, when from somewhere there came a comforting presence in the midst of the pain. It was as if my father was there in spirit, soothing things in the best way he knew. This presence stayed with me for a month or so, until I realised my father had to continue on his own journey and that I had to let go. I wrote my farewell letter to him here at Killydonnell Friary.

I went down the lane and crossed the stile into the friary; it was totally quiet and peaceful. It had not changed in the twenty years since I was last here. The graveyard was tidy and the ruined friary was still more or less as I remembered it. The last time I was here I had perched on a large windowsill in a ruined wall to do my writing. I went over and sat down on that same windowsill and gazed down in the sunlight at the sweeping Swilly waters of blue, silver, grey and white. The wind occasionally brushed through the trees and the ivy made the odd rustling noise. Crows cawed in a nearby copse and seagulls squawked in the distance circling over the estuary. Everything else remained quiet. I was alone there, though accompanied by many peaceful presences, which were encased by broken slabs and verdant growth. There were all sorts of graves there, old and new, big and small all together, all decaying, all a monument to distant memories and to their relatives' love and pride.

Here are extracts of what I wrote to my father at the time.

*Death is like a piece of burning paper, crinkling, blazing, blackening, shrivelling up and changing. The black ash disintegrates and falls into the hearth no longer recognisable as to what it once was."*

*Do you remember the time before you died, when you realised that you were going to go? You told us to take care of each other. I saw the calm and acceptance in your eyes but at times I also saw the fear and fright there. It made me realise for the first time what a big step there is between life and death. Before this I did not think about it at all. We should see life and death as the ebb and flow of the tide, not so much a change in essence as a change in direction.*

*I am sorry father that I did not give you more help with that last step. I would not answer your question 'Am I dying?' I spurned an opportunity because of my fear. I did not trust the next step – for me it was a step over the precipice into nothingness. However you did believe and it was you who helped me. I remember your humour before you died, the humour we shared. It was a while since we had shared humour so nicely and gently, and it was nice to share it one last time, at least in this reality. We have a similar sense of humour; a humour that refuses to take things too seriously and at the same time is not too harsh.*

*I got so many things from you and for all of them, thank you.*
*I miss you.*
*See You?*

I climbed over the stile and headed back the way I came. Upon reaching the main road again I hitched a lift back into Letterkenny. A young man in his late teens/early twenties stopped to give me a lift. He was dark haired with a slight stubble on his face. He had friendly (I hoped), open eyes and was extremely chatty. The first thing he told me (rather reassuringly given the previous day's conversation about young drivers) was that he had been in an accident six months previously, and that he still had pains in his legs and back from the resultant injuries.

'Just my luck to get a lift from one of those young Donegal rally drivers,' I thought. Of course I was foolish enough to get in with him. Well, if the truth were known he was the only one willing to give me a lift – all the sensible folk continued serenely on their way. Some with a conscience pointed vaguely to the left as if they were trying to convince me that they were turning off at the next junction. All I can say is it must have been a very busy back road if everyone who pointed left went that way. So the option was walk into Letterkenny or take a drive, possibly on the wild side.

We zipped along the road into Letterkenny, so our conversation was short. However he had time to tell me that he missed playing football, and that he hoped to be able to play again in the next six months or so when his injuries healed. In Letterkenny I thanked him and wished him well. I duly headed into a café for a cup of coffee to recover!

After leaving the café I headed off walking for the oldest part of the town. Letterkenny was buzzing as preparations were in place for the arrival of a ten-kilometre road race and walk in aid of local charities. This was a community event, featuring a continuum of competitors from serious athletes to people out for a Sunday stroll. There were marshals in yellow bibs everywhere whose job it was to control traffic, give water to competitors, tend injuries and deal with any emergencies. There was music in the streets and some balloons were drifting in the air, striving in vain to warm the atmosphere and to lift the gloom of the increasingly cold and damp grey skies. A few people with pints in their hands were hanging around outside the pubs waiting for the action to begin. I drifted along with the swirling litter to the bottom of the street, where I stood talking to an ambulance man from the Red Cross. He told me that we had a good vantage point, as we would be able to see the athletes on the way out and the way back again. We had waited for a while, when around the corner came a police motorcycle followed by two runners. One was a young man in his early twenties, the other was a grey-haired man possibly in his late thirties or early forties. They passed me with muscles straining, sweat glistening, breathing laboured and with faces contorted by effort as each strove to reach their limit. It seemed to me that the younger man was going much the easier.

"They will be coming back in that other road," said the marshal, pointing at a road across the small roundabout. It just showed how good a judge of athletes I was, because when they came back it was the older grey-haired man who was in the lead – and by a considerable margin at that. A group of about twenty athletes, which included the first two female athletes, followed these two front-runners. The energy expended by all the athletes was tangible. It felt like being in the midst of a stream of churning white water impatient to get to the sea. After that sudden initial swell of activity, there followed a lull with the odd bob of energy representing a struggling athlete drifting in the wake of the main surge. These runners were wilting, having taken on more than they could achieve. It is human nature I suppose, to be optimistic about our abilities especially when these abilities are not often tested. It is this blindness that makes us persevere and challenge the boundaries of logic. A new wave of energy arrived, the fast walkers and slow joggers streamed past, equally intent on getting to the finish as quickly as possible. Another lull descended and then one could hear a hum coming closer to us like the sound of a swarm of bees on the wind. As all the social walkers and families approached us and streamed past, the sound of human interaction and laughter filled the air. People were walking and talking together in groups, children were running about, some dressed up in various mad costumes. I spotted somebody I knew in the crowd, so I joined him as our routes went for a while in the same direction.

Shane always has a smile on his face, which blends into slightly jowled features and twinkling blue eyes. Joining Shane was a costly decision, because he wheedled a financial sponsorship from me for one of his charities.

"Sure €20 will not break you," he said, and then added while awaiting my response, "It's all in a good cause."

He just laughed when I jokingly wondered out loud whether he could sponsor me in return, as I was going to Ballybofey, which indeed was much farther than he was walking? His face creased in a grin.

"It's all in a good cause, it's all in a good cause," he said as if to comfort me.

His head was nodding enthusiastically as he said this. He told me that he had collected €600 so far for his charity, and that he was pleased with himself for having surpassed his €500 target.

"If everyone here collected the same as me," he said, "there would be a lot of money collected."

"You should be ashamed of yourself," I said.

"Why is that?" he asked.

"For all the money you have duped out of people, you should have had to run the whole distance."

"The ould knee is playing up," he said with a laugh.

At the next junction we parted ways and I left the mass of bodies to follow my own route. There is something infectious about following the same route as everyone else. When together we get a sense of comfort and security, a sense of belonging and the feeling that everyone is on a shared adventure. On the other hand there is also a need within us to escape from the conformity of the crowd, and explore where our curious imagination takes us. Probably all the great explorers possessed this curiosity to a high level, thus helping to spread human influence and to shape our inner and outer worlds. Exploration is always followed by the development of physical routes and mental routines, which are essential for our survival especially in relatively new uncharted waters.

From a slight hill I looked back at the town of Letterkenny. Silhouetted on the sky were the cathedral, the bishop's palace and the secondary school once run by the Church. This was a visible testament to the Church's past power and influence. As I looked at the landscape however, it was obvious that a new power was now arising, as evidenced by the fact that rows of housing estates have spread like a low growing dense fungus over the hilltops and valleys of the surrounding countryside. All in blocks of uniform colour and design, they are laid out in straight lines, which are in direct contrast to the flow of the landscape.

A feeling that everything is temporary and fleeting came over me. All these buildings from the palace to the humblest house were but an ephemeral growth on the land. Like all growths they will wither and die. We humans have this great need for symbols of permanence because we inhabit a world of transience. In facing the abyss we build a wall behind which to hide. Perhaps this is one of the driving forces of our species, a cussedness in the face of blinding fate, a determination to fight the odds. Sometimes however all we can see is this wall. We become blinded by the prospect of temporal power. The cathedral and palace are symbols of this arrogance. It was a structure that did not respond to the landscape but strove to control and overpower it. It dominated the hilltops but forgot about the valleys.

Farther on that same road I got an enthusiastic welcome from a horse, who upon seeing me galloped the length of the field to get his nose rubbed. I do not think I would go as far to get my nose rubbed or maybe then I am thick and I am missing the point. Maybe though on reflection it depends on who is doing the rubbing.

'Is he lonely?' I wondered. 'Is he expecting something to eat? Is he just used to human company or does he just want me to let him out of the confines of the field?'

I gave his nose a final farewell rub and moved on. He followed me in a determined manner to the end of the field and continued to watch me until I disappeared around a corner. I felt guilty somehow, as if I had failed or disappointed him in some undefined way. Maybe he was just waiting for the next sucker to come along?

I wandered on until I came to Newmills. There I decided to take a narrow forestry road up through the hills. At the beginning of the road there were a few houses scattered here and there, but soon all signs of human habitation petered out and gave way to Sitka spruce forestry that encroached from all sides and soon became the whole world. A little respite from this dreary denseness was achieved when I came across a stand of airy Japanese Larch trees. As I looked along the rows of larch, dappled light reached and illuminated parts of the forest floor, revealing old rocks, mosses and ferns. Some of the trees had toppled sideways and were leaning against other trees for support. All these long slender bodies were pushing skywards in fierce competition, searching for any available light. As these trees were closely planted together they are being forced to conform to the fashion of having long slim bodies, bearing few branches and consequently having no awkward knots. The goal is uniformity – these trees have dispensed with their natural habit because of the lack of light. They are symbolic of many aspects of our own world. We all need to be suffused in light in order to flourish and grow to our potential, knots and all.

I came across an old abandoned two-storey house that lay right on the edge of the track. There were two burnt out cars on the opposite side. All the windows in the house were broken and the front door was slightly ajar. I had to push hard in order to open the door, as its swollen timbers caught on the floor; stepping inside I was assailed by mouldy scents of decay. This was once a place full of order, which was being reabsorbed into chaos by the forces of Nature. Layers of wallpaper were peeling off the wall; some parts of the walls were black and putrid where water was leaking in through a hole in the roof. Furniture, tables and chairs lay scattered around the floor. Holding on stubbornly to centre stage, as it has done for many's the long day was an old Stanley range. A blue dresser stood in a corner and the red remnant of a carpet still clad the banisterless stairs. I could only guess at the lives and events that unfolded under this roof. There are many houses like this one in the rural countryside, decaying and disintegrating back into the soil. As people congregate in towns and cities they are prepared to pay higher and higher prices for smaller and smaller accommodation. Other houses are abandoned, disintegrate and disappear.

As I stepped out of the house a deer emerged out of the trees in front of me. Like a silent shadow it crossed the track and disappeared into the forest on the other side. These glimpses of wild animals in Nature are such precious things. It is usually a fleeting glimpse, full of intensity that leaves you yearning for more. After such a moment you are often left with the wonder and the feeling that it might not have happened at all. However you remember the intensity and then you know it was real.

After the house the signs of human habitation ceased altogether, at least to my untutored eye. However, a little bit farther on I came across a prominently displayed sign, which declared 'No dump here'.

I found out later that the local authority had planned to open a dump here, in what they thought was a remote spot. The idea was to impact upon as few people as possible. However a very active anti-dump campaign suddenly arose and was successful in halting the development of the dump. All over the country there are numerous campaigns similar to this one. What we should do with our waste is now a real issue and likely to become a bigger one in the future. Should we bury it, burn it, export it or dump it at sea? Of course the level of our waste does not increase in direct relation to our numbers but has increased in proportion to our greater affluence. We have learned to consume relentlessly, but we turn a blind eye to the consequences of this consumption. We all know however that someone has to cope with it. If you live near a dump or an incinerator it is you who has to cope with the consequences of other people's waste. It is usually the weak and the powerless in society who are forced to do this. The rich and the powerful try to insulate themselves from the negative aspects of the environment they create. Rich individuals increasingly strive to lead 'healthy lives' and to eat healthy food and drink bottled water. They try to create environments which are conducive to their physical and mental health at their own individual level; that some other people are living in less than healthy circumstances does not overly bother them. People are obsessed with health in an increasingly unhealthy world; the tendency is to avoid making the obvious connection.

Of course the answer lies partly in all our hands. I consume as much as the next person. The real question is; Am I willing to drive and fly less? Am I willing to buy less convenience foods, fertilisers, weed killers, televisions, lawn mowers, computers etc., etc. Am I prepared to grow my own food (*hmmm*)?

One of the features of this day's walk was the sound of male cuckoos singing their distinctive notes across the hilltops (if 'singing' is what you would call it). Every spring it is with delight that I await the cuckoo call. There is an informal community competition as to who hears it first. It is great to be able to ask someone 'Did you hear the cuckoo?' and receive their slow reply 'no, not yet'. You can then affirm your superior connection to the natural world by informing them that you have already heard the cuckoo two weeks previously. It is also useful to say that you heard it early in the morning, thus suggesting to your acquaintance that they do not get up too early in the morning either!

However, as we all know, our delight in hearing the call of the cuckoo heralds the death of a nest of small birds. How can we feel delight in hearing this bird when we know that they will deposit their egg in the nest of a small bird such as the robin or dunnock, for these small birds to rear at the expense of their own hatchlings? The manipulative cry of the fledgling cuckoo not only entices the new foster parents to feed it but also entices any other passing adult bird as well; this certainly gives a new meaning to the concept of an extended family. Even when it leaves the nest the young cuckoo needs no help from the parent in navigating its way to beyond the Sahara desert. In fact the natural parents head on the journey long before the young cuckoo is able to go. I suppose the adult cuckoo regards coming to Ireland as a bit of a holiday: who wants to be doing mundane things like building nests, feeding hungry mouths or teaching fledglings to fly and navigate successfully when you are supposed to be enjoying yourself? In some ways cuckoos are the heralds of the modern hedonistic age.

I saw two cuckoos flying at different times during the day. A small bird closely pursued one of these cuckoos. The flight of the cuckoo is similar to a hawk, and it is really only by their call that you can tell them apart. On this day the cuckoo calls all had perfect tone, except for one who sounded as if he had the hiccups or was slightly inebriated. He always managed to get the *cuc-* part out OK but the *-koo* part sounded like it was being strangled out of a constricted throat. Every time I heard him I laughed out loud. They say that the best pleasure is the simplest pleasure. I suppose that's why they lock up so many people who enjoy these simple pleasures; after all you can't have people enjoying themselves for no reason whatsoever. Perhaps this cuckoo was taking pity on me and was keeping me entertained for a while on my walk!

The cuckoos brought back memories of an elderly neighbour, who told me some of the superstitions in relation to cuckoos. He told me that when you hear the cuckoo you are supposed to say the following for good luck:

'Thanks be to God and may we live to hear it again.'

He also told me that if you hear the cuckoos call in the right ear it is supposed to be lucky, though he didn't say what would happen if you heard it in the left ear first! However if there are omens for good luck there are equally omens for bad luck. Beware if you hear the first call of the cuckoo indoors as it will bring bad luck in its wake. It gets worse! If you hear the first call of the cuckoo before breakfast you will have a hungry year ahead and woe betides anyone who hears the first call of the cuckoo from a graveyard, as that means a death in the family before the year is out. So now you know what to listen out for next spring, and the places not to hear it!

Soft blankets of mist washed my face as I walked along; I sought protection against its persistent intrusion through keeping my head down. Why do people walk with their head down in the rain I asked myself. What difference could it possibly make? You are going to get wet anyway. It is a bit like soldiers in an army attacking enemy lines with their heads down against the incoming fire. After leaving the track I came onto a small road. Out of the heavy mist there came towards me a small lean elderly man. He was sauntering towards me with his hands clasped behind his back, head in the air, wearing just a pullover, obviously unconcerned about the misty rain. He was the first person I had seen in hours. He was not bothered with 'Lowe Alpine' raingear or anything sissy like that, but he did have a cap on his head that I am sure provided ample protection. There was no house to be seen anywhere so it was difficult to figure out where he was coming from and where he was going. Of course he could have said the same thing about me! A few fleeting words were exchanged about the weather, and the mystery man and I went our separate ways, neither too much the wiser about the other.

About an hour later as I turned on to a larger road, farm houses started to appear on the landscape. Opposite a farmhouse in a field full of sheep and rocks I spotted a sign on top of a small hill.

'Ah a national monument,' I said to myself. I debated whether I should go and have a look at it. 'Would the farmer mind?'

I answered the question myself by opening the gate and walking to the top of the hill. When I got there the sign informed me that the site contained a National Monument, which was not to be tampered with in any way whatsoever. I presume that if you did meddle with it there will be dire consequences of one type or another. For example a crow might dive bomb you or a sheep might attack you. There was no information about the monument itself, no clue to its significance.

'Bloody typical,' I thought.

One would not be able to find out anything about this site without undertaking extensive research in some dusty archive. The monument consisted of a grass-covered mound of rocks. I thought to myself that I could erect as good a monument as this one and claim that it was a National Monument as well. I suppose it all depends on the definition of National Monument and of course who defines it. Looking at the monument more closely, I thought to myself that it was probably a burial chamber.

Did you ever wonder why so many rocks were placed on top of dead people? In this instance it seems that they were making sure that the person would have great difficulty in rising again no doubt! I think all these fabulous burial chambers are not a statement of the high status of the dead person but rather a statement of how much they were detested. Our Celtic ancestors understood this perfectly, as they also cremated the dead before placing the rocks on top, thus making doubly sure that they could not come back. I wandered down the field and out the gate, making sure that I tied the rope on the gate, and left everything the way I found it. If the sheep got out it was not going to be my fault.

I was nearing Ballybofey when I spotted two men talking in a shed, with a red and white setter lying at their feet. I saluted them as I went past. In reply they just stared in silence at this bedraggled specimen of a human being.

'They must be town people,' I said to myself. 'Country people would always return a greeting'.

I passed a cemetery, famous locally because it is the burial place of 'The Drumboe Martyrs' who were executed not by the British, but by the Irish Government forces during the Civil War, following our Independence from Britain. The four people executed were Charlie Daly (26), Daniel Enright (23), Timothy O'Sullivan (23), all from Kerry and

Sean Larkin (26) from Derry. These men and some of their colleagues came to Donegal to continue the fight for a thirty-two county Republic. In the autumn of 1922 the then-Free State Government initiated their policy of official executions, by establishing a three-man Army Council and military courts under the provision of Emergency Powers. These four men were captured in November 1922, tried by military court on 18th January 1923 and sentenced to death. A firing squad executed them on 14th March 1923. Their final letters to their families before their death showed a calm resignation, an acceptance that it was worthwhile to die for their beliefs, and a belief that they would be going straight to Heaven. Their only seeming sorrow was the pain their death might cause their families. This civil war between people who accepted a twenty-six county independent State and more extreme republicans who wanted to settle for nothing less than a thirty-two county Ireland is one of the more inglorious episodes in our history.

Every Easter this graveyard is the focal point of local celebrations by Sinn Fein to mark the anniversary of the 1916 uprising and rebellion against British rule. It is held on the spot where the executions took place. In the tribal tradition speeches are made and music is played to yet more silent stone epitaphs. All the perceived wrongs of history are recalled and somehow we are supposed to feel better because of it? To deal with the future it is better to live in the present.

I arrived in Ballybofey coming in along the picturesque wooded walk beside the river that is undoubtedly the jewel of the area. Swathes of glistening bluebells illuminated the way, as it was time for them to celebrate their part in Creation. They have to make sure and appear every year before the leaves come on to the hardwood trees. It is a marvellous time of the year to be walking in woods, as one can sense the life force surging just underneath the skin of the Earth, getting ready to emerge in all its chaotic and frantic glory. I stopped for a moment beside a large tree, with a hollowed out trunk, in order to let a group of joggers go by.

'Are they mad in the head or what to be out in weather such as this?' I thought to myself. The old tree I am sure has seen more unusual behaviour than this.

I crossed a footbridge over the swollen river and headed into the town. This is roughly the spot where Red Hugh O'Donnell crossed the river on his way south on his triumphal march to fight the battle of Kinsale. This was to utterly change the way of life in Ireland over four hundred years ago. Defeat at Kinsale marked the end of Celtic authority in Ireland and allowed the British to extend their control over the whole country. This march was the last hurrah of Celtic rule in Ireland. If only there had been a flood in the river that day!

After watching parades, listening to cuckoos, and battling the rain I felt I deserved a pint. I dropped, dripping into the nearest pub I could find, which was Jackson's Hotel. There were only a few people in the bar. I had just sat at the counter with my pint when a man stood beside me and ordered a pint as well. He was a tall, big-boned man, about forty years old, wearing a suit with a blue open necked shirt.

"Do they serve a good pint here?" he enquired of me in a Co. Mayo accent.

He had a weather-beaten face and had a cast in his left eye. Whenever I meet someone with a cast I never know where to look. If I look at them in both eyes I worry that they might think I was staring at the bad eye and take offence. In this instance I pointedly kept my eye contact on his good eye.

"I am enjoying this one anyway," I replied.

"Are you a regular here?"

"No, I am just passing through, like yourself?"

He clasped his pint and told me that he had come to Ballybofey for a job interview as a salesman. He assured that he was "a right good salesman".

Some men like an audience and my Mayo friend was no exception. For the next half-hour or so, or to be more precise for the duration of two pints, he told me about the main exploits of his life. He stretched out his big hands in front of him, gazed at them with admiration, and looked at me.

"These hands killed two Doberman dogs," he said. He waited to see my reaction.

When I dutifully wondered how that happened, he took great pleasure in telling me the story.

He had been working in a mine in England when one night on leaving the mine with a friend he suddenly remembered that he had forgotten something. Telling his friend that he would be up in a few minutes he went back down the mine. The security firm, thinking that the mine was empty, locked the gate and set two Doberman Pinscher dogs loose to guard the area. My Mayo friend certainly got a surprise when he encountered the two dogs.

"They made for me with their bared teeth," he said.

By luck he got into a confined area, which meant that only one dog could get near him at any one time. He caught one of the dogs by the throat and started to strangle it. In the meantime the other dog was not idle. It had clambered up onto the roof of a container. As he killed the first dog the other dog launched an attack from above, however after a struggle it met the same fate as the first. Bloodied he made his way to the gate and shouted for the security guards. Astounded, they asked after the Dobermans, and he replied that those dogs were "asleep on the job".

It was not the only time that those hands were called into action. He told that one time he was in a pub and spotted a man whom he felt had stitched him up and stopped him getting a job he was entitled to. He followed him into the toilet, caught him by the throat with those self-same hands and pinned him against the wall. He then told him politely not to interfere in his life again.

"He did not come out of those toilets for a long time afterwards," he said with a glint of self-satisfaction in his eyes.

These exploits were only the start of it he told me about all the fights they (the Mayo men) used to have with the men from Connemara in England, while declaring that the Connemara men were easy to defeat because they could never agree among themselves. He finished off by telling me of how he played in a Co. Mayo club football final with a broken collarbone. He certainly left me in no doubt that they would not have won the game without him.

My head full of his exploits, and feeling I had lived a very uneventful life I headed to the bathroom, which I locked behind me! When I came out again he had abandoned me for sunnier climes. He was sitting in a small alcove of the bar beside a woman still in full linguistic flow.

## Ballybofey to Glenties

The route from Ballybofey to Glenties follows the valleys, etched out by river and stream through the mountains and hills of the centre of the county, an area known locally as the "Heart of Donegal". This walk leads you into one of the most remote, rural areas in the whole of Ireland, where traditional culture still has a foothold.

Leaving Ballybofey and heading toward Glenties, I had the misfortune of looking at a signpost; this indicated that it was a journey of 45 kilometres and as my route was through the back roads it could be much further! Why do people have to put up road signs with bad news on them? It is probably a mistake however to pay too much attention to an Irish signpost because they have an inbuilt tendency to interpret distance in a confusing manner. Many walkers past and present have looked at Irish signposts and wondered ruefully whether they should take them seriously or not. In nineteenth century Ireland the first thing you would have had to establish was whether it was an Irish or the standard British mile that was being referred to. The Irish mile was invariably longer, with the added complication that there was an element of subjectivity in relation to its measurement.

Nowadays when looking at a signpost, the first thing to be solved is whether it refers to a mile or a kilometre. In this country we are seemingly never one thing or the other, we are always making plans for the transition to a new standard that never gets fully completed. The tradition of subjectivity in relation to the measurement of distance was still alive and well on this day. After walking for half an hour, presumably in the right direction, I was thrilled when I came across another signpost which informed me that I still had 45 kilometres to travel to Glenties! Thereafter the signposts were in miles, which added further clarity to the situation. There is always something reassuring about tradition?

This small road on the outskirts of Ballybofey had a long line of bungalows on each side of the road, in a ribbon type development so detested by planners but popular with the people. The area had the feeling of being a cosy, close-knit community. Outside one of the houses two young boys were on their knees looking in an intense and purposeful manner through the grass. I surmised that they were looking for those ancient, adaptable relics of evolution called frogs, as they each had two big basins of water with them. Their faces were friendly and open, as the faces of young boys usually are. They called a greeting as I passed and then immediately resumed the important work at hand. What they would do with the frogs when they caught them is anybody's guess.

Talking about frogs reminded me of a conversation I had with a colleague about health service managers. She was describing her work and how the rise of the manager class impacted upon her world. This world was full of busy suits with mobile phones and laptops producing the latest grand strategy that had little or nothing to do with the lives of ordinary people. They spent their time croaking to and meeting each other on different committees and being very busy going essentially in circles in a self-absorbed and pretentious manner. She said that their only interest was the search for power and an obsession for controlling the staff below them in the pecking order. She colourfully described their activity having the same effect as "small fat frogs farting in the long grass". All energy expended clouded the issue and produced more noise than substance! I do hope the boys treated the frogs gently because you never know if one might be a manager in the health service?

I came onto the main Ballybofey/Glenties road, which was a lot busier than the road I had just left. In this context busy is a relative word, as a vehicle every 30 seconds or so would hardly count as busy in other parts. However it was busy enough to be annoying so the search for a quieter route became the immediate quest. It was a workday and all the houses seemed empty but I finally spotted a house with a car outside which was a good omen of possible habitation. I walked down the driveway and inadvertently glanced into a bedroom where a matronly woman was assiduously powdering her nose. Fearing I was intruding on an intimate moment, I briefly considered turning back! I hastened forward with averted eyes and knocked at the door. After a delay, the same woman hesitantly opened the door, probably wondering who was around so early in the morning. In my most reassuring manner I passed the time of day with her, explained that I was walking to Glenties and was looking for directions. She initially looked at me slightly suspiciously, but this thawed into a slightly nervous good-humoured laugh, as she came to the conclusion that I probably was a harmless sort of being. I then asked her if she knew of any quiet back roads on which I could walk? This query was greeted with a very perplexed look indeed. I could see her thinking, 'why would anyone want to take the awkward way when there was a perfectly good main road, which was signposted all the way'. Thinking it might clarify matters I produced a map. This induced a look of complete panic on her face and she said.

"My husband is much better at maps than I am."

With that, like a knight in shining armour, a healthy-looking, grey-haired man appeared around the side of the house. Dressed in a bright green jumper, he walked with a slight limp as if he had hurt his leg recently or suffered from an arthritic hip. On his arrival the woman (relieved of the responsibility of guiding lost strangers), hurriedly retreated into the sanctuary of the house. I turned to the man and explained my quest to him. He understood immediately that I was in search of the road less travelled.

"Be sure and walk through the Croaghs," he said, enthusiastically.

He explained that the Croaghs was a beautiful area at the bottom of the Blue Stack Mountains, which though once a thriving community, was now relatively deserted. We had a short conversation on politics. We scouted along the fringes both unwilling to take the step that would commit us to a potential crossing of swords. We contained ourselves to wary words. I was thankful for their help and continued on my way.

The sound of the River Finn bubbling and gurgling its way through the countryside provided a pleasant backdrop to this stage of the walk. I stood for a while and watched a large flock of crows, feeding in a green field, on the other side of the river. I spotted two crows on sentry duty; one crow was perched on a high post, with the other was stationed on the branch of a small tree. As crows feed, there are always a few from their ranks delegated to this protective role. I wondered how they organised this. Does the sentry ever get a break? Do they operate a rota system or do they pick the same individuals time in time out? What happens if the sentry is unobservant of danger – is there a system of punishment? Is there any dissension in the ranks over roles and responsibilities? Pondering the structure of crow society and listening to the sounds of the companionable river enabled a few miles to painlessly pass by. Whilst such idle thoughts rolled around in my mind, I spotted a sign in a field:

## BE AWARE OF RAM

'What's this?' I thought. 'There must be a very angry ram on the loose.'

I had visions of one innocently stooping over to tie one's shoe and suddenly ending up headfirst in the river. A few likely candidates deserving that fate immediately came to mind.

Obviously perplexed at my fascination regarding a seemingly innocuous sign in a field, an older man of perhaps seventy pulled his car over opposite me. I saw him busily moving objects out of the front seat of his car into the back in preparation for giving me a lift. I indicated to him that I did not want a lift, as I wanted to continue walking. He looked incredulous and before I could thank him properly for stopping he zoomed off. He must have thought, 'Has the world gone mad?' No one in his right mind would walk when he could get a lift. He could have been right of course.

Shortly afterwards a delivery van slowed down beside me and the driver offered me a lift. I again declined. I wondered to myself, perhaps I was walking with a limp or something, as everyone was being so thoughtful? Later on in the day, when I was definitely walking with a limp, nobody offered me a lift. But sure isn't that life for you? I met this van a few times during the course of the day and every time I got a friendly wave and a beep of the horn. It was easy to see that we were in a truly rural area and that here at least the old friendliness and courtesy remained intact. On 'main-road Ireland' people would avoid giving you a lift because of the fear that they might get assaulted, or the passenger might claim on their insurance if in an accident, or because they are in too much of a hurry. If one saw a person walking on the main road they would certainly never stop voluntarily and offer a lift. It's a bit like walking down a street in the city where no one will acknowledge your presence or pass the time of day with you. In such overcrowded situations the engaging part of the mind seemingly shuts down suffering from stimulation overload.

The walking was pleasant, as the sun reached its full height in the sky. I settled into the rhythm of the road and mile after mile tumbled by, or was it kilometre after kilometre? Voices filled my head reliving old roles from my past, sometimes a hero, sometimes a victim, sometimes a romantic, sometimes just remembering.

March can be such a beautiful time of the year when the weather co-operates. There was a slight breeze blowing against me, which gently massaged my face and neck. The river was still flowing beside me and its tinkling music filled the air in a symphony full of birdsong and the bleating of sheep. This was only occasionally interrupted by the noise of a car or a van. I stopped and took a photograph of three newly born lambs lying on a slab of rock underneath a boulder. One of them got up, stretched himself and lay down again. How interesting is that! I suppose there are different ways of looking and seeing. If I were a fox, I might be very interested in that scene.

I passed a sign proclaiming 'Gaeltacht'. I was now officially in Irish speaking territory, where most of the population was supposed to be native speakers and not only that but supposedly use it as their everyday language as well. This is a border full of significance in some people's minds, but like most borders one side of it was indistinguishable from the other. Three teenage girls sitting on a wall outside a house said 'hello' to me in English. I heard them laugh softly as I walked by.

I came to a small shop and Post Office. I had competing inclinations; I knew that the route was long so I felt that maybe I should press on with the journey. But how many small shops in the middle of the countryside is one likely to come across? Not many, is the answer, so I opened the door and walked in. Coming in from the bright sunshine outside, it took a few moments for my eyes to adjust to the dimmer light. This was definitely an old-time, multi-purpose shop. There were all sorts of goods catering for the needs of the household and farm scattered around in an ad hoc manner – on one shelf, baked beans were placed beside boxes of nails and electric fuses. All the shelves were fully laden and the corridors in between were full of cardboard boxes and bags. The shopkeeper, a trim, slightly built woman extended a friendly greeting as I entered. The older woman whom she was serving at the counter also turned and smiled an acknowledgement. I was aware that another man was standing in a dim light at the back of the shop.

'What will I buy?' I asked myself. I was tempted by the thought of a bar of chocolate. The usual internal dialogue then took place. Chocolate in small amounts, I told myself, is good for you. It contains anti-oxidants, which help prevent heart disease and cancer. I was taking so much exercise that a little bit of chocolate would do me no harm at all, at all. I pondered deeply about the predicament for a few moments. Suddenly a wave of inner strength possessed me, as I picked a solitary orange up from the shelf and took it to the counter. As I stood there the little bell on the door of the shop rang as other people entered. The woman being served was rooting in the depths of her bag for money, opening compartment after compartment. The woman behind the counter recognised that it might take some time for this search to be concluded. She turned to me.

"I will let you go," she said.

She must have known that I was the last of the big spenders! I paid and turned to go out.

"Are you walking then?"

The question-come-statement came from the man at the back of the shop. I turned towards him. The voice continued.

"I saw you earlier on, walking on the road."

I recognised then that it was the old man who had stopped to give me a lift. He was a small but solidly built man in his seventies, smartly dressed in a light tweed jacket and hat. He had a cane in his hand, which he was tapping gently on the floor. He wore a large cream hearing aid, which dangled from his ear. On closer inspection the hearing aid may at one time have been white but now it had coloured with age. I took the opportunity of thanking him for stopping earlier. The hearing aid must not have been working too well because he ignored my gratitude.

"How far are you going?" he asked.

"Glenties," I replied.

He nodded thoughtfully.

"Where are you from?"

"Mountcharles."

He now had something to hang onto, and he immediately went into a story about a man in Mountcharles, who had overcharged him for a small item. He said that he would have nothing to do with this individual ever again, because he was the greatest scoundrel about. He lifted the cane to emphasise the point. I deemed it wise not to mention that I had been to the States with this same individual on a holiday, visiting a mutual friend of ours. He then asked me if I knew any fiddle players in Mountcharles. Without waiting for a reply he rhymed off a host of fiddle players from my parish, only a few of whom I knew, much to my shame. He made a comment about the qualities of each of the fiddle players as he went along. I won't repeat his pronouncements here, as I have to live in the place!

"I play the fiddle myself," he said.

"Ah," I said. "Have you ever played down around our way?"

"Often," he said with enthusiasm.

He then spent some time describing to me in detail the memorable sessions he could remember. This led into a general discussion on the quality of Donegal fiddle players.

"Paddy Doherty," he stated, "is getting great recognition now, but I always preferred his brother Mickey."

He looked at me with serious eyes and continued, with a slight wondering shake of the head.

"When either of them were in the humour they could put on some performance!"

He went on to tell me that a fiddle player needed the right conditions in order to perform. One of the crucial ingredients – he assured me – was a shot of whiskey. However having the right conditions didn't necessarily produce a virtuoso performance, because the fiddle player still might not be in the mood. A good performance is a gift given; it is not to be expected all the time. In an era of standardised performances and standardised living, there is something reassuring about unpredictability. Perhaps one can only hit the heights of virtuosity every so often.

At this stage I took out my map and inquired from my fiddler friend about the road through the Croaghs.

"Oh no don't go by the Croaghs," he said. "The best road is the straight road."

At that moment a fresh-faced breadman was walking past us with tray of bread.

"Are you thinking of walking in through the Croaghs?" he asked, on overhearing our conversation.

"I am."

"Hold on a second until I leave down this bread."

Leaving the tray of bread on top of a box of Tayto crisps lying on the floor, he came back and with a friendly engaging smile, took the map from me, and examined it for a few moments.

"I walked in through the Croaghs a couple of years ago and I really enjoyed it. If you are thinking of walking in that direction, that is the way you should go," he said, pointing to a thin squiggle of a line on the map. He then shouted across the counter to the shopkeeper, who was still talking to the customer whom I presumed had found what she was looking for in her bag.

"What do you think Ann, what route do you think he should take?"

Ann obviously was up-to-date on our deliberations. She came from behind the counter, and together with the woman customer, she ambled over to look at the map. The map now became the centre of attention of the whole shop, everyone looking at it from different directions.

"I agree with you John, she said. "Definitely that is the route he should go, but it is a long walk."

She looked at me and gave a gentle laugh.

"I am sure you will manage it though."

There was a tap on my shoulder. I turned around and a young man who had a learning disability offered his hand.

"Hello, I am Tom," he said.

His eyes were immediately engaging. I shook his hand and he laughed and grinned.

"Tom is John's assistant, on Wednesdays," Ann said.

Tom's face broke into an even wider beam on the public proclamation of his role as apprentice bread man.

"I would be lost without Tom's help and his company," said John, smiling.

After a few more minutes of friendly conversation I said thanks to all the people, shook hands with the fiddler and Tom, refused a lift with John, waved to Ann and the customer and went on my way fortified in my resolve to walk through the Croaghs. As I walked, I wondered what reply would I have received, if I had gone into a supermarket in a town or city and asked the same question. I certainly would not have engaged all the staff, deliverymen and customers in my deliberations. As this hypothetical question went round in my mind, the bread van with John and his assistant Tom on board passed me. Tom gave me an enthusiastic, friendly wave and John beeped the horn.

After another hour or two of pleasant walking in the company of a nearby river, I came across a spot that I thought would be nice for lunch. At this point the road lay more or less directly above the river. In between there was a small birch wood with a few tree stumps, which would make excellent seats. As I approached the first stump a smell of rotten fish assailed my nose. I looked down and spotted the head and a part of the body of a trout. It seems that some other drama had been played out in this spot between either an otter or mink and the trout. The mink is a more probable culprit. Mink were introduced into Ireland from North America at the beginning of the twentieth century, in order to be farmed for their valuable fur. When in captivity forced breeding ensured that a variety of colours could be produced. Some of these ingenious animals managed to escape and adapt successfully to the countryside. Once back in the wild their coats revert to their natural colours. They are fearless, versatile hunters that can run quickly, climb trees, burrow into holes and swim strongly. They can operate in any natural setting. Rats, stoats, birds, eels and fish are all on their menu. There is a strong debate about whether they attack poultry and lambs, with strong proponents on either side. At one time it was feared that their numbers would increase so much that they would upset the balance of wildlife in the countryside. This fear has not materialised; as territorial animals, they naturally control their own numbers.

I kicked the head of the fish to one side but the smell remained. However this was the best seat in the house and after a while I did not notice the smell anymore. Just shows you can get used to anything. People who have smelly feet are the only ones who are oblivious to them. Just to prove the point, I took the shoes and socks off my aching feet and took great pleasure in rubbing them on the moist cool grass. I sat there for a while, relaxing and listening to the tinkle of the stream as it flowed over and around small stones, weaving and gouging its way inexorably onwards. A van with a Dublin registration went up the road, turned, came back and stopped directly beside me. I was sitting below the level of the road in the wood and I wondered if the driver had seen me. Maybe he was looking for directions? The driver's door opened and a young man got out. He must see me, I thought. I was about to shout to him but I decided to wait and see what happened. He went to the far side of the van. I heard a door opening, a dragging noise and then the sound of the door closing again. Shortly afterwards the man came back to my side of the van, quickly hopped in and drove off. I finished my lunch whilst pondering what he had been up to. Perhaps he had been dumping a body?

"No, I have definitely been watching too many 'whodunits' on television," I said to myself.

Eventually, however curiosity got the better of me – maybe, just maybe I was witness to some dastardly deed. I got up to investigate but I found nothing so dramatic, just two black bags of rubbish. I gave the rubbish a small kick just to be sure.

One of the most notable things about this day's walking was the amount of rubbish to be seen, especially old abandoned cars and vans left to disintegrate in this beautiful countryside. Sometimes though what we classify as rubbish is a relative thing. We consider an abandoned car to be rubbish and to be highly objectionable, while we often consider a new car to be a thing of beauty and a desirable object. In real terms however the shiny new car is far more harmful to our environment than the old abandoned car ever could be.

This brought back memories of an old van that a neighbour (with my father's permission), had dumped on a piece of wasteland on our small farm. For a while it was a great place for my friends and I to play. We headed off in many adventures in our imaginations in that old van. It went on expeditions to far off lands, it raced around rally circuits, bad guys chased our van, it survived bombs and bullets, it was our place to talk. Eventually however the love affair waned, doors fell off, windscreen and windows got broken, metal rusted and disintegrated. The steering wheel and handbrake came off, rubber perished and the old van was left to its own devices as it withered into the soil. Forty years later, it has more or less disappeared; it is just a tumble of briars, nettles and vegetation. In some ways it is made up of the same stuff as us.

After lunch I followed the path of the Reelin River as it wound its way through bog and stone. On arriving at a crossroads, I realised that I could not decipher where exactly on the map I was. Seeing a tractor coming towards me, I walked over to the left-hand side of the road and proceeded to wave it down. As it was slowing a sudden gust of wind came from the glen and swept the baseball hat off my head and on to the road. I chased after it in a most awkward manner. The cap, just to be contrary, kept on eluding my grasp. The small man behind the tractor steering wheel was laughing heartily when I eventually returned after capturing the elusive baseball cap. He opened the cab door, his friendly face not only creased by laughter but also by age and weather.

"It's hard to keep on caps such as those on windy days like this," he said shaking his head, giving the impression that he had never seen the like of it in his life.

My new acquaintance had a cloth cap on his head, which probably hadn't moved much in years! If I hadn't known better I could have believed that it was he who caused the wind to rise, like some prankster fairy, hell-bent on causing merriment. There was a bit of devil in those eyes. I tried to cover my slight embarrassment through showing him my map and asking directions. He must have thought that maps were not much good to this man, if he could not even figure which of the two roads he should take. After he told me the right way to go, I asked him about the state of farming around those parts, which was a safe enough opening gambit for a conversation.

"Ah sure the farming isn't much good on this land," he said. "But," he continued, looking me directly in the eye, "there were times when it was worse. One time people around here had next to nothing, now they only think they have nothing."

He elaborated further.

"I'll not ask how much money you have and I am sure you will not ask how much money I have, but I am sure both of us have plenty. Ah I could tell you stories about the poverty there was here but I'll not get into that now."

The intimation was of course, that if he started talking about it we would be there until dusk.

"But when I tell young people what it was like," he continued, "they think I am pulling their legs."

At this stage he went on to apologise for his use of the English language, as he said he usually conversed in Irish and sometimes found it difficult to find the right words. I thought to myself if I had half the flow of language of this man I would be doing well. His eyes now settled into conversation mode.

"Around here in the past you'd only go to the shop for tea, salt, sugar and maybe sometimes, sweet cake. You'd produce all the other food yourself. Now nobody grows anything and young people are eating sweet cake until it comes out their ears."

He then asked me why I was walking. I gave him the best explanation I could, saying that I wanted to explore the back roads of the county, as I was the curious sort. This answer seemed to meet with his approval. He said that it was truly amazing that the faster people went from A to B, the less time they had.

"If you were in a car and had asked me the way," he said, "you would have been gone long ago. When you are walking you have time."

He recounted that in times past the door was always open to a passer-by, and at the worst of times a cup of tea would always be on offer. I went on to tell him about my mother and her attitude to a good cup of tea. During the Second World War tea was rationed. When my mother got her tea rations, she would put all the tea into the pot at the one time, declaring that she would rather have one decent pot of tea than spend a month drinking "coloured water". Not to be outdone my new friend started on a story about tea. He had just started when a car came down the road, and he had to pull the tractor in closer to the ditch. When the car had passed he told me that he remembered once, years ago, a visitor called into a house in the area. Of course the tea was produced as was normal for any passer-by at that time. The newcomer's reaction to the tea was unexpected.

"The visitor passed out with the shock it was so strong!"

He told me that he might have died but for the fact that a neighbour who was passing knew something about reviving people. I think the agreed antidote to the effects of strong tea is a large shot of whiskey – whatever it was, it seemed to work anyway, so the visitor went away having received all the courtesies that a traveller should be offered and receive. He elaborated further, that the man in the house did not believe in using spoons of tea. Instead he put it in by the handfuls.

"He had brave big hands too," concluded my acquaintance. The tradition of having a bigger yarn than the previous storyteller was alive and well here.

It turned out that my new acquaintance had only left this area once, to go to Scotland. He stayed there for a few weeks but he failed to settle so he returned home. I sensed there was a story here too but he did not continue further. He added that he seldom left his local parish now. Here was a man who was content in his way of life and in tune with the area in which he lived. Many Irish emigrants had left their home area over the years and never coped with the change. Lives of quiet desperation, loneliness and alcoholism were often the result. This man had the wisdom to recognise that such a life was not for him.

"I had better not keep you any longer," he said, as he shuffled back into his seat, tugged at his cap (which did not move), restarted the tractor and with a nod he headed off at a leisurely pace, down the road.

A bit farther along, I met a man who was working with cattle beside an old rusty shed. A disinterested sheepdog was lying at the side of the road – the only thing that moved in the dog were his eyes, which followed my every move. The man headed in my direction and thus another long conversation ensued. I was wondering if I would ever get to Glenties! He was another small man who had the look of bachelorhood about him. He was unshaven and dressed in an old jacket, which was tied with a rope around his waist. He told me that he had been born in a neighbouring valley but when his family were unable to take care of him he came to live with relatives here, and he has been here ever since.

"The only time I leave the area now is when I am going to the mart to deal in cattle," he informed me.

To my acute embarrassment, despite this lack of travel he knew more people in my own parish than I knew myself. It is amazing how the webs of contacts spread out across the country and indeed the globe. He said that life had been full of hard work and that along with working on the farm he had worked for years on the forestry for the mighty pay of four pounds, eighteen shillings and nine pence, (£4 18s 9d) old money. I said to him that they were stingy that they would not even give him a fiver. He laughed. Subsequently, when listening to BBC Radio 5, I heard that there was a mini crisis in the British Treasury because of the poor standard of £5 notes in circulation. It seems that people now have very little regard for £5 notes and consequently they roll them into balls and stuff them into all sorts of pockets and bags and nooks and crannies. In contrast £10 and £20 notes are folded and put into purses or wallets. My friend on the side of the road had a different perspective on £5 notes.

This man told me that the road into the Croaghs was about a quarter of a mile farther on. He was slightly unsure of its exact location. The last time that he been on that road was in the 1950s when he had to go to a wake. My initial thought was that it was amazing that somebody should live near a road and not be on it for nearly fifty years. Then I thought of all the back roads near my home, and I am sure there are some I have never been on. We are definitely creatures of habit.

He said that at that time there were a few hundred people living on the road to the Croaghs, but now there were only three or four people left, the youngest of which was about forty-five. It seemed that nobody wanted to farm in such a remote spot anymore, even though, he informed me that the holdings, were well over a thousand acres each. Not bad, I thought even if the land is poor and mountainous. It is certainly likely to improve in value in the future, given the rate of population increase on the planet and the fact that more and more people are valuing access to wilderness and semi-wilderness to a greater and greater extent. Some person will probably buy up the land and make a fortune out of it. I bade farewell to the man and as I picked up my rucksack to go, the eyes of his dog continued to follow my every move. Awareness combined with stillness is what some people say life is all about – anyway it was embodied in this dog. As it is often said that dogs resemble their owners, these were probably qualities that the man also possessed. Such attributes would serve a cattle dealer excellently I am sure.

A short while later I came to the rural equivalent of 'Spaghetti Junction'! A number of roads were heading in varying directions with no apparent indication of the right way to proceed. Which road to take? An elderly man on a Honda 50 motorbike solved the problem for me. He wanted to talk as well, and was disappointed when I did not delay. After all I did want to get to Glenties in the same day! I was finally on the road heading through the Croaghs.

This was one of the highlights of the whole journey. I had a feeling that I was entering a sacred spot, a place not only of natural beauty but meaning as well. I looked below to a beautiful valley heading into the base of the hazy Blue Stack Mountains. The Reelin River was glinting like a steel cord in the sunshine as it cut its way haphazardly through the brown, boggy terrain. The road itself tracked the river through the valley. I have thought of this road ever afterwards as 'the road where trees grow out of boulders'. Everywhere I looked there were trees perched on the top of big boulders. Their roots twisted tenuously yet insistently down the face of the boulders en route to the thin soil below, strangling the stones, like a hawk grasping its prey. On closer inspection some trees were surviving on an extremely thin layer of soil on top of the boulders, while others had forced their roots through narrow rocky crevices to the soil below. The roots of a tree on top of one of the largest boulders had followed a split through the middle of the boulder, and had probably opened the crack even wider. As I stood there and looked one could only be struck by the tenacity of these trees in adversity. I thought back to when the parent tree had dispensed it seeds across the countryside. Some seeds would have landed on open soil and some less fortunate seeds (you would think) would have landed on the top of boulders. If the parent tree could have pondered the future, little would it think that it would be the seeds that landed on top of the boulders, which would survive, prosper and grow to maturity. The grazing sheep had taken care of any of the seedlings that had dared to put up their head in the open soil below.

All the houses along this road were of similar design and construction, built of stone with a long rectangular single story design, just one room wide and set low into the hollows and contours of the hillside for shelter and protection from the elements. At one end of the house there was usually an adjoining barn or byre where the cattle would have been kept during the winter. This building usually had a window-sized hole in the gable so that manure could be easily cleaned out. This was a sunny day but one would have no difficulty in imagining that this landscape would not be such a pleasant a place to be, in the driving storms and rain. In order to further protect them from the elements, strands of misshapen sycamore trees bent by the prevailing wind sheltered all of these houses. Most of these houses are now abandoned and the children who once lived in them are scattered over the globe. I hope they all have landed on fertile soil or on top of the boulders, if that is more auspicious.

After forty minutes or so of walking along this road which had now turned into a gravel track, I saw what seemed like an old man with a bag of feed on his back making his way up the hillside. He was a bit like the Pied Piper as he was followed by a flock of sheep and three redundant sheepdogs – there must have been something really good in that bag! The bag was full and seemed heavy as he walked slowly upwards and onwards without stopping. I admired his fitness, There is nothing like treading day after day up a mountainside to keep you fit. After a while he must have sensed my eyes upon him, because he stopped, turned and looked down the mountain straight at me. One of the dogs stopped and looked as well. The sheep stopped too but didn't look down; their sole interest was the bag – they didn't know what they were missing! (Or maybe they did?) He then turned and went on his way. I think people have some innate sense that alerts them when they are being watched. We are not able to identify this sense in scientific terms as yet, but most of us have felt this uneasy feeling when under scrutiny. It makes perfect sense in evolutionary terms; in fact it would be a surprise if we did not possess this survival ability.

The walk after that was beautiful but it disappeared into a blur because of a blister on my left foot. I passed waterfalls, new valleys and small rivers until I came onto the tarred road, which led through the Glen of Glenties. Despite this attractive environment, my only concern now was to get to Glenties and get some respite for my feet. It is amazing how easily the sense of wonder and awe disappears in the face of discomfort.

Dusk had descended, a slight chill had come into the air and some parts of Nature were getting ready to shut down for the night. Birds were busy in the hedgerows and a flock of crows passed overhead heading home. There were a few cars on this road and in a moment of heresy I considered hitching a lift from them. This would have amounted to cheating of the highest order, because I had promised myself before leaving that I would not take a lift on any of the back roads during the journey. There is nothing like a bit of suffering to energise a cheating soul! The Lord must have been looking after my conscience however, because nobody stopped to offer me a lift, unlike earlier in the day. I reached Glenties in the darkness with my honour intact.

I spotted that the church was still open so I went inside. It was pleasantly warm and like many churches it had that sense of quietness and prayerful calm inside. I sat in the back pew, took off my shoes and relaxed in the quiet and the warmth. When one is tired I think one is most open to the spiritual side of ourselves, probably because we don't have the energy to be distracted. I stayed there until people started to come in for a prayer service. With that I put on my shoes and socks and left. I wonder what all the people thought of the new brand of incense in the church that night – I hope it helped them concentrate on their spiritual side!

I headed off to the comforts of home.

## Inver to Killybegs

Today the walk started in Inver, a small traditional fishing village about ten kilometres from Donegal town. Inver is one of those places that for generations has looked to the sea rather than to the surrounding harsh soils for its sustenance and survival. Experience of the sea and its moods has left a mark on the psyche of the people living here. The relationship between the people and the sea is like the life of the small fish that groom and feed off the shark or the large whale. There is the understanding that this unequal relationship could spell doom at any time.

This is a place where small boats have headed out onto uncertain seas. For well over a thousand years the ebb and flow of the sea has exerted its pull upon the people. Every year young men have set forth with excitement, exuberance and expectation upon its waves. Just as the sea enchants people with its mysteries it can also suddenly, callously consume lives as if by a fickle whim. From every generation of young men who set forth, the sea takes its quota and sometimes more.

One such day was 8th December 1904, when in the early morning a twenty-eight foot open yawl with oars set out from Inver village to fish for herring. It was called the *Evening Star* and it had a crew of seven on board. The crew were all neighbours. Their names were Peter Kennedy the skipper, his son Pat Kennedy, John Gallagher, Tom Sweeney, Charlie Keeney and the Brown brothers, James and Patrick. A sudden storm arose causing the boat to capsize. Five men were immediately lost but two held on grimly to a part of the boat and were washed ashore on the nearby headland of St Johns Point. Both survived for a short while but died later of exposure. The loss of seven people in circumstances such as this must leave a large mark on a small community. Fate always seems to play strange hands at moments such as these. One of the crew, George Rose, could not go out on that day because of illness but nineteen-year-old Pat Kennedy decided to take one last trip before he took up the job of salesman in Dublin. Thus one man was lost and one man saved by a seeming random throw of the dice.

Another disaster occurred just a few miles away, at Bruckless in 1813, where over sixty fishermen lost their lives. This disaster was attributed to the power of a witch. Bruckless was the centre of the herring fisheries for the county at that time and fishermen from all over came to work there. One night all the boats set out, but a fierce storm unexpectedly arose, destroying nearly all the boats and drowning scores of men. The blame for this was placed on a travelling woman, who had come to the area some time previously. She had made a habit of going down to the port every morning for a few herring. After a time the fishermen grew tired of giving her the fish: they all agreed that she was too demanding and would consequently get no more free fish. They told her 'to be on her way' so to speak. Little did they know that this woman was a witch! As she was banished she swore vengeance on the fleet. The next night when the fleet went out after a shoal of herring, a young girl observed the traveller woman filling a basin of water into which she put a small vessel. She then started a powerful incantation that caused the water to agitate and boil. Eventually the vessel flipped upside down in the basin. At that very moment the fleet of fishing craft was destroyed in the bay. The witch (wisely!) left the area the next morning and was never seen again. It is interesting to wonder why a poor traveller, woman who was a stranger in the area should be considered to be a witch. In a time of misfortune we all tend to blame the outsider for collective misfortune. The fact that this 'witch' was a female, living in poverty and a traveller to boot were real characteristics of an outsider.

The fate and destiny of the people left behind, after tragedies such as these, was also intimately bound up with the sea. In the future more fathers, sons, neighbours and friends would be undertaking that same journey. In order to justify taking such chances it was certainly easier to blame someone for the disaster than to cope with the possibility either that a mistake was made in going to sea on that particular night or that such a disaster could search them out again. Seafaring communities such as Inver village put a lot of effort into moderating and explaining the power of the sea. Boats were blessed, amulets were taken on board, all in an effort to ensure good luck and good fortune. The yearly 'blessing of the boats' is still a strong tradition in the Inver area. I think the feeling is 'it will certainly do no harm anyway' to have the blessing. Rituals like this are still important in bonding people together and in reminding them that life is uncertain.

It is also natural that the sea should give rise to folk beliefs, which is a way of dealing with overwhelming and uncaring power. An example of this folk belief is that if you meet a red-headed woman on the way to fishing, it is regarded as a bad omen and one should return home immediately. Another belief is that if by chance you are on board a boat you should never whistle as it calls to the powers of the deep with unknown consequences. Within Inver village as in other fishing villages it was also considered unlucky to be able to swim, because such obvious mistrust would provoke the anger of the sea. Fishermen often felt that knowing how to swim would potentially make crew careless and cause more accidents. It is interesting to note that only one person on the boat in the 1904 shipwreck could swim.

Out of trouble there springs strength. According to a cousin of mine, Cora Herrity, Inver is still a very close-knit community, a place where every door is still open to neighbours and passers-by. If you are a neighbour you do not have to knock to enter, you just walk on in and take the place as you find it. It is a place where if you run short of something you ask a neighbour rather than running to the shop. A close-knit community such as this is shaped out of adversity. The sea seeps into the stories and music of this place, it gives expression to the joys and sorrows of people's experience and gets its outward celebration in the traditional music and storytelling festival held in the village every year. Music holds a resonance for the people here, a sharing of experience and meaning. As Ludwig van Beethoven said, "Music is the mediator between the spiritual and the sensual life".

This world is now of course draining away. The large boats have mopped up the fish farther out at sea leaving little for the small fisherman. As I looked out over Inver bay, I saw lines of salmon and trout farms owned not by fishermen but by business interests. Small boats with divers on board now head out to these cages to feed the captive fish. Some people argue strongly that these farmed fish pollute the surrounding area, and fish that escape from the cages destroy the genetic knowledge of the wild fish.

At the edge of the village, I looked across at the scenically situated monastery that was originally founded in St Colmcille's time by St Naul. This is situated on a nook of the river and looks out over the small estuary to the sea. It is said that St Naul had to get the permission of St Colmcille to be able to build his monastery here. St Naul certainly had an eye for location. The walls of the monastery are now crumbling, and the surrounding area is peppered grey with gravestones. On leaving the village I met a local man who had spent a lot of his life working on voluntary groups for the good of the community. He was in his late fifties with a strong thatch of grey hair, but his main characteristic was a boyish enthusiasm for life. He bubbled up with ideas on how to improve life within this community; his eyes held the hope of an idealist who had not yet surrendered to the call of cynicism or apathy. He told me of his plans to get the pier upgraded, to improve the physical infrastructure of the village, to make safe the old walls of the monastery and to organise fishing trips for tourists. This was a total grand vision of how this community might move forward. As one way of life ebbs away, maybe a new one is flowing in?

The first person I met after Inver village was a woman on a bicycle. She nodded a friendly greeting as she passed by. She then meandered at a slow rate into the distance in front of me, until she faded out of sight. She was obviously not obsessed by any modern notion of speed, because I estimated that if I walked harder, I might have been able to keep up with her. I contrasted this with my own attitude to riding a bicycle. The consumerist culture is very evident in my life as a leisure cyclist. I have all the gear – a lightweight bike with more gears than is possible to use, 'Bollé' cycling glasses, gloves, jackets, shorts, helmets and any other contraption you can think about. In fact I am a living advert for the fitness industry, the only drawback being that I don't get paid for it and I am not very fit. When not riding with the club I am pushing myself to the limit (well nearly anyway) in order to keep up a fast tempo and in order of course to look good. It would be a blow to my pride to be seen riding a bicycle at a slow rate. It is also a matter of pride to race any tractors that are on the road, and to try and break the speed limit through towns – helped immeasurably by the fact that there are steep descents through some of them. The appearance of a person on a racing bicycle is also an immediate challenge to any young person in a town on a bicycle. Once they see you they take off after you shouting appropriate war cries. If they see you coming in the distance they will head off in front of you pedalling as fast as they can to see how long they can stay in front of you. I remember once

I was cycling through a small town and much to my dismay a man riding a bicycle with a pair of wellingtons passed me. His head was down between the handlebars and his legs were going round like billy-o. I told everyone I was taking it easy that day, as after all one needs recuperation time!

I realise now I should have been looking at how older people, generally, ride bicycles. Not for them the mad frantic revolution of the wheels. Rather, the bicycle is used as a glorified walking stick, or indeed as a type of container truck. I know one man who takes his bicycle everywhere, but only rides it going downhill. In fact he never bothers to throw his leg over the bar; he stands on one pedal and lets the bike freewheel for him. On the bike he carries all sorts of things: bales of hay; buckets of nuts for animals or indeed even the shopping. Another man I know cycles around using an old yellow construction hat as a cycling helmet. As often as not he has a flower in his hand, freshly plucked from the countryside, which he gives to the first eligible woman he meets. The combination of a yellow hat and a red rose is I am told a near irresistible combination. If he added in a box of chocolates he would be guaranteed success every time!

On the remote, small roads lying between Inver and Glenties I passed a lot of old houses that have been converted into byres for cattle. The roofs of these houses, which were originally thatched, are replaced by rusted tin. Outside the front doors, there were usually clumps of daffodils, which were persistently poking their heads through cattle manure and hoof marks. The daffodils, those sprigs of colour in the landscape, are a reminder of how people tried to make the best home from what little they had. It was recognition that aesthetics in life were important and it was a symbol of hope for a better future around the corner.

A person cannot walk the back roads of Ireland and not come into contact with dogs in all their shapes, forms and attitudes. Almost every house has a dog, and there is usually a cacophony of noise when you approach. A message is then seemingly passed on from one house to the next. The first dog that I met on this day was a part-Alsatian who advanced towards me with his tail held high in the air. I cursed myself for having forgotten for once my big, stout holly stick. I had always been told not to show fear to a dog, and to keep on walking as if you don't have a worry in the world. It was also said that you have to watch most closely the dog that approaches you from the rear and does not bark at all; they are supposedly the most dangerous and unpredictable. I suppose they are a bit like people, in that it is the ones that threaten you all the time are the ones least likely to cause you bother. This dog was not barking and the position of his tail in the air told me that he was having aggressive feelings towards me. However as I got closer to him, the tail lowered somewhat. Did I even notice a slight wag? I now figured he was not all that bad, though I wasn't prepared to trust that judgement too far. I pressed on and went past the dog. As I did so the dog came in behind me and followed me.

'Oh, oh,' I thought to myself.

I looked closely at him and still figured that he was all right, even though I would not like to be the person to startle him suddenly, as he might react aggressively. We then walked down the road together as if we were literally glued together, with his nose stuck in my calf as he sniffed some interesting odour or other. After a while he gave up and triumphantly trotted back to his own territory to see if there were any other interlopers whom he might be interested in intimidating.

Later in the midst of the hills I came across a stretch of road on which there were a lot of thatched houses. I had thought that this type of house had more or less disappeared from the landscape. These houses were still inhabited and were unusual in that they were not tourist cottages. The thatch roof is nearing extinction because of the obvious bother in re-thatching, and also because of the increasing difficulty in getting adequate insurance at a reasonable price. This is another piece of evidence that the conforming forces of globalisation are in full swing. The insurance industry, the banks and investment houses are determining the shape of our lives by controlling the spaces in which we live.

One of the thatched houses had a byre, with a midden outside it. This midden lay directly in front of the door, a reminder of times gone by. The roof of this house was sagging and in urgent need of repair. I had a sudden urge to go into photograph snapping mode. I resisted this temptation however, when I remembered how in my youth people laughed at Yanks taking photographs of thatched houses. What possessed me that I would now consider doing the same thing! Had I lost touch altogether with my background? (I sneaked a photograph later, unknown to myself!)

I remember my father coming home one evening after helping a neighbour with the hay. A number of people were visiting in the house that night, and my father started telling them a story about Yanks taking photographs. Seemingly earlier that day some American tourists were driving along a road in the neighbourhood when they came across a donkey grazing on the long acre. On seeing the donkey they stopped the car, got out and cajoled the donkey to put his head in through the window of the car. They then took photographs of the donkey in this ignominious position. The trouble only started then, because the donkey having being bribed by biscuits to cooperate, was strangely reluctant to take his head back out again. Obviously the grass was not as sweet as the biscuits. A whole night's entertainment was conjured out of this image.

Another person then told the story of Yanks that visited the local tweed shop in search of a tweed hat to take home as a present. The shop owner was delighted to see them coming, and he brought out all his very best hats, displaying them proudly on the counter. On seeing these hats, the customer was distinctly unimpressed, because he considered the price to be very cheap, and therefore he surmised that the quality must be suspect. The American visitor asked if there were any more expensive hats that he could look at. The shop owner thought for a moment, and said he might have the very thing for him. With that he went upstairs and took out another hat of the same quality as those on the counter. He doubled the price on it and brought it down to our American friend. He told him it was the *crème de la crème* (or words to that effect) of hats and it was the only one that was left. The price was agreed and both parties went away extremely happy. The one thing that local people of my parents' generation really resented was visitors taking photographs of people who were considered to be 'characters'. A 'character' in this instance was usually a person who was drunk, never washed himself or his clothes and had maybe one tooth in his head, which of course was stained brown from chewing tobacco. If he was generally agreeable and was trying to sing that was a bonus.

All these stories coloured my perception of American people until I went to the States a good number of years later and found out that these selfsame Yanks in fact are among the most generous people on Earth. I suppose that in retrospect the idea of people taking photographs of 'characters', houses and donkeys and things like that had a slightly uncomfortable feel to it. It felt as if these visitors were sentimentalising our poverty and consequently belittling us as people. They of course probably thought that they were experiencing authentic Irish culture. The trouble was it was a culture everyone was trying to get away from at the time. Now Irish people go abroad: and what do they do? They take photographs of everything that they think is unusual. They go mad taking photographs of 'characters', camels, shacks, monkeys, donkeys, people working on the land etc., etc. The camera is always on hand, for the more cultures we can capture on it, the supposition is the more interesting we are as people. What do these people think about us, with our obsession for taking photographs and video footage? Do they feel resentful or angry? The wise ones of course charge tourists for the privilege.

The walk for the next two hours went through hilly countryside, consisting of seeming endless heather, conifer plantations and sheep. Cresting a hill, I suddenly stopped and blinked in surprise, when confronted by a most unexpected sight. I stood as if transported to the Riviera or to the Algarve. Situated in front of me was a large caravan park laid out in neat rows, into a heathery hillside. Of course unlike the Algarve there was a not a person to be seen in the whole place. Such an incongruous sight! What mad optimist would locate a caravan site in the middle of nowhere on a remote hillside in the rainiest part of Ireland? Then again, I thought, maybe it will be the coming thing. Maybe people don't always want to be surrounded by the sea and a myriad of other facilities. Maybe they want to relax in the mountainy, midge-infested, wet Donegal countryside?

Some years earlier the same charge of 'madness' was levelled at a Swiss man who built a hotel a few miles from this spot, on what everyone considered to be a swamp, in the middle of nowhere. This swamp just happened to be situated beside a beautiful lake, surrounded by the Blue Stack Mountains. All the locals agreed that he was mad and there was much nudging and winking.

"More money than sense," everyone said.

His subsequent success just goes to show you that a definition of madness is limited by other people's perceptions and understanding. This hotel has now become the 'in spot' for weddings and meals in the area and also caters for the luxury end of the tourist market. A scenic spot in the middle of nowhere is its main selling point. There is also the story of a hotel in the west of Ireland: when marketing in the Middle East, it guaranteed to all the guests who came to stay that it would rain during their stay. If it didn't rain they would get their money back. What an ingenious idea! If other people sell on the basis of guaranteed sun, why can't we sell on the basis of guaranteed rain!

Leaving the caravan site aside, the most interesting thing around was sheep. One of them said *Maaah*. I said *Maaah* back. Suddenly there erupted a chorus of *Maaah*s. This is what solitude does to one, I thought. I was supposed to be freeing the mind, tapping into the unconscious rhythm of life etc., etc. What was I doing then, communicating with sheep? The worst thing was the fact that they seemed to understand me! As I went on I tried out different tones and lengths of *Maaah*. The answers came back, and the more you listen to sheep bleating, the more you recognise their individual voices and accents. Some were high-pitched, some were deep and others were what only could be described as rough.

As a boy, one of the things that fascinated me was the fact that everyone had their own distinctive, unique voice shaped out of a melting pot of family, locality, language, culture, history and race. I could tell the identical twins who lived next door apart by the sound of their voice. It seems now, that the same applies to the myriad of creatures that surround us. The world is filled with these unique voices; the sheer scale of this is mind-blowing. The song of the thrush that we listened to last year is not the same as the one we listen to this year. We just haven't learned to spot the difference.

Later in the day as the sun started to disappear behind a nearby mountain, a low musical humming noise came to me on the wind. It seemed that it was coming from a lone hawthorn tree at the side of the road. In my childhood hawthorn trees were considered to be places full of magic. It was often said, semi-jokingly by my father's generation, that these trees enjoyed the protection of the Fairies. Having also heard that fairies often play enchanted music under these trees, I decided to investigate further. The only clue to be found was a piece of sheep wire attached to the tree. It seemed possible upon investigation that the humming was coming from its vibration against the tree – though to be truthful I could not be sure. In the middle of the world's deserts there are some sand dunes that emit a humming noise and despite intense scientific investigation no scientific explanation has been found for this phenomenon. Holy men or shamen have for thousands of years regarded these spots as centres of religious experience and healing energy. Listening to the sound of this tree, a truly brilliant(!) Zen paradox came into my mind:

"Is it the wind or the tree that creates the humming sound?"

There probably was some little fairy there, blowing hard on a miniature trumpet, or rubbing the wire with his fiddle bow and shouting in his loudest voice:

"It's neither the wind or the tree, it's me. It's me."

It is funny how fairies have suddenly become invisible; they get little credit for anything now, such as the abduction of babies and children or the stealing of milk and butter. Everyone believes every strange event now is caused by extra-terrestrial beings from the other side of the galaxy.

If you are driving along a country road late at night and see strange lights shooting across the sky, you can ponder on how long it may have taken these extra-terrestrials to get here just to see you! All in all, I think, we would be as likely to encounter fairies as extra-terrestrial beings.

When I was building my house I hired a man to do some excavation work with a digger. I told him to avoid touching an old hawthorn tree that was growing directly behind the house. He replied that he had no intention of going near it, because he had a bad experience when tampering with a hawthorn tree in the past. Intrigued, I asked what happened. He told me that he was once clearing scrubland, rather ironically in order to prepare this land for forestry. During this operation he came across a single hawthorn tree in the middle of the field. He did not think much about this, until the bucket on the digger touched it and there was a sudden flash of flame and smoke out of the engine of the digger. He said that he did not go back near the tree as someone told him that it was a fairy tree. They left the tree there and planted the forestry around it. I wonder how this tree is doing now in the midst of all that forestry? I hope it is getting enough space and light in order to survive.

The road finally meandered into Killybegs, which is Ireland's largest fishing port. It is said that there are more millionaires to be found in Killybegs per head of population than in anywhere else in Ireland. About two miles outside the town I saw one of the biggest private houses I have ever seen. I stopped for a while and endeavoured to count the number of windows to the rear of the building. I tried three times and got three different answers. My headmaster in National School would have been ashamed of me, after all the effort he took instilling mental arithmetic skills in my brain! Taking an average, there were in the region of thirty-five windows to be seen. I didn't bother trying to count the number of windows in the rest of the house as my brain had enough for one day.

Killybegs is a natural harbour and has been consequently associated with the sea from earliest times. The Saint associated with the town is St Catherine, patron saint of seafarers, who died in Egypt in the fourth century. Killybegs has been associated with St Catherine since the sixth century and there is a holy well dedicated to her in the town. This well is still used by people looking for divine intercession. She has not disappointed over the years, with many cures attributed to her.

Before conquest by the British, Killybegs was a trading port with Spain and France and was also attacked by pirates at various stages of its history. After the defeat of the O'Donnell clan by the British at the beginning of the seventeenth century, arrangements were made by the conquering forces to bolster the defences of Killybegs due to its strategic importance. It became one of the 'garrison' towns of the north west and officially became a Borough under the 'Plantation of Ulster'. The Corporation of the Borough according to T.C. McGinley was: 'To consist of a provost, twelve Burgesses, and a commonality of cottagers and other inferior inhabitants'!!

Was the establishment of this Corporation an effort towards achieving democracy? I asked myself. As long as one agreed with the powers-that-be, was the answer. We would never use a phrase that included the words 'inferior inhabitant' nowadays. However the reality may not have changed as much as we suppose because power, control and influence is still vested in the few to the exclusion of the majority. All that has changed is the definition of the ruling class and the type of language they use.

After Independence in 1922 Killybegs grew to become the biggest fishing port in the country. Killybegs is now also the home port of the largest fishing vessel in the world. The *Atlantic Dawn* was built in Norway. It was greeted with great fanfare in its home port before it sailed to fish off the coast of Africa. The local population were invited on board to have a look; parties were held in the town, there was free booze and politicians arrived with their entourages and made grand speeches about how all of this was a symbol of progress. Their crew have become the latest additions to the jet-set age as they are flown out there, from Ireland to work their stints on board.

There are of course a number of ironies about Ireland having this huge boat. The first is that for years we used to complain that the big Russian trawlers used to hoover up our fish and leave small pickings for local people. Now we are inflicting the same circumstances on the people of an African country. The local small fishermen of Mauritania are finding it increasingly difficult to make a living. Short-term gain for some people in Mauritania will lead to destitution for many. The second is that the big trawlers in the Irish fleet are driving the smaller trawlers out of business because the big trawlers get the bulk of the quota of fish allowed by the European union. The reality is of course, that more and more of these huge trawlers are being built to chase fewer and fewer fish. Traditionally popular fish such as cod and haddock are in danger of being wiped out. The European Union regularly puts a quota on the number of fish of a particular species that can be caught, in an effort to preserve these species for future generations. What happens in practice, according to a fisherman friend of mine, is that when such fish are caught they are dumped dead back into the sea. This enables the boat to stay within quota but does nothing to preserve fish stocks. We have a lot to learn from the Icelandic fishing industry, which is closely monitored and ensures that all fish caught, are landed. Of course Iceland's wellbeing as a nation depends on their collective care of their fish stocks, which is a great advantage in ensuring preservation and ecological balance. Within the EU the ethic is 'catch as much as you can because if you don't somebody else will'. This is short-termism at its worst. As fish become scarcer the boats head into deeper and deeper waters fishing for new and to our eyes strange species of fish. One of the popular fish now being landed is the 'orange roughy'. This deep-water fish lives for one hundred years or more. They mature late and consequently have low reproductive rates. This means that they are extremely susceptible to over-fishing and no doubt these fish too will be endangered in the near future. In the meantime new fish will appear on our menus such as blue ling, siki shark, redfish and black scabbard – enjoy it while you can! The long-term outlook for fishing around our coasts is bleak indeed.

Bigger boats have also meant that fishermen spend longer out at sea. Many fishermen are gone months at a time from home which means that a lot of the families are virtually lone parent families for long stretches of time. When they come back to shore it is often not easy for fishermen to integrate back into the daily family routine, as a different structure will be established in their absence.

I went into the Bayview Hotel in the Killybegs main street for a coffee. There were not too many people about, just one other couple having a pot of tea. There were certainly no fishermen at the bar drinking. The manager of the hotel kept us going in conversation, obviously hoping that a few more people would come in, if only to relieve the boredom. After finishing my coffee I walked down to the harbour in the town to have a look at what boats were tied up at the pier. As usual the gulls were flying in squadrons overhead. Killybegs is the only place I know where no matter the weather it is advisable to bring an umbrella with you. It would be useful if you had another implement to ward off the articulated trucks, which also congregate here to carry fish all over Ireland and the Continent.

Killybegs is recognised by 'twitchers' (people who, to my mind, who have an unhealthy obsession with observing birds) as the main port of call for seagulls in Europe. Hence there are often conferences and seminars in the town where the ins and outs and ups and downs of bird watching are discussed in detail. A few years ago a Thayer's gull normally resident on the west coast of Canada appeared here for a while, much to the excitement of bird watchers on this side of the pond. The residents looked on in amazement as bird watchers from all over Europe arrived to get a glimpse of this rare specimen. Well, I suppose whatever turns you on. To me one gull looks much the same as another! These gulls of course all come to Killybegs for a free lunch. The free lunch in this instance comes from two sources. One is the abundant supply of fish and the other is the raw sewage being pumped into the bay. The bird watchers are up in arms because there is a proposal to set up a new sewage treatment plant in Killybegs, which will curtail the supply of food to our feathered friends. The other unintended consequence of this reduction in food and consequently in the number of gulls will be a sharp increase in heating bills for factories and any houses along the shoreline. It seems that seagull droppings make excellent roof insulation and also ensures that one does not easily lose slates in a storm.

I left Killybegs back towards Bruckless by a back road. The entrance to the road bordered the shoreline that was covered in layers of rubbish. I wondered why there was so much dumping there, so I resolved to ask the first person I met. This person happened to be a woman who was out for a walk. She was of medium build and had blonde hair. She also had a young child in a pushchair. I stopped and asked her about the rubbish. She rather angrily blamed it on the fishermen in the boats who, when they leave the port dump their rubbish overboard. It is then washed up onto this shore by the tide.

The landscape here was hilly, the road was up and down, my feet were sore from a long day walking and I was feeling sorry for myself. I was passing a house that was etched into the hillside when a red ball of quivering energy bounded over a hedge, onto the road, right beside me. There is nothing quite like a Red Setter that epitomises so well the notion of perpetual motion. This was a young dog perhaps a year old and like all Red Setters he was anxious to make acquaintance. He lay down on the road and then sort of crawled up to me to say hello, still quivering all over, energy seeping out in all directions. After a short enthusiastic greeting, which included an unexpected leap into the air to lick my face, the dog adopted me as a convenient companion for his walk. The road was wooded on both sides. With a bound he again cleared the ditch and disappeared noisily into the thicket. Moments later he reappeared on the road in front of me. He looked back to see if I was still coming and then after sniffing the wind for a moment he disappeared over the other ditch. This pattern went on for a while; occasionally he would come up to me to receive a quick pat before he went off again. Being experienced in the ways of Red Setters I knew there would come a point when his common sense would overcome his natural exuberance and would point him in the direction of home again. This point came after about two kilometres of walking. He finally came to a standstill beside the ruins of an old house. As I walked on he stood there and looked after me. One could see the conflict within him pulling him in both directions. He was still watching me as I disappeared down the road and around the next corner. My feet were aching when I met the Setter, but I can truly say that I never noticed my feet whilst he was with me. To me Red Setters are the greatest dogs in the world, but if you take responsibility for one you have to have loads of energy. They are truly at home when on the move in an environment which is of interest to them. They should never be kept as ornaments, which, because of their looks and colouring, they too often are. Also the owner of a Red Setter has to be able to share them with the world. They are so naturally gregarious they have a welcome for all and as in this case they will 'adopt' you if it is opportune. If you are the sort of person who wants total loyalty from a dog – don't get a Red Setter. You will only ever be the first amongst equals in their lives.

## Killybegs to Glencolmcille

Leaving Killybegs it was my objective to walk the coastal road to Kilcar, as it is one of the most beautiful coastal roads one is likely to find anywhere. This narrow scenic road twists its way up and down through the shadows of Crownarad mountain with spectacular views of the sea. From its highest point there are beautiful vistas of Ben Bulben, the Sligo Mountains across the bay and of the Blue Stack Mountains stretching in a semi-circle across the horizon. Progressing further along this road the magnificent mountain of Sliabh League unfolds its splendour before the appreciative eye.

Here the houses are hewn into the mountainside and if this place were located in the south of France or indeed in any spot where sunshine persists, these houses and fields would be worth a fortune. One could easily envisage terraces of vines layered up the slopes of the mountain. If global warming ever worked to our advantage then it could be the fashionable spot to live – however we might have to wait a few hundred years – too long for me anyway.

After ascending another steep hill I spotted below me a small deserted pier, which extended out from the rocky shore. A number of small fishing boats (punts) were pulled up onto the slipway and onto the heathery fields behind. A nearby house had a large piece of driftwood erected in the garden, which had the shape of a demented bird, at least to my untutored eye. It was situated like a sentinel alongside three large stones, which were erected in imitation of a dolmen. To complete the scene and to add a slightly eerie dimension, a solitary crow perched upon the top of this dolmen gazing out over the sea. Maybe he too was enjoying the spectacular view – why indeed should this just be the preserve of humans? The sudden sound of conversation dragged my attention to two men with a small Jack Russell dog, who were in a byre beside the side of the road examining a sheep. I got the impression that one was a vet but the only evidence I had for that observation was that he seemed to be adopting the pose of an expert, but then I suppose in any group of two there is always an expert! A sheepdog was tied to a nearby fence by a chain and looked rather disconsolately at all the activity around. I suppose he was thinking it was rather an unequal world when a Jack Russell dog could run free while he was tied up. As this was sheep country a lot of the dogs were tied up outside of houses whilst their owners were away at work. Some of them gave muffled barks or disdainful glances. There are some advantages to being a Jack Russell in the freedom stakes.

I heard the thud of metal upon rock and soil. I passed a man who was energetically digging a large hole in a field. He was down nearly at head height and all one could see was the rise and fall of the pick as he dug ever deeper. I presumed all this effort was for a purpose, but if it was, it remained a mystery to me. White houses and sheep were speckled through this vista of heather, rock, mountain and the odd green field. All around on these hills and mountains there are whole, vast landscapes of rock, which have been stripped of their peat and laid bare over the aeons. In other places big boulders and rocks emerge out of the remaining fields like a crop in bloom. In the distance sheep and rocks are sometimes indistinguishable. If it doesn't move it is probably a rock.

On the way into Kilcar I was in a bit of a quandary about which was the best way to go to the next village. The road was really quiet, there was no one to be seen and all the houses had their doors closed; it seemed as if there was no one around from whom I could ask directions. I eventually spotted a man who was walking with a rolling gait towards me. As he came nearer I saw that he was a man in his fifties, with a strong crop of grey hair. He carried his rather large stomach, by leaning backwards as if carrying a bag of cement. He audibly puffed along.

I stopped in front of him and asked the best way to Carrick village. With a vague wave of his arm he told me to follow the road and to be sure and keep left all the way. If I had followed his directions God knows where I would have ended – I don't think it would have been in Carrick anyway. We passed a few pleasantries about the weather.

"This country has gone to the *f..k*," he suddenly announced. "The only thing anyone is interested in is money!"

I perked up my ears, thinking that I was going to hear some strong thoughts on the impact of the Celtic Tiger on our quality of living. Was this a conscientious objector to the materialistic way of life? Maybe he was going to talk about how greedy people are nowadays, and how little time they have for each other. I was just going to ask about this.

"One hundred Euro will buy you nothing these days," he vehemently exclaimed, "and a pint costs €3 10c. You can't live on the dole at those prices."

It seemed the main factor in determining the adequacy of his income was the cost of a drink. This burst of heartfelt energy seemed to leave him breathless, so I stepped into the breach, agreeing that three Euro and ten cents was an awful price for a pint, and it was a given fact that the pub owners were making a fortune at our expense. Having caught his breath again, he proceeded to tell me about most of his drinking exploits and binges (when drink of course was obviously cheaper!). After filling me in about his (numerous) escapades, he fixed me with a steady gaze, and delivered a grand account of what he regarded as the pinnacle of his drinking achievements.

"One night about twenty-five years ago," he said, hitching up his trousers, "a friend of mine and I drank three bottles of poitín and a bottle of vodka."

He let that sink in for a moment before continuing.

"After that, at about three in the morning we went to a wake house to get more drink, and we stayed there until the man was taken for burial – two days later!" He laughed out loud with the memory. "Those days are gone now," he said rather mournfully.

It was his belief that wakes now seem to be but pale imitations of the wakes long ago. To cheer him up, I recollected the times that my wife used to get bottles of poitín, which we drank together at parties with some of our friends. A comradely look emerged into his eyes and he immediately quizzed me about where she had got the poitín and how much it cost.

"Nobody makes poitín around here any more," he said, rather forlornly.

I told him that my wife was from Tipperary and that she got the poitín from a neighbour for nothing. I really had grabbed his interest now.

"Is your wife still around?" he asked.

Seeing the drift of the conversation I explained to him that, once I got married, the flow of poitín dried up. He looked at me knowingly. His demeanour showed that he had the implicit understanding that once you married a woman, life changed utterly, usually to a man's disadvantage. The sparkle went out of the conversation after this and we went our respective ways.

Four cars came snaking in a row towards me. Wow! This narrow back road had suddenly become busy. I stood in on the grass verge to let the traffic go by. As each driver passed he acknowledged me in a customary rural way; a momentarily raised index finger from the steering wheel, accompanied simultaneously by a slight nod of the head. A Land Rover with a trailer, which was going in the same direction as myself, pulled into a lay-by behind me to let this convoy of vehicles pass. When they had all gone, the round-faced, moustachioed driver drew up beside me, rolled down the window and asked if I wanted a lift. His eyes were engaging and generous but at the same time probing. This farmer, I thought to myself was well practised in the art form of friendliness and information harvesting. I thanked him for stopping and told him I was walking for my sins. He laughed cast his eyes to the heavens and reckoned, in that case, he should be walking himself. Then, of course, ignoring his new-found insight, he drove on off up the road.

I walked through Kilcar village; I was tempted to go into the Tír Boghaine office to say hello to work colleagues. I resisted the temptation however as I thought 'I am trying to get a change of scene'. The Tír Boghaine project is a community project in south-west Donegal, which endeavours to establish vibrant social networks in the community. The project is named after an old chieftain from the fifth or sixth century called Boghaine. He was one of the sons of Niall of the Nine Hostages, who was responsible according to legend of capturing a young lad called St Patrick and taking him into slavery, thus instituting more changes than he bargained for. Anyway the county of Donegal was divided between Niall's seven sons and the part that Boghaine got became known as Tír Boghaine – the country of Boghaine.

I ascended a steep hill out of Kilcar. This road later turned into a track that was ideal for hiking. I came back onto a small road and after a while I sat down on a large rock near a house for my lunch. A man appeared at the door of the house with a dog behind him. He looked at me with a non-engaging curiosity and then, seemingly satisfied that I was not an obvious threat, he went back into the house. A piece of my sandwich fell on the ground. I looked down between my feet at the heathery humps and I saw a whole new world there. Here was a miniature world of scaled down mountains, forests and lakes, which was teeming with all sorts of weird and wonderful creatures that roamed there. These creatures usually had many legs, tough armour and fierce expressions. In this world, other large creatures buzzed about, above the heathery tree line before settling and resting in those trees. If disturbed, whole armies of various shapes and colours would rise and fly out. This was a world prone to fierce cataclysms as immense forces from above (my footstep) compressed whole mountain ranges. Lakes could be displaced in the blink of an eye and all creatures had to be continuously alert for danger. A sudden unnatural darkening of the sky was usually an omen of cataclysmic change. The only thing to be done was to curl up and hope that the force did not descend on you. Sometimes when confronted by the power of Nature, one feels like this. If you are hiking in the mountains or kayaking in the sea you realise that one chance event could in an instant snuff out your life. In some ways it heightens the experience of living.

I came into Carrick, which is a small village best known as the access point for Sliabh League. On the same road out of Carrick is another small village called Teelin, though 'village' might be too strong a word. There has been a lot of dissension over the last few years between some people in Teelin and other people in Carrick over fishing rights. One group has been granted the angling rights to the river; another group reckons though that this arrangement interferes with their traditional fishing rights. They feel that they have fished the river and estuary for generations and how dare anyone try to interfere with or regulate their access. The resultant feud has split the community. In some ways this is fairly typical of small village Ireland, usually bristling with deep-seated animosities towards their nearest neighbours.

On the main street in Carrick a woman was sitting on a seat. Beside her a little girl of about three or four years was busy playing trying to put a toy in a box. A man in overalls was sitting in a car, with the door open, and with Raidió na Gaeltachta (the local Irish language radio station), blaring out across the village. Details of deaths in the locality were being announced. I presume he was carrying out a public service just in case anyone might miss the news. Outside of the car an assortment of work tools were strewn on the ground beside a broken pavement. Presumably the man was on his lunch break. He looked fairly relaxed anyway.

As I passed the woman, the little girl looked up.

"Why does that man not cut his hair?"

Her mother managed to avoid answering the question until I was at least out of earshot. I justify the following passage by saying that I was annoyed at yet another comment about my hair, especially since it is now starting to go grey and, even worse, to fall out.

Society is full of conformity enforcers, probably necessarily so if we are to survive as a civilisation. Children however are amongst the most enthusiastic 'conformity enforcers'; they take to it with a real relish, focusing in on any point of difference. I have always thought that we have too sentimental a view of childhood. The image of innocent little darlings cuts little ice with me, and in fact I think it is slightly patronising to think of children in this way. We should treasure them as complex beings full of the same attributes as ourselves.

Hair was always an issue for me. When I was a child I used to pray to God, to the Virgin Mary and to any saint that I thought might have any influence so that I might get, by some magical intervention, straight black hair. I admired intensely the black hair of the local tractor driver and any time he came into the house I would look enviously at his hair. My prayers were never answered, well at least not yet, for hope springs eternal – even if hair does not! I was left with a mop of fair curly hair that I never succeeded in taming. The nearest my hair ever got to being tamed was by the Salesian priests in boarding school. Every few weeks the barber would come to the school. It was then a battle of wits between the priests and the boys, who would endeavour to go into hiding until the barber left. Any announcement of the barber coming to the school near holiday time used to cause all sorts of trauma, as it would certainly not be cool to be parading around in short hair during our holidays. This was the time when long hair and more to the point, long locks were the height of fashion.

The time we were most vulnerable was at study time in the evening, as it was not possible to evade the vigilant priest who took great pleasure in searching out the hairy deviants. The fact that he was bald himself, I am sure had nothing to do with his fanatical approach! When the barber was there you never saw such an avid bunch of students in your life. Each one would be totally engrossed in work, elbows on desk, head cradled in both hands, collars worn high covering any stray locks, eyes glued on book and ears listening for the footsteps of the conformity enforcing priest as he rounded up the last victims. One dreaded the hand on the shoulder, followed by a wordless indication that you were for the chop. When you met the priest the next day, he would invariably comment that the barber had "not taken half enough off you". As I disappeared around a corner, out of the village I wondered what the little child's mother said in reply to her question. Was she a proponent of conformity or diversity?

From now on the mountain slopes of Sliabh League dominate this part of the walk. Sliabh League is recognised as one of the beauty spots of south Donegal and is famous for claiming the highest sea cliffs in Europe. It is also one of Ireland's three holy mountains, along with Croagh Patrick and Mount Brandon.

However on the walk the part of Sliabh League that is visible is not the sea cliffs but the extensive land-facing slopes of the mountain that are at times dark and threatening and at other times soft and sensual. This depends upon the play of light, cloud and shadow on the gradients. This is one of my favourite places and I have often walked its slopes. It was here that I introduced my children to mountain hiking, though I am not sure that I would recommend cliff walking with children as a pastime for nervous protective parents (which I am). The first time that Cróna my youngest child climbed it (aged four) she surprised me with a burst of speed near the top and nearly stepped over the side.

It also has a special memory for me in that it was the place that I brought my friend Paul who was suffering from motor neurone disease. Paul and I grew up and went to primary school together. He was a great sportsman and athlete and in fact in his youth he would run up mountains for sport. He neither smoked nor drank in his life and he was a picture of fitness. After college he went to live in the States and became a professor of epidemiology in the University in Minneapolis. He was diagnosed with motor neurone disease in his early forties: for such an active person this must have been the prospect of hell on earth. However he turned the illness into a positive experience for all those around him. and fully engaged with life and living until the moment of his death. This was helped immensely by the support he got from his family, neighbours and friends in Minneapolis. We pride ourselves on our community life in Ireland, but I can honestly say that the greatest example of community life I have seen was in the so-called 'materialistic United States' where Paul lived. Neighbours and friends were there twenty-four hours a day when needed.

One of the only mountains in Donegal he had not climbed was Sliabh League. On a visit home a few years after his diagnosis he asked me if I would accompany him on the climb. We started up the pilgrimage route, which goes up the land side of the mountain to the top. Even though his legs were weak he battled his way upwards. His was a spirit that would not be quenched. His was a remarkable determination – a determination that would achieve the maximum out of his body for as long as he could. When we got to the top we were blessed with sunshine and a still air. This is one of the great views of dramatic cliff scenery one is likely to get anywhere. Far below the seagulls circled above the glimmering sea. They were rising and descending on invisible currents of air. A small fishing boat was near to the rocks, two thousand feet below. On a day like this I thought what better way than to spend your life as a fisherman. Then I thought of the other three hundred and sixty four days when winds howled and rain came out of the heavens. Paul sat there and pointed out all the areas around. He loved to be able to figure out the names of all the visible headlands, islands and mountains. This was a new perspective on the landscape, and sharing moments like this is a way of rekindling friendship. This place was something beyond and greater than both of us and we would be joined forever in a shared mutual awe of this place.

On the way down we came across a little lamb beside a rock. On impulse Paul lifted this tremulous new life into his arms. I teased him that the lamb now may have bonded with him, as he may have been the first living thing that the lamb had seen.

"You will have to adopt her," I said.

The lamb and Paul both took the prospect of this seriously until the ewe arrived. The lamb then scuttled off to get real sustenance and meaningful attention and we beat a hasty retreat in case the ewe got real annoyed.

Sliabh League was also the place that I came to see the first light of the new millennium. I failed spectacularly in convincing my family to get up in the middle of the night so that we could climb the mountain in order to celebrate that first dawn. Fired with the hype about the millennium I headed off by myself. I again climbed up by the pilgrimage path, which is relatively safe, until one gets near to the top. I got to three-quarters of the way up the mountain in loads of time only to be confronted by a line of mist, which clung to the mountain. As I went through it the starlight disappeared. I now faced a choice. Stay below the mist and see the coming of the dawn or proceed to the top and risk falling off the cliffs or being stranded up there until the mist cleared. I decided to go to the top because it would not be the same to welcome the dawn halfway up a mountain especially on the land side. As I climbed higher the mist got thicker and became nearly impenetrable. I climbed on until I had to leave the path and head for the summit. As I climbed the last part I formed small triangular mounds of stones to act as markers for me in the mist and to enable me to retrace my steps. I had enough experience on mountains to know that mist is potentially lethal, especially on cliff faces where to go the wrong way is not to be advised. Using this laborious method I finally got to what I judged to be the top. As I got there the sound of the sea and the slightest of breezes welcomed me. I got as high as I could, then I sat down brought out my flask and sandwich and waited for the dawn. I am not sure that I saw the dawn but the mist became increasingly grey. However at no time could I see more than a few yards in front of me. There was no chance of seeing the sunrise but I would not have swapped my position with anyone. There is something magical and otherworldly about mist, something that contains the hint of other realms. Up there the only hint I had of any other existence or reality was the murmur of the sea far below. There trapped in that world I welcomed in the new millennium.

Every time I go to walk on Sliabh League I take some food and water with me in case I step on one of those dreaded hunger spots on the mountain. These places can be identified by circular piece of light green grass where it is said that people died during the famine. If you step on one of these spots then you are seized by the terrible hunger experienced by the person who died here. If you don't have some food with you, you too will die of the hunger. I have never stepped on one of these spots yet but one never knows!

There are two roads into Glencolmcille. I took the road that goes via Malinmore. This passed by the gentler aspect of Sliabh League where the slopes are more sensual and rounded. After a while walking along this road what struck me most forcibly was the absolute quietness of the place. There were no sounds from machines or traffic, just the sounds of Nature. I did not feel alone however. There was a sense that as I was watching the landscape, it was watching me. Watching something is not a one-way process: it is a relationship. I stopped to eat a sandwich and chose a perch overlooking the lake, which had as a backdrop the slopes of Sliabh League. The water of the lake viewed from above had small ripples in it, forming ever-changing, interweaving designs. In the centre of the lake a large group of birds flurried about, obviously energised about something important – food or maybe even sex. In the distance all their activity was silent to me.

From this vantage point I had a view of the road for a few miles in every direction. In the distance I spotted something moving towards me. I watched it coming until I could see and hear that it was a quad bike. There were two shapes on board, a burly man with a dog (obviously the navigator) sitting beside him. It reminded me of one of those cartoons featuring a dog riding a motorcycle, complete with helmet, goggles and up to no good. I saluted him (the man), but he just looked at me with no acknowledgement. He was probably thinking, 'Who is that mad idiot out in the middle of nowhere?'

I am sure he didn't think I was from Donegal anyway. Probably some daft German or Australian I could hear him think. It's a wonder the skills you can get when out walking: mind-reading is certainly one of the most entertaining ones around.

I walked down over a field to the next small lake I came to, and stood there for a while listening to the sounds of Nature. I stepped onto a large flat stone at the edge of the lake and looked down into the water. I saw a fragmented image of myself staring back. This image did not live up to my self-perception, but was an image full of ripples and disturbance.

Was that really me staring back through those ripples or was it a different 'me' entirely? Did it reflect some different aspect of myself, which is usually hidden? What happens when one looks at a mirror image of oneself? When you raise your right hand, the image lifts its left hand; the mirror, it seems, does not know its left hand from its right hand. Then I wondered; if a mirror reflects left as right, why it does not reflect images upside down as well? Maybe that is just the preserve of soupspoons. It would be great in the morning to get up and have an upside-down image to help shaving under the chin, though I have some acquaintances who swear they see themselves upside down in the morning anyway. There could be other mirrors for seeing yourself back-to-front and mirrors which reflect the inside out. These last mirrors would do away with our need for psychologists, psychiatrists, and all New Age therapies. We could have our daily dose of painful self-examination along with our cold shower first thing in the morning.

I looked into the lake and again saw the ripples crossing my image, changing it, transforming it, or maybe then again all I was seeing was my wrinkles. 'Hold on,' I thought, 'that ripple has stolen part of me and is escaping…come back, come back and return to me my past.'

On the road, near to Malinmore, I met a woman out for a walk. She was pushing a child in a buggy and had a boy about seven years old in tow. She looked to be in a bad humour. It brought back to me a description my mother would often use – "she had a face on her that would stop clocks". The woman ignored my greeting and proceeded to berate her son for walking on the grass verge of the road, which incidentally was, full of sheep droppings.

"Stop walking on that grass, you will get your shoes filthy."

With that the young boy jumped up and down on the verge, completely ignoring his mother. The one-sided argument was still raging as I went out of earshot. A short time later I turned and looked around. The mother had given up the battle and was walking in a bad-humoured way as fast as she could. The boy walked after her still on the grass verge, in an equally determined manner.

Houses now appeared in the landscape. A man was out digging in his vegetable garden. A car came up the road, whereupon the man in the garden stood up and looked to see whom it was that might be driving past. He looked after the car as it went around the corner seemingly lost in thought. This is a part of the world, where generally speaking, one will recognise the people in the cars that pass by. You could nearly see the man wondering about the people in the car: 'Where are they off to now?'

It would be equally easy to speculate that this conversation would continue in his own house at the next meal with the rest of the family. A whole dinnertime conversation could ensue from this observation. Some people might call this 'nosiness' but in rural life this information might be vital. His neighbour might have tapped into some new network or resource, which might be beneficial to him and his family. If you in turn are to benefit you have to find out the information. In a tribal society it might be a new place to collect food. In an agricultural society contact with a new market or supply source might bring benefits. Thus many work games and strategies were played out within the context and setting of friendly conversation. The next time that they meet, the man in the garden might say, 'I saw you heading up the road today?' in the hope that he might find out some piece of new information. New information was not extracted easily and such a query often received a vague reply. This charade could go on for weeks. Of course the same information and observation game is played in nearly every office in the land, where the goal is the search for power and influence. Everything is watched closely and meaning is attributed to every word and interaction.

I passed by the Malinmore Adventure Centre, turned right at the crossroads and headed towards Glencolmcille. To my back there was a small clustering of housing called Malinbeg and also Raithlin O'Beirne Island with its lighthouse in the distance. This is a small bare uninhabited island off the coast. My Uncle Kevin from Co. Clare in the south of the country used to work as a lighthouse keeper here in the 1950s. He spent months at a time out on the island with only the seagulls and the sound of the wind for company. Every time he came to do his stint on the island he used to stop off at our house to visit. He had a big motorbike on which he would rev up to the house before parking outside the front window. He would march in the front door with a roguish grin on his square face and stand in front of the fire warming his back; his big frame would seem to fill our small kitchen. If I were playing on the floor he would look down at me with a mischievous smile and push out his false teeth with his tongue. The first time he did this it must have terrified me because every time he came afterwards, he always performed the teeth ritual. He would then proceed to throw me into the air and catch me (usually) on the way down. Uncles must have these strange ways of communicating because I had another uncle who engaged in another connection ritual. Every time I met him he would shake my hand and he would then proceed to squeeze my knuckles until I grimaced sufficiently or gave up. Of course my feeble efforts to squeeze back had absolutely no effect. I had to resort on occasions to punching him in the stomach with my free hand that had the same negligible effect. Maybe there is a physical ritual of communication that men engage in which transcends words and tells boys that they belong and are important. The probability is that this type of communication would seem to be disappearing because of the greater suspicion associated with touch.

The road into Glencolmcille was full of holiday cottages and beautiful views of the sea cliffs. In front of me were the cliffs of Glen Head with a tower on top, which was built for observation purposes during the war. Behind that were the spectacular crags called 'The Sturral' which sweep vertically down to the sea. If one is to do a cliff walk in Ireland, the hike from Glencolmcille to Port via the Sturral crags is the one to do. Of course I might be biased, so you will have to find out for yourself by undertaking it. I guarantee you will not be disappointed.

Farther on I was accosted by the dirtiest-looking sheep I ever did see. Like bandits and bushwhackers they charged from the rocky hillside in my direction. I was exceedingly lucky that there was a good thick sheep wire fence between them and me; otherwise the prospect is too horrible to think about. There was one of them in particular who had a wild glint in its eye. After the wild sheep I came upon a rock that had a sound like a waterfall coming from it. It was only audible within a certain distance of the rock. This is a huge boulder that overhangs the road into Glencolmcille from Malinmore, so you cannot miss it. (Well you had better miss it if you are driving). I could not make up my mind whether the noise of water was an echo from the sea pounding into the cliffs below or whether a small stream was flowing down behind the rock from the mountain.

I must really have been suffering at this stage of the evening because two Canadian students stopped and offered me a lift in their hire car. They told me that they stopped because they took pity on me, as I was limping so much. I indignantly disputed the quality of their perception and claimed that they had been drinking too much whiskey, or God forbid something stronger. It seems they must have been spying on me because they said that they had seen me on the road earlier in the day and that I was not limping then. We got into a conversation about Colmcille and I told them some of the stories about his adventures in Glencolmcille. When I had finished and completely bored them they told me that they really loved coming to this area out of the tourist season when it was so quiet. Both of them were flying back to Canada in a week's time in order to sit their final exams.

One of them was an anthropology student. It seems that Glencolmcille is a real magnet for anthropology students, as there have been a number of books written taking it as an example of typical traditional Irish rural life. I told them to be sure and see Sliabh League. As the car disappeared into the distance my feet got sorer. I arrived into Glencolmcille some time later, went into the shop and bought a banana and a bar of chocolate. I then thumbed a lift home.

However I cannot leave Glencolmcille without some mention of the man himself, Colmcille – after all, the place is called after him. Some people dispute whether he came here at all, but I am not one of those 'Doubting Thomases'. There are a whole range of sites, folklore and traditions connected with Colmcille in the area. Just to give you a flavour of this, I mention briefly his encounter with demons in the area.

It seems that when St Patrick came to Croagh Patrick in Co. Mayo he banished the demons from there. The only trouble was that he only managed to banish them to Glencolmcille where they resided quite happily for a period. It was left to Colmcille to come to the rescue. He collected a force of his holy followers and banished the demons from here in a fierce confrontation, utilising the forces of magic and prayer to prevail. Colmcille's valet called Cearc was killed in the battle and consequently the river where the foul deed was done has been named after him. There is also a townland in Kilcar called Sraith Na Circe (field of Cearc). *Star Wars* and *Lord of the Rings* are only in the tuppence place in comparison to this confrontation. In the conflict the demons hid in thick clouds and had turned the river into a wall of fire. However Colmcille with the aid of magic drove the demons back. Then with the aid of a green stone and a bell he banished the demons onto a small rocky island off the coast. With the further aid of his holly stick, Colmcille finally banished the demons to a small rocky island off the coast. Not contented with that Colmcille then with a final wave of his sacred holly stick drove the demons into the sea and turned them into fish. This was not any old fish mind you, but one-eyed redfish, which the local fishermen afterwards knew to avoid like the plague.

Over the years however people of the area must have forgotten about demon fish, as the disagreement between the fishermen mentioned earlier has become a bitter issue in the area. The resulting disagreements have resulted in families not talking to each other. In some ways the demons have returned yet again. Like in *The Lord of the Rings* the demons hide in the wasteland, waiting for the right conditions to re-emerge. In the routine of everyday life demons are always presented with opportunities to wield influence, and they insidiously worm their way back into your daily life. You want to be a better person but it is hard to break the routine. They become very comfortable to live with and at times enjoyable. It is easier to hold on to them than waving the powerful holly stick all around you in righteous anger. Of course then there are some people who take it on themselves to banish other people's demons whether they have them or not, conveniently forgetting about their own.

# Glencolmcille to Ardara

The Irish Public Bus Service is well renowned for being a law unto itself; it is a little bit like the infamous Italian rail system before Mussolini came along.

Talking to people they say things like: 'It's never on time'; 'It takes the scenic route'; 'You can never depend on it' or 'It goes the long way round'. Stories abound of buses stopping in the middle of nowhere waiting for passengers to emerge. My intention was to get to Glencolmcille and to walk to Ardara, so with sandwiches under my arm I headed for Donegal town to catch the bus to Glencolmcille.

At the bus stop the sign told me that in springtime this bus service only operated three days a week. I panicked on seeing this, thought the worst and berated myself for not having checked the times beforehand. *Phew!* I was lucky, for on reading the notice further it said that there was a bus in fifteen minutes. The question now was whether to believe the sign, for there was no one else around. Gradually a few more lost souls gathered at the bus stop so I reckoned I was safe enough, and that the bus would turn up eventually.

The bus was only fifteen minutes late and as it pulled up beside the bus stop, a straggle of people headed towards it. The majority of people getting on the bus on this day were young women in their twenties. Amongst them an extremely thin young woman whose face was creased with worry and anxiety caught my eye. There was a deep uneasiness in her eyes.

'There are generations of pain harrowed into that face,' I thought to myself.

Sometimes, people's faces reflect not only their own sorrows, joys and preoccupations but those of their ancestors as well. Immediately she got onto the bus she put her head on the seat beside her and fell asleep in an unnatural and uncomfortable looking position.

Predictably a few latecomers came rushing. A young man with a sports bag slung over his shoulder got on board and manoeuvred his way to the back seat of the bus. A portly, ruddy-cheeked middle-aged man emerged out of the nearby hotel and rushed towards the bus in obvious fear that it would leave without him. He clambered on board with heavy footsteps.

"Is this bus for Killybegs?" he asked in a Scottish accent.

Satisfied that he was not going to end up in Galway or Dublin, he relaxed and plopped into the front seat. The last arrival was a twenty-something female in hipster jeans and a short top that revealed a slightly pudgy midriff. She sat opposite the sleeping young woman with the harrowed face, whose physical demeanour immediately aroused her concern. Leaning over, she gently shook her and showed relief when the other woman woke up and indicated that she was all right.

Even though he was already late, the bus driver satisfied himself that there were no other potential passengers by waiting another five minutes. The bus then headed off through very familiar countryside, a road that I often travel by car. One often assumes that if you view a place from the same location every day that you know that place. However on a bus you get a slightly different, elevated perspective on the world. Just as walking can give you a new way of looking at the countryside, travelling on a bus provides additional though fleeting glimpses of the landscape and impact of the people living in it. Glimpses of old sheds, private gardens, warehouses and cattle in fields all slipped by. Buses have lost a lot of their character, since the age of efficiency has exterminated the bus conductor. Conductors added to the colour and quality of our lives (well, most of them) and made buses a lot more human and safe to travel on.

When this bus reached Killybegs every other passenger got off. The girl with the worried face woke up and, acknowledging no one, headed off into her world. The bus driver got out and I watched as he headed into a local shop. I sat there feeling sort of guilty that I had a whole bus to myself. After a few minutes the driver got back in and we took off again. I wondered for a moment: if I had not been on board, would the driver have bothered going on into Glencolmcille at all that day? Being the only other person on the bus I felt that my privacy was now exposed. I considered getting up out of my seat near the back of the bus to go up and talk to the bus driver. It would have been only good manners to go and talk to him, however a lazy feeling came over me, so I sat back and looked out at the countryside instead. Perhaps the driver was also relieved that he did not have to expend energy in making conversation – or perhaps he felt that I was rude and selfish for not making the effort.

On a narrow road about two miles from the village of Carrick the bus stopped for two women in their seventies who were standing beside the gate pillar of a house. They clambered awkwardly on board, waving their free bus passes as they came and sat into the front seat, in order to pass a few words with the bus driver who obviously knew them well. These people did not hide in the cloak of privacy, they were engaging fully in the world. They both got off a few minutes later when the bus arrived in Carrick village, with their shopping bags at the ready. For these two older women the bus provides a service, as they can be flexible enough to fit into the bus's timetable. How they get home again is anybody's guess though! Alone again with the driver and feeling specially chauffeured, I finally arrived in Glencolmcille.

There was a friendly buzz of activity around the village, with people interacting with one another on the street. A car stopped in the middle of the road, as the driver wished to speak to a man standing outside the Post Office. A few people were talking in a doorway. An elderly woman and a younger woman were walking slowly along the street talking. A woman pushing a buggy stopped to talk to a man who was coming out of the local shop. Both spoke to the breadman who was carrying a tray of loaves into the shop. An elderly man drove away with his small bag of groceries, accompanied by a tan-and-white dog sitting in the front seat beside him. The conviviality of village life was apparent here and extended to the visitor in their midst. Everyone said 'hello' as I passed, and all this combined to drag me out of my solitary, private mood.

Glencolmcille is a haven for tourists – especially those who are interested in learning the Irish language and music. Residential courses are run all the year round in a purpose-built cultural centre. Many visitors come year after year and thus develop a relationship with the local people, avoiding the indifference towards tourists seen in many other centres. In Glencolmcille as well, tourists are called 'visitors', reflecting a different nuance in the relationship. As I left the town my attention was taken by a traffic jam: a lorry could not get past a builder's van that was parked at an awkward angle on the road. A short beep of the horn resulted in a man appearing out of a new house being built at the side of the road. With an affable wave of the arm he moved the van. Both drivers then shared a few friendly words before parting with a laugh. In some others parts of the world they might have started haranguing each other!

Farther on this small road just outside the village boundary an elderly man came out to the door of his house to greet me and to obviously see who was going by. This reminded me very much of my father when I was growing up. If my father was in the house and somebody walked past, he would be out the door like a shot, to see who it was and to speak to them. This needless to say caused me great embarrassment, and I would be exhorting him to "sit down and stop annoying people". At that stage of my life I had no real appreciation of traditional information-gathering strategies and exchange of civilities!

The elderly man, walking stick in hand, smiled a greeting.

"The rain has forgotten about us," he said.

"Long may it be so," I replied.

We both laughed, as we knew it would be back with a vengeance soon. Having satisfied some of his curiosity I went on my way, until I came to a small bridge under which flowed a bubbling river that trundled down through the remnants of a wood now confined to a line of trees on each bank. The sound was so melodic that I nearly felt like waltzing around the road. There really is something about the sound of flowing water that energizes the spirit. The old trees on the river bank added an extra dimension, giving it the feel of a special spot. As I climbed the narrow straight road up the mountainside there were remnants of far more ancient forests. Stark ancient stumps of pine stuck up in the bog like columns in some ruined temple. These had been preserved and enveloped by the warm deadly embrace of layers of peat laid down over generations. The trunks were in turn rendered free by generations of people harvesting turf. The cycle is now complete, as this four-thousand-year-old wood is now gathered by artists, who polish and sculpt it with an imagining eye and then sell shapes to our fancy.

The road climbed steeply beside a stream that made a tinkling noise as it murmured gently down the mountain. My legs were too sore to dance! A short way up the mountain four men were plastering a construction, presumably a sheep-dip. Two of them were standing in the back of a pick up truck sporadically mixing cement into a cement mixer on board. Another man was carrying the cement to the oldest man, who was the one doing the plastering, and indeed most of the work. For the others effort was interspersed with talk and laughter.

Half way up the mountain I stopped and looked behind me. The scene below was like a panoramic painting; in the foreground was the boggy mountain soil spread like a blanket across the membrane of the earth. In the distance below I could see Glencolmcille nestling into the hills and beyond the village the blue sea with white waves breaking on the cliffs. The individual waves were not distinguishable in the distance; the scene was like a photograph capturing one white static wave at a moment in time.

The stream kept me company to the top of the mountain road; its gentle voice soothed my senses and my runaway mind. There was just the feel of my step on the road and of my breathing, responding to the severity of the climb. At the top a surreal sight greeted me. A man was sitting on a turf bank in front of a small fire. Even though he was a man in his late fifties he had a boyish, roguish aspect about him. He was small and of a sturdy build; a healthy tuft of grey hair splayed about wildly on top of his head. When I got up near him I shouted across the bog to him and he shouted back. In this rather odd manner we conducted a conversation. He told me that he worked in the local fish factory that was located a few miles from here in the middle of the countryside. You may well ask why should a factory be located in the middle of a sparsely populated rural area? Would it not be more profitable to base their operation in a large town? The answer of course is that this is a Gaeltacht area, which means that it is a place where the Irish language is the primary language of use by the people in every day life. The Irish language is clinging on precariously in certain rural areas of Ireland most of which are on the Western seaboard. These are the very communities that are threatened, because of their geographical isolation and the increasing urbanisation of life. The local authority for the Gaeltacht area give incentives to industry to locate in areas such as this in order to maintain the viability of these threatened rural communities and also as a means of preserving Irish as a living language. Whether such a strategy works is questionable because this policy is not backed up by other policies such as providing the physical infrastructure necessary for these communities to thrive. This however did not seem to be bothering my friend on the mountain. He described what he thought was the ideal working arrangement.

"I have three days for work and four days for myself," he said. This sounded like a good deal to me. This train of common sense continued.

"I don't like working indoors on a good day," he said, "because I spend my time wishing I was outside."

I could really empathise with this viewpoint, as good days are so rare in this country that one feels that one should make the most of them. He explained that people who are used to living outdoors, like small farmers and fishermen, feel entrapped and imprisoned when working inside all the time.

"Whatever about anything else," he said, "the important thing is to be content in life."

By chance I was talking to a businessman a few months later who employed workers for indoors and outdoor work in a rural community. He said that it was near impossible to get workers for indoor factory work, even though the work was far less strenuous. By contrast he had no difficulty getting workers for outdoor work.

"Rural people don't like to work indoors," he said.

Of course the other factor is that there is probably a lot less scrutiny of outdoor work, there are probably a lot more opportunities for what euphemistically be called 'flexible working patterns'. I left my new acquaintance sitting serenely in the bog.

After walking a little farther I came on another strange sight. On a hillside to my left a big quarry full of machinery was in full operation, busy buzzing about like ants excavating a food source. The strange thing was that right in the middle of this quarry stood a small house, outside of which was sitting an elderly man. He was in conversation with a younger man who was leaning against a door post. They both seemed to be oblivious to the diggers, loaders, tractors and lorries that were moving around them, changing the shape of the environment in clouds of dust. I suppose for the old man those machines might have been humming a sweeter tune than the most melodic songbird? He is probably getting well paid for the stone in the quarry.

I descended into Meenaneary, which is an amalgam of houses, a church, a pub, a large community centre and the huge factory mentioned previously. Meenaneary means 'Plain of the Shepherd' or some people claim 'Plain of the Fairies' and there are countless stories of fairy lore in this area. Children were always warned to keep away from certain spots for fear of being kidnapped and hauled away to the land of the fairies.

At the crossroads I passed a small school. All the children were out playing in a small yard circulating in seeming random swirls of energy. However the energy in this school yard was in no way a random happening but rather a closely choreographed, interrelated dance with patterns of energy centring around dominant individuals. As I passed by, I became for a fleeting instant the focus of this swirl of activity. All the children stopped playing momentarily and shouted hello. A few girls standing nearest the wire fence asked me where I was going. I told them I was going to Ardara. They laughed, and one of them wistfully said, "we have to stay in school". This communication was completely natural. One of the advantages of rural living is that there is a lesser segregation of the generations; children grow up with the knowledge of how to interact with adults in appropriate ways. Imagining another school in a different setting, it would be likely that one would get a totally different, more suspicious reaction.

The road afterwards became narrower and quieter. I sat down at a small bridge to have something to eat. In the distance I observed a man spreading artificial fertiliser by hand onto a field. Beside me there was another field stretching up the hillside. On this field, there were tractor loads of cow manure scattered around in a seeming haphazard fashion. This was the winter harvest, which was now ready for distribution. A graip was stuck into one of these lumps of manure with a deserted wheelbarrow beside it. A man had been spreading this manure manually around the field. This is a procedure that has gone on for generations in an effort to build fertility into the reluctant soil. Comparing the two fields it was no real surprise to see that the field with the natural fertiliser was the greener field. All was quiet here; even Nature seemed to be taking a rest. The man who was spreading the artificial fertiliser climbed into his jeep and headed to a house across the road, probably to get his dinner.

I looked at a clump of mountain ash trees growing in a ditch at the side of a field, and marvelled at their beauty and tenacity. The ancestors of these trees emerged in the mist of time, millions of years ago. These trees have now adapted to this landscape; the frequent high winds here carry salt spray, which is damaging to many plants. This tree has remembered how to survive here; it has drawn on the experience of its ancestors. When a new seed falls upon the earth it is the collective memory that guides it to maturity, telling it what minerals to take from the soil, how many branches to grow and how to preserve itself when it faces adversity. The mountain ash seed contains all this knowledge within itself, adapting it to present circumstances. On top of all that it delights us with white flowers in the spring and red berries in the autumn.

As humans the past is within us as well: knowledge of the past comes to us culturally. Are we in the process of eradicating much of our cultural knowledge as we build a global culture based on consumerism and the sating of the senses? We need to ask ourselves what useful memories are we extinguishing in this process. The knowledge of native peoples are being destroyed, the memories and connections, which have helped get us here, are being undermined. We ignore the signals from a world that is becoming increasingly toxic for us.

Farther on I came across an older woman who was kneeling on a mat weeding her lawn. There were many lines of experience set in this woman's strong square face. I said hello; upon seeing me, she struggled to her feet commenting on her bad knees.

"You are doing too much praying," I said, in consolation.

She laughed and asked where I was going. I told her I was going to Ardara.

"You have a ways to walk yet, and you might be saying prayers yourself before you are finished," she joked, neatly getting her own back on me.

She then told me that she loved to walk but is not able to go too far now because of "these bad knees". She with a softening smile stated that her grandchildren come to see her every day and that keeps her going. She talked fondly of her young grandchildren and all the activities they engage in together each day. Perhaps there is hope for human culture after all?

I faced a choice of two beautiful routes going in the direction of Ardara. Either choice involved walking through a spectacular valley, but would of course mean missing a walk through another spectacular valley.

'Will I walk thorough Glengesh or Granny Glen?' I asked myself.

In this part of the world there are two passes through the mountains, both of which are steeped in history. For thousands of years they provided ample reward for brigands and outlaws who waylaid the unwary. These outlaws were generally speaking outcasts from the Clans, who congregated together to pursue their self-interest. First let me mention the Glen that I chose not to walk through. Travellers and other walkers have always remarked on the beauty, wildness and grandeur of Glengesh. It is a glen of varying moods. In good weather it is picture-postcard tranquil, but when the wind blows and funnels down through the Glen it is best to keep your head low, taking the example of the traditional houses in the area which lie crouched behind any bit of available shelter. The name Glengesh is loosely translated as 'The Prohibited Glen' which indicates that in olden times this Glen was a dangerous place to traverse and was to be avoided if at all possible. It was full of obstacles, natural, human, animal and even supernatural. The clear message was 'go there at your peril'. According to Lochlann McGill in his book *In Conall's Footsteps* one of the main place names on Glengesh is 'Alt Na nDeamhainn' which means 'the precipice of the demons'. So you can see that it was with reluctant steps and trepidation that the traveller set forth.

Maybe it was because of this ancient taboo that I decided to go by the Granny Glen. The other reason is that now a switchback road comes up Glengesh, which has a constant level of traffic. The road up the Granny Glen is lightly used and is but a glorified track, far more peaceful for the walker. You might be wondering why this place is called the Granny Glen. It has nothing to do with elderly women, but Lochlann McGill tells us that it is so named because the word in the Irish language used to describe the gravel on the bed of the river ('grean') sounds like 'Granny'. The valley is bounded on one side by Sliabhtooey, which means 'the mountain to the north' and by a gentler mountain on the other side. Sliabhtooey arouses feelings of danger when one looks at its slopes and aspect. The mountain has a certain majesty and mystery about it, especially if clouds cling to the mountain top. It is not a mountain that you should approach lightly; it is likely to punish you for such arrogance. It has known its fair share of tragedies over the years. This mountain was one of the last haunts of the Golden Eagle in Donegal, and one has no difficulty in imagining its cry as it soars high over the slopes of this mountain. Perhaps now that the Golden Eagle has been reintroduced into Glenveagh Forest Park in north Co. Donegal it will eventually spread back, to nest high upon the slopes and cliffs of Sliabhtooey.

I sat down at the top of the Glen with my back to Sliabhtooey and gazed in wonder at the stone walls rising in straight lines up the face of the mountain facing me. It beggars belief how people could have the energy to build such walls on often-precipitous slopes. What levels of need and perseverance drove this endeavour? In the valley below me in the midst of a sweep of bog lay a small field with stone walls as boundaries. Perhaps its purpose was to provide shelter for animals, or else was used to contain them at certain times of the year or at night time. The river flowed over the neck of the valley and descended in sweeping curves onto the plain at Maghery and then joined the sea. Maghery itself is in fact a large area of sandbanks, which in turn lead onto one of the most beautiful beaches in south west Donegal. It is not only beautiful but deadly. This is a place where swimming is definitely not recommended, unless you want to be swept out to sea on an adventure trip from which there is little chance of return.

In times past this coast was deadly for other reasons. There were many shipwrecks off this coast, which added to the local economy when the goods were washed ashore. Stories are told of how local people assisted this process by lighting fires on the slopes of Sliabhtooey, thus luring ships and sailors to their doom. A local woman I met told me a story of one such incident, when after a shipwreck brought about by such mischief a body of a sailor was washed onto the shore at Maghery beach. The treasure hunters repeatedly threw the body back into the sea so that the tide would take the body back out again. However every time they threw it into the sea it was washed ashore again. There was to be no easy way of cleansing their conscience of this deed. They then decided to bury the body deep into the sand, as no one wanted to bury the body near or on their own land. However after burying the body the tides exposed the evil deed again. So began another process of trying to bury the body even deeper. It was all to no avail; the body kept reappearing, part of a living nightmare. Some of the locals got so worried that they called a priest to help calm the spirit of the dead sailor. The priest duly did this, but only at the cost of invoking bad luck on the family who had caused the shipwreck in the first case through lighting those false beacons. The family left the area for good shortly afterwards.

I descended now down the valley on the rough road. A four-wheel drive Land Rover with Northern Ireland number plates passed me. I saw a man coming out of a field at the bottom of the valley with a sheepdog at his heels. It was as if they were joined together by an invisible thread. This brought into my mind a saying I once heard which speaks of the connection between people and dogs.

'God went forth to create the world and took his dog with him.'

I arrived at a cluster of houses, which is Maghery village. I stopped to talk to a woman in her early sixties who exuded good health, who was busy emptying rubbish into compost bins. She told me she was big into gardening and that she recycled everything she could. She pointed to a row of about eight compost bins of different designs and told me that the cheapest bin was in fact the best one to make compost. It was in reality just a plastic top with no bottom; this allowed the forces of Nature to help with the work, which is always a good idea. The woman asked me where I had come from on my walk. I told her. She laughed and told me that when she was a girl she regularly walked that route as they drove cattle from Maghery to the fair in Glencolmcille. Any cattle they did not sell at the fair they drove home again that evening. This was a world where walking was the way of life with nothing thought of it. I believed that I was great, being able to walk from Glencolmcille to Maghery in one day. This woman as a slip of a girl walked it both ways in the one day and probably fitted in a day's work on either side of the journey.

A little bit farther on I came to a car park, which seemed a little bit incongruous in the middle of the countryside. Maghery is not only a beautiful spot – it is famous for its caves and many people come to see them. To get to the beach and caves, however, requires crossing a person's land. It seemed fair to me that people should pay a small fee for parking and access. There are three large caves that are only accessible when the tide is out. If you visit them you have to be sure and come out before the tide comes back in again! No one knows for sure how far the various tunnels and passageways stretch though there is a story of a dog that having got trapped in one of the caves was seen coming out of a hole in the ground near Glencolmcille.

These caves were also the scene of a massacre of the local population by British troops following the 1641 rebellion. The rebellion was brutally put down in the area and as usual in war it was the innocent who suffered the most. A few hundred men, women and children sought refuge from the British forces in the caves at Maghery. It was winter time and very cold. One of the women started to give birth and a small fire was lit in order to keep her warm. This was spotted by the British/Cromwellian forces across the bay, who then came and killed all the people, bar one man who found a hiding spot on a ledge high up in the cave. Imagine being that person and seeing your family, relatives, neighbours and friends being slaughtered. Was it bravery or cowardice that kept him on that ledge? It was definitely the logical thing to do; revealing oneself would just have added one more casualty to the list. What was life like afterwards for this man? Did he thank the heavens? Did revenge burn in his heart? Did he lose himself in drink or turn to religion? Did he have sleepless nights? How did the event mark him?

A little farther on one comes to a large waterfall that cascades down the steep mountain. It is called Easaranca loosely translated as the 'wrinkled waterfall'. This spot is a magnet for people drawn to the song of the water and its cascading power. As I stood there listening to the 'wrinkled one's' roar, a car pulled up and a man, a woman and a young child got out. The child rushed to climb a rock, then excitedly clambered down again and started throwing stones into the pool at the bottom of the waterfall. His parents joined him; we are all drawn by the voice and power of the water.

The walk along the estuary here to Ardara is very pleasant. It is illuminated by rows of silver birch, which have as their backdrop the blue water of the estuary. Their white silvery barks have an otherworldly radiance about them. The first tree I planted when we moved into our new house after marriage was a silver birch tree. I remember dreaming about that tree one night. I was standing under the tree and a golden light was coming out of it, which surrounded and infused me. I felt peaceful and contented. I go back to that dream every so often when the need arises.

The silver birch is known as 'the lady of the forest', a tree of healing and mystery. I look at one of the trees now silhouetted against the water. It has two trunks, each entwined around the other like a lover's embrace. It is sensual yet elegant.

I reached the outskirts of Ardara and as I walked on the long footpath into the town I passed by a rather plump young woman who was strolling along. She probably thought what was that wee squat man doing passing her? As soon as I had passed her she upped her pace and pressurised me all the way into Ardara. This was her sprint. I felt like pleading for pity, and would have reminded her that I was completing a marathon walk – if I only had the chance. Manfully, however, I did not let her pass; every time she caught up with me I put on a spurt. However the first shop I saw I suddenly decided that I needed an ice cream. I dived into the shop and managed to get into it before my adversary passed. My honour was salvaged!

# Mountcharles to Rossnowlagh

On this day I headed out walking from my home. The very first house I passed is where I was reared. It is one of those very old, small rectangular houses, which initially consisted of two bedrooms and a living room, with a fireplace in each room. At a later stage a flat-roofed extension was added, which included the luxury of a bathroom. This house was fairly typical of a home belonging to a small farmer in the west of Ireland in the nineteenth and twentieth centuries.

My father was one of eight children – four brothers and four sisters born and reared in this house and small farm. He was the only man who stayed at home and thus he inherited all. Two of his brothers emigrated to the United States. One became a sailor, sailed around the world and died of malaria in New Orleans. The other brother worked in odd jobs all around the States. I think he essentially lived the life of a hobo, and became over fond of the drink. Another brother had a mental disability and died relatively young. Two of his sisters were nurses; one died from tuberculosis in her twenties and the other again emigrated to the States. One sister stayed at home, became a teacher and married locally. The remaining sister worked as an au pair for a lot of her life and as a consequence travelled the world – as she said herself: "It is one of the advantages of working for rich people!" In the long run however I am not sure it was a great advantage, as she never seemed to be overly content with life. She seemed to be full of superficial pleasantness accompanied by obvious internal strife and worry.

I don't know exactly how my mother and father met; my mother was a Jubilee nurse who came to work in Co. Donegal as part of the Lady Dudley Nursing Scheme, a voluntary organisation. This scheme was later taken over by the Health Service. She was from Kilrush in Co. Clare, where her parents owned a number of shops. At a young age she went to England to train as a nurse. Upon completion of her course she came initially to Gweedore to work and then to Frosses, where she met and married my father. This encounter was never fleshed out in any great detail for me. They had one child before me but he died at childbirth. I have been told that there was great jubilation when I came along, all the more so because I must have been a last gasp: my father was fifty-one and my mother was forty-one when I was born. I think the whole community did not think it was going to happen, and as it transpired I was their only surviving child.

My mother had to give up work when she got married. The law stated that married women could not work in the Public Service, which is unimaginable in today's society where everyone is 'encouraged' to work. We were poor, like everyone else, and there was not a lot to spare – there was a not a great return from twenty-five sparse acres. We used to keep cattle, we milked the cows by hand, sold a few calves and for fuel we went to the bog for turf. The sheepdog (Fionn – named by me after the Irish mythological hero) would go out to the fields and take in the cows for milking on his own. We also kept pigs and poultry. In the late 60s the legislation on married women working in the Public Service changed. This enabled my mother to go back to work again as a public health nurse. She had a hilly rural area to cover, which she did on bicycle. The extra money was used to educate me (one of the advantages of being an only child) through secondary school and ultimately university.

Our house was always full of people as all the neighbours used to call. My father used to love to chat and argue about religion, politics, farming etc. My mother was a very practical person whereas my father was more a people-person, very friendly and welcoming. He had very little formal education but he was very well read and loved debating topics, especially history. He also had very good 'hands' and traditional skills. His pride and joy was drama and he used to produce stage plays every winter in the local community. Initial rehearsals always took place in our kitchen (which was very small). People were packed in everywhere and there was a real buzz around the house. I knew everyone's lines and was totally engrossed in the action. If any of the actors paused to even catch their breath I was in like a shot with the appropriate lines. However because I was young (or more probably because I was a right pain in the ass) I was sent off to bed at my official bedtime, which I resented with a great intensity. A battle of wills was fought out which I usually lost. I wanted so much to be part of things, to be grown up and to be able to join in this adult world.

Later in the night I could hear them all leaving the house laughing and joking. The main actress was Hilda Griffin who was blonde and was usually the centre of the action in terms of banter. I could not wait to grow up! The plays were one of the only forms of entertainment locally, as there was no television. Our part of rural Ireland didn't get television until the late 60s or early 70s. I remember the first television that came into the community: we used to all gather in the poor unfortunate person's house to watch it!

My mother said that the first thing that struck her forcibly when she came to work here was the extent of the poverty in Donegal. People had nothing. Tuberculosis (TB) was rampant, and very often people who had TB were put into outhouses, banned from human contact and even had their food left outside the door for them. People were *that* afraid of TB. When I first heard this story I was appalled that people could be treated in such a manner by their own family. On reflection, families with a TB sufferer living in the house with them faced a real conundrum. How to do the best thing for the person who was ill and cater the needs of the rest of the family. My mother insisted though, that despite the poverty, the generosity of the people was remarkable. Even if they had little they would share it with you. Every home had a welcome for you.

She told me about the travelling dentist who arrived every month armed with his only tool, a pair of pliers. When he arrived, all the people who could no longer avoid him would collect outside an old barn, converted to his operating theatre for the duration of his stay. In trepidation – and only because of desperation – they entered the shed. My mother said that the roars of the people inside the barn were something else. She had to attend to all the casualties. No wonder we have an aversion to dentists; it is probably some classification of genetic memory!

My mother delivered all the babies – some older people still tell me that my mother delivered them – and laid out all the dead in the locality, so I guess she got a balanced perspective of the important things in life. I remember one Christmas morning she had to go and lay out someone who had died. When she came back I remember looking at her hands as she served out the dinner.

'How could I eat that food after those hands had touched a dead person?' I wondered.

Hunger must have got the better of me because I still ate my dinner! I later helped her lay out a few people; the first person was our next-door neighbour. My mother saw me staring at the face, and asked me to help move the body in some way. When I started to lift the body one of his eyes popped open! I nearly ran out the door and my mother burst her sides laughing. Memories. Where do they come from and where do they go?

As I continued walking towards the sea at Mountcharles I passed Hilda Griffin's house. She now has a whole gang of grown-up children and even a grandchild or two. I am sure there were many dramas played out in her house afterwards, I wondered if she had retained the role of leading lady? She had lots of competition as she had four daughters.

I walked along the shore road at Mountcharles, which is a beautiful two-mile walk on the edge of the sea. When I arrived at the end of the seaside walk, I decided to walk on the beach for a while. There is nothing as tranquil as a beach walk. It was one of those warm days without a breath of air. There was a hint of thunder in the air and the sky was grey. As I walked along the beach it started to rain lightly, falling straight, which was rare in this part of the world as the wind is usually blowing. I sheltered under a solitary tree and looked out over the bay. A man was walking along the beach with a dog, framed against a backdrop of sky and sea was blended together in subtle variations of grey. As I stood there, the head of a seal suddenly popped up through the water just out in front of me – I think he was taken by the antics of the dog charging up the beach after some invisible object. The seal disappeared after a few moments and popped up again quite a distance away, still curious, still watching. By this time the dog had upset a bird, which was sending out a shrill warning call. A heron rose from the rocks and flapped slowly across the still water. Oystercatchers scuttled along the sand and took off as one swooping entity across the water. Dunlins, their small silver bodies flashing, whooshed low across the bay; their every movement synchronised to the melody of some invisible orchestra. The sea lapped its way across the shoreline and murmured through the shells and stones. The only 'fly in the ointment' was those blasted midges which kept on taking lumps out of me as I tried to remain serene – the midges won. So much for mind over matter! Did you know that it is only the female midge that bites?

I walked up through my home village of Mountcharles. Like a lot of Irish villages Mountcharles has gone into decline over the last twenty-five years, with commercial activity now concentrated in the bigger towns.

Mountcharles once had three hotels, amenities and a variety of shops from grocery to hardware to tailors to butchers. Now it has one or two shops, a fish and chip shop and a selection of pubs. Many of the houses are derelict and falling into disrepair, and the resident population is growing old. The village is full of school-day memories, of places where we played street football and marbles, had fights and wrestling matches, where we cogged homework before we went in to face the teacher. The 'Master', as we called him, took it as a personal affront if children did not learn, and to have something wrong was to face the direst of physical consequences. It was always a toss-up whether the cane used was the thick fat one or the *whishy* narrow one. To have one's ears twisted was commonplace, but when his face went red with incandescent rage…that was the most frightening thing about him. When his bald scalp went red we knew we were in for it. We used to call him 'Baldy' – behind his back!

Another teacher, Kathleen Carr tried in her own gentle way to introduce music, culture and poetry into children's lives – not to much success in my case. We got off school on fair days that came on the 22nd of each month. The main fair day of the year was the harvest fair, which was held in September. On that day the street was full of salesmen and gaming machines, as well as the cattle and sheep.

Today the village was quiet. The only person on the street that I met was an old woman in her eighties. To call Mary 'old' is however a bit of a misnomer, because if there is a world champion walker then it is she. All her life she has walked everywhere, and is still walking strong despite having been struck and injured twice by cars in recent years. For most of her life Mary had been the sacristan in the local church. She lived two miles from the church, which meant that she had to walk to and from the church three times every day: in the early morning, to get the church ready for half-eight mass; in the middle of the day to do some cleaning, and last thing at night she had to be on hand to lock up. This she did every day hail, rain or shine for what I am sure was little or no money. All the walking obviously did her no harm as she still has a glow to her cheeks, and a sharpness to her tongue that has never dulled.

She stood back and looked at me as I came up the street.

"My God, where are you going to with that bag on your back?" Mary asked.

"I might go up Drimarone way, Mary," I replied.

"There's no settling you at all."

"Maybe you would come with me," I said.

"Sure you wouldn't be able to keep up with me," she replied. "Anyway I have to go in and see my boyfriend."

Jim Brennan is one of the local shopkeepers who has a word for Mary and anyone else who goes into his shop. Every time Mary calls in there is a lot of banter, usually about money and who is getting the better end of the bargain.

"Well, you better not keep him waiting," I said. "He is an impatient man and he will be looking to make a bob out of you."

"Hmphh, he will be trying to rob me as usual," she laughed.

However she must have decided that it was good to keep Jim waiting for a while, because she continued talking about her nieces and nephews and what they were doing now.

"I hope those shoes of yours aren't letting in," she said as I left.

This was a direct dig at my new 'Merrell' walking shoes, which eagle-eyed Mary had spotted.

"Maybe I should have brought the wellingtons with me," I replied.

Saying goodbye to Mary, I left Mountcharles village and passed where the lazy bush used to grow. This was a solitary hawthorn tree that grew at the side of the road. The sign of a fairy tree was that though very old, the tree remained small and stunted. As we grew up we heard many stories about the fairies who used to dance around that particular tree in the dead of night. The tree of course disappeared when the road was widened, reflecting the regard that centralised planning had for local stories. One of the local pubs in the village was called after the fairy tree, and sure enough some funny dancing goes on there late at night too! In the same field as the fairy thorn there are some standing stones that are monuments to other memories that now only exist as nagging traces in the firmament.

Further up the hill in Drumkeelin I passed the old stone quarries which once provided cut sandstone for Buckingham Palace. Many of the stone carvers who worked here died early deaths because of inhaling of dust from the carving of the sandstone. The stone was carried down to the pier by horse and cart to the pier in Mountcharles where it was loaded for export. Paris may have plundered one of the Egyptian stone obelisks from Karnak Temple in Luxor but London plundered sandstone from Mountcharles.

I decided that one of the objectives for today would be go and see the three new windmills on a hilltop in Diseart. These are (we are told) the next big thing in terms of a power source for electric supply, as they are seemingly a perfect fit for our windy climate and our increasing need for power. To get there I had to walk through a real jewel of a place called Drimarone. If there is magic in a place it is here. Drimarone is situated at the bottom of the Blue Stack Mountains in a remote rural valley with a river trundling through it. As I walked up through the hills my favourite mountain, Carnaween emerged directly in front of me as if springing up from the road; it was a friendly, familiar signpost on the way. Frogspawn and tadpoles mingled noisily in the drains at the side of the road but when I bent to have a closer look the noise disappeared into a watchful stillness. The postman stopped to offer me a lift; we talked for a few minutes before he continued on his round. I eventually got onto a rough track that seemed to head towards the windmills. About half a mile up the track a Land Rover came towards me. I knew that it would in all probability be the farm owner, who would stop to check out my credentials. In other words a polite way of asking 'What the heck are you doing here?'

Sure enough the Land Rover pulled up beside me. The lean angular man of about fifty and he had a dog sitting on the passenger seat beside him. He rolled down the window.

"That's a fine looking dog you have," I said.

"Aye," he said. "He is a great dog after the sheep."

"You would need him on these mountains right enough."

"I suppose you are going up to the windmills?" he said.

I told him that I was curious about them, as I had never been up close to them before.

"A good lot of people go up to have a look," he said.

I told him where I was from and sure enough he knew some of my neighbours. We spent about thirty minutes talking after that about every subject under the sun. He told me about the area and all the people who used to live here one time.

"See those houses over there?" he said, pointing to six small ruined houses that were in a cluster. "All those houses were full of families one time."

These small houses of a maximum of three rooms provided for big families of between twelve to fifteen children. It was amazing to think that so many people could live together in such small houses. We now live in a time when people are building bigger and bigger houses but they have smaller and smaller families. It does not seem to add up. And not only that of course, there is an increasing trend that when all the children leave the house to make their own way in life, a new extension is then built to add further to the house.

My farmer friend told me that most of the children emigrated from these houses, very often never to be heard from again. Those who stayed behind on the land or to care for ageing parents never married, and the houses fell into disrepair after their death. The family connections had dissipated to different parts of the globe and lost connection with the locality. He told me that one time this whole valley had been full of people and families. Now, the only one remaining was a ninety-two-year-old woman who lived on her own, farther down the valley. The authorities had wanted her to go and live in an old people's home but she refused point-blank, wanting to die in her own spot. And what a beautiful spot it is too. Standing here you could appreciate her point of view.

Now new families want to build farther down the valley, as they recognise this as one of the most beautiful places that one could find. However my friend told me that they were finding it difficult to get planning permission, as the rules and regulations have 'got very tight'. Groups like the environmental group An Taisce are objecting to people living in the countryside, as they feel that it blights the beauty of the area. However, it also blights an area if there is nobody living in it. Communities die out and people congregate in cities and towns. The function of these areas is then to provide a leisure experience for an urban people. The ownership of the land transfers to big business interests, whether it is large farmers, or insurance/pension firms who buy up the land for investment purposes. Give me houses any day.

He informed me that he used to run cross-country races up until recently, and that now chasing after sheep kept him fit. His lean weather-beaten face broke into a grin as he told me about the times that he used to run on these back roads while training. He was the only one in the locality who took up running, and he got real enjoyment out of it. Most of the people around of course thought he was mad in the head, he said, to spend so much time running. They thought he would have enough exercise chasing sheep on the mountain.

In full flow he started talking about how unfit young people were, and that most of them in his experience take little or no exercise. How could they be healthy and take no exercise, he wondered. Whilst on the topic of schools he told me about National School when he was young. He said that fellows would often stay on there until they were fifteen or sixteen because they mixed schooling with farming. In the school you would have all these big strapping young fellows who were fit and active from their lifestyle.

"Yet," he said, "we were all terrified of this small fat teacher."

The teacher spent his time giving out to them, twisting their ears if they did wrong and walloping them around the place with a cane. All of these lads could have easily clobbered this teacher if they had wanted. He wondered what had changed now and why had young people no fear or indeed respect for teachers. I had no answer for him on that one.

His conversational range included asylum seekers and refugees, who are now coming into this country in increasing numbers. He was knowledgeable and sympathetic to their plight, as he had worked with one on a building site in a remote rural area. He said that he had found out a lot about Nigeria from this man. He shook his head with amusement and said that his friend from Nigeria would often go 'blue with the cold' when working on a bleak Donegal landscape in our winter. It was a far cry from what he was used to in terms of temperature. Looking around me this sympathetic understanding should not have been surprising, because in this spot the desolating effects of emigration surrounded us.

"I had better not detain you any longer," he said, putting his jeep into gear. With that the dog and himself took off down the track.

I continued on up the track to the windmills. There are only three windmills at this site. Their sleek lines and silhouettes reached into the sky; their blades whooshed powerfully through the breeze high above me. Across the country these windmills are spreading especially in mountainous areas and are becoming a feature of our landscape. There is even one located in the middle of the fishing village of Burtonport, creating much discussion as to whether it enhances or detracts from the character of the place. I sat down at a small lake for something to eat with the sound of the windmills as a backdrop.

As I came from Drimarone in the direction of Donegal town I met a man in a tracksuit who was power walking. Power walkers are somewhat like 'whirling dervishes', though come to think of it I have never seen one of those in real life. There seems to be a specific technique to proper power walking. First of all you have to hold your arms rigidly straight at 45° to the body. You then proceed to swing these arms as fast as you can. At the same time you propel your legs as quickly as possible in the direction you wish to go. However you have to ensure that as your right arm swings forward, your right hip swings backwards and then vice versa for the left side. The upper and lower parts of the body swivel around the waist in opposite directions as fast as they can go, thus creating the peculiar motion of the power walker. If we could only connect all this energy into the national electricity grid we would definitely do away with the need for windmills!

This power walker was accompanied by a boy of about ten years on a bicycle, who was seemingly offering him encouragement, though to be honest I did not see any sharp needles. I think this must have been the first man I ever saw power walking. Well, on further reflection, I have seen those fellows who walk in a funny way at the Olympics. But they don't count in real life, because they can walk harder than I can run. When one sees a power walker coming in the distance you can nearly always be assured it is a female. Maybe the men now are going to catch up and express themselves. Around every town and village you are likely to bump into an array of people taking exercise in a very determined manner.

We are sometimes obsessed with putting off the inevitable decline of the body. To be ageing in this youth oriented society is a complete no-no. The older people that we look up to are those who are praised for their ability to remain young. What we should be doing is praising them and valuing them because they are older. They should achieve status because of their age, not by trying to negate it. The message is 'keep young at all costs – it is good for you'. Even if we understand that we should be ageing gracefully it is still difficult to go against the stream of youth culture – After all, we should remember it is only dead fish that go with the flow.

A little while later as I was standing taking photographs at a small bridge, a woman I knew stopped her car and wound down the window.

"Are you all right?" she enquired.

By this I presumed she was asking me did I want a lift? She stopped to talk for a while. She told me that she had a stiff shoulder for the last six months, which was causing her a lot of discomfort and that she had utilised all the conventional medical approaches to no avail.

Abandoning conventional approaches she was now on her way to a fourth Reiki session in a month, in the hope that it would bring her some relief. I asked her if she thought the Reiki sessions did her any good. She replied that after a session "it either feels a lot better or a lot worse". The practitioner told her that even if it felt worse that this was a good sign of the body healing itself. 'Wow,' I thought to myself. 'The Reiki master can't lose here. No matter what way the treatments affect the other person it is claimed as a success. That's the way to do it!'

I met an old man at a crossroads who was shuffling along the road with the aid of a walking frame. His clothes were dishevelled and his face was full of dirt and grime. I asked this man the direction to the next village. A sudden look of panic came into his eyes and with a dismissive gesture he scurried away on his walking frame as quick as it was possible for him to go. I wondered why should I have engendered such a response? Was it because I frightened him in some way and he was afraid of being attacked? When looking for a scapegoat, it is useful to blame the media, with lots of stories about older people being robbed and at times murdered. These stories probably transmit a mistaken impression of the scale of this type of crime and which in turn creates an unnecessary feeling of vulnerability within older people's lives. Not so many years ago people would always leave the key in the door so that people could come in and out at will. Now this is no longer the practice. There were other potential explanations for this man's behaviour – maybe he had a hearing impairment or had got out of the habit of speaking to people. Why, indeed, should he feel that he was obliged to talk to every Tom, Dick or Harry he meets?

After meeting the old man, my walk took me into drumlin country, featuring short steep ascents and descents; this countryside was pleasant walking territory especially when the sun shone. I came to another house with a small front garden. In this garden there was an intense, noisy game of football in progress involving a redheaded woman, a man and four young children, all of whom I estimated were under ten years of age. The game was so all-consuming that no one noticed me as I walked past. The ball fell to a small girl and immediately her father came in with a strong challenge, which sent the girl flying to the ground holding her leg in agony. The father set off on a mazy dribble, accompanied by a running commentary. This featured an impressive account of his own consummate skills and touch. The felled daughter contemplated her sore shin and tears welled to the surface of her eyes. However the excitement was too beguiling; she thought better of it, hopped up and gave chase to her father. As I walked on past the house and up the road I could hear their laughter interspersed with flashes of commentary and lots of shouting – a family at play.

Approaching Laghey, I was in familiar countryside, as my wife Terry and I had lived in this area for a year after we got married. I stopped outside the small house that we lived in. For old times' sake I sat on a wall near to the small house we had once lived in, and I let the memories flood back. The house still had its tin roof. As I looked at the house, I remembered winter nights sitting in front of the fire, dog lying at our feet, glasses of wine in our hand, the wind howling outside, the sound of hailstones and rain battering on the tin roof. Our dog called 'Dearg' disappeared one night, sparking a frantic search for a number of hours in the darkness until we finally found him caught in a snare nearby. By good fortune his paw was caught and not his neck. He was one grateful dog when I found him. Some individual around used to set snares on animal trails in the roadside ditches. Our dog loved to gallop in the fields nearby, following those same trails. A war ensued between the snare layer and me, for I made it my business to destroy snares whenever I went out walking. Snares are a barbaric way of hunting as the animal usually gets their neck caught in the wire. They then usually choke themselves when in panic they try to escape.

Memories and appetite sated I ventured on into the small village of Laghey, bypassed by the main road and overlooked by a large quarry that dwarfs the village. I went into the petrol station for a bar of chocolate and nearly got run over by an impatient driver. I crossed the main road and went down the small road in the direction of Murvagh beach.

Further on down this road I came on a woman with two small adventurous children in tow. She was saying goodbye to an older couple, probably her parents, who were standing outside a house in a well-kept garden. I must have looked quite a sight with my holly stick in hand because the older man spoke to the children with mock alarm in his voice.

"Watch out for that man with the stick. He might take you away."

The myth of the dangerous stranger was certainly being perpetuated here. The children dutifully took no heed of this warning. Both continued climbing on to a wall and proceeded to walk precariously on top of it. I thought it would be more in his line to warn them about the dangers of the wall. (Too much walking brings out the worst in me!) I stopped anyway to talk to the man.

Ever the diplomat I praised him on his garden. He looked over it for a moment as if surveying the wreck of the *Hesperus*.

"I can't do much work on it this year," he proclaimed, "as I did my knee in when I fell off a ladder six months ago."

I wished I had that excuse, as his garden was perfect compared to mine. I consoled myself with the thought that it is hard to beat a real wild garden because of the wildlife it encourages; there are far too many of these well-manicured gardens.

Recognising that I was a captive audience, he proceeded to tell me of all the things he couldn't do in the garden because of his bad leg. With every mention of a job uncompleted, I shrunk further into a feeling of gardening inadequacy. He then said that he was going into hospital soon "to get his knee sorted out". In the meantime he was not going to do anything too strenuous, just take it easy and rest. We then started into a conversation about leg injuries. This surely was my day on health topics!

I suggested to him that exercise sometimes helped injuries. I told him that exercises like cycling and swimming, which were non-weight bearing, could help build up the muscles around the knee. He considered this rather 'preachy' advice for a moment.

"Oh, I wouldn't be able," he declared, "to cycle or anything like that with this knee, but the funny thing is I can dance like the devil and do it with no pain."

Well, I thought to myself, exercise needs the appropriate motivation. Probably in this instance a woman! I have been working in the Health Service too long!

I sat up on the next small bridge to eat my lunch thinking that simplicity is everything; in this case there is intense pleasure in just walking, looking and eating when one is hungry.

Later on I looked down upon a lake between Murvagh and Rossnowlagh. Two swans were swimming away from me, around a bend. I watched for a while as they swam into the distance. Like a good cyclist all their momentum was created from the legs, with no unnecessary body movement. They looked so elegant and poised; like a lot of us they may just be presenting a good exterior to the world. Swans have a special significance for me since the time of my father's death. On the day he died two swans came to the lake near to our house like a portent that his time had come. On the day of the funeral as my father's body was being taken from the house for the last time, I saw the two swans in the lake. I thought that they were the link between this world and the next for my father. It was as if they were there to guide him on the next stage of his journey, to a world that was not visible to us.

The other vivid memory I have of swans is when a group of friends and I were hiking in the Blue Stack Mountains. It was a mild winter's evening when suddenly a thick mist descended stealthily upon the mountain. It was getting dark and we were totally lost. The mist had enveloped and enshrouded everything and there was a strange otherworld, luminous light. We came upon a small lake when suddenly we heard the *whoosh* of wings through the silence. Three swans flew out of the mist and landed beside us in the water. I was transfixed; I could only stand and stare at the scene, which for a moment was like a scene out of a mythological story. It was a moment of startling beauty.

One of the important things that defines and gives expression to our humanity is the ability to appreciate beauty, especially the beauty of natural things. The opportunity to do this is becoming more and more important in a world dulled by our addiction to gratifying the senses. This addiction permeates all our worlds, of work, leisure, media and relationships. It does not satisfy but leaves a deep ache within us that depresses and dulls our very being. We have to make an effort and search out the beauty in all things, especially people. Beauty in people is an indefinable quality that springs from the inside. It is not associated with fashion or glamour; it transcends these. It is a radiance, a searching, a contentment, a heartfelt laugh, an unquenchable spirit. All of us have beauty within us; what we need to do is learn to release it into the world so that others can connect with it.

I was totally lost in this moment in the mountains. I was pulled out of my reverie by a colleague's worried words. He pointed out to me that it was now nearly dark and we were totally lost in the dense mist. The not very subtle message was 'Would you not cop yourself on and hurry up'. So feeling admonished but unrepentant I joined the rest of the group and we ploughed on through the gloom. The nearest to disaster we came was when one of our members, just back from climbing Mount Kilimanjaro, disappeared up to his waist in a bog hole. I bet he didn't encounter too many bog holes on Kilimanjaro! We had difficulty in pulling him out; he was just very lucky that it wasn't deeper. Another one of our party on this expedition appointed himself as rescuer-in-chief and chief scout even though he had never been in these mountains before. This involved him disappearing totally in the wrong direction and resulted in us having to go searching for him. The more unsuccessful he was the more stubborn he became. No sooner would we find him than he would disappear again in search of the route out. As we got more concerned about our situation, the more impatient we got with him. His only excuse was that he was a medical person, and like most medical people was not the best at listening too closely to other people. Any criticism he received seemed to wash off his back like water off a duck's back. Such a single-minded spirit had got him this far; it is always those who think they are always right who have such positive self-esteem. We finally proceeded together as a unified though disgruntled band, and found our way off the mountain by following a mountain stream. The rule of course is if lost 'follow water as it will lead to more water'. The only problem with this rule was that the stream disappeared underground for periods of time. This meant we had to follow it by sound alone, which is easier said than done in a land of water and bog. We finally got out of the mountains and back to a warm fire.

I finally came to the main destination for the day, the Franciscan friary at Rossnowlagh that has acted as a retreat for people over the past century. The Franciscans as a religious Order have been in Ireland for a long time. St Francis of Assisi, their founder died in 1226 and at that time some of his followers were establishing themselves in the south and east of the country. In the next one hundred years, forty friaries were established. However they did not get as far as Donegal until 1435 when the local chieftain Niall Garbh O'Donnell invited them to establish a friary near Donegal town. A number of other friaries were subsequently established in other parts of the county such as Killydonnell, Kilmacrennan etc. Franciscan fortunes over the next centuries flourished or fell according to the fortunes of the O'Donnell clan. The final defeat of the O'Donnells by the British in the seventeenth century caused the Franciscan order to fade out in Donegal. However like a plant under pressure they did not fade out before producing their greatest flowering. The Franciscan presence in Donegal at that time produced one of the great books of Irish literature called the *Annals of the Kingdom of Ireland* or more commonly known as the *Annals of the Four Masters*. The Four Masters were four Franciscan religious brothers. Their leader was Brother Michael O'Cleary and he had three assistants called Conary (nothing to Sean) O'Cleary, Cucogry O'Cleary and Ferfeasa O'Mulconry.

Michael O'Cleary joined the Franciscans rather late in life at thirty years of age. It was during the course of his studies in Louven in France that he came under the influence of an Irish priest from Donegal called Hugh Ward. Intensely interested in Irish history, Ward sent Michael O'Cleary to Ireland in 1626 to research and write the definitive Irish history from earliest times. Michael O'Cleary and his team travelled around Ireland collecting, collating and copying documents and sources that might be relevant to Irish history. In this sense the work is not original but a compilation of available works. The seven volumes are a real storehouse of history and are a most valuable resource for the nation.

The *Annals* began in 2958BC and finish in 1616AD. The first entries talk about a time forty years before the Great Deluge when Noah's granddaughter came to Ireland. I personally would like to see their sources for this fact, but it just goes to show you how central this wee country was in the global scheme of things – well at least we were as good at storytelling as the rest of them. The first battle in Ireland is said to have happened in 2510BC between the Partholonians and the Formorian invaders. History keeps on repeating itself ever after with the arrival of different groups such as the Firbolg, the Tuatha De Dannann, the Celts, and then invasions from the Vikings, Normans and English. The only ones we missed were the Romans and Genghis Khan. The account finishes with the story of Hugh O'Neill, one of the great Irish chieftains who very nearly defeated the British and the might of Queen Elizabeth I.

In the wintertime the 'Four Masters' came back to the Donegal town friary to write up their findings. The work was finished in 1636 and brought to Louven. The work was not published, due primarily to the death of Hugh Ward in 1635. It was finally published in 1851, over two hundred years later. The Franciscan influence in Donegal faded from the end of the seventeenth century until the twentieth century. Then in a celebration of the tercentenary of Michael O'Cleary's death it was decided to reopen a friary in Donegal. The seed that had lain fallow for so long finally bore fruit again when the new friary was opened here in 1946. Ever since it has been a centre of healing and recently has been dedicated since 1993 as the Franciscan Centre of Peace and Reconciliation.

As I came in the gates I first went into a peaceful sunken garden, which had as its centrepiece a tulip-shaped fountain. The bed of the fountain was full of coins that glistened in the clear water. People had hoped that the very act of throwing these coins into the fountain would lead to altered and richer events in their own lives. The supposition being that if you give up something of value then you might get something back from an otherwise callous fate. I had a different idea altogether for the water in the fountain. I sat on its rim and bathed my feet in its waters. In my own way I was giving something and getting something back. I left the garden with my feet fully refreshed, went into the church and sat there in its cool serene interior. This was a popular spot and other people were in there as well; a few were on their knees immersed in prayer and a tourist with a backpack was walking around the church having a look.

The door on one of the confessional boxes was open and a green light indicated that there was a priest available inside who would hear confessions. When someone went into the confessional a red light came on – little did we suspect that there was a 'red light district' in the local monastery! All these lights take the sport out of things, as it makes it difficult to 'accidentally' wander into extremely private conversations. Two women came into the church and went immediately to kneel outside the open confessional box. After a few minutes' prayer one of the women got up and went into the confessional. A few minutes later she came out with a very reverent look on her face, and went to a side altar in the church in order to presumably to say her penance. It was then the turn of the other woman who duly emerged with an equally contented look on her face – whatever goes on in there, seems to work.

The last time I had been in this church was when I was a boy. My mother brought me here occasionally to go to confession. I much preferred coming to the Franciscans for confession, as the priests were friendly and seemingly more tolerant of my list of childhood weaknesses. I presume that this was why it was also so popular with adults as well! The confession regime in our own church could be a bit unpredictable at times. Once when I confessed as a young boy to having stolen apples out of an orchard, the priest (who was a relative of mine) roared and shouted at me in the confessional. I came out with my head low, and I felt the eyes of all those waiting boring into my soul as I left. If I had looked more closely I suspect I might have seen some fear in their eyes. I suspect that the calibre of sins confessed later on that day by all the other people present were fairly minor indeed. I found out afterwards that this priest had an orchard himself and had suffered somewhat from opportunistic (or was it hungry?) children. Oh, the events of heaven and earth are continuously intertwined.

There is often great relaxation to be found in a church and I sat there for a while taking in the quiet. I resisted the temptation to go to confession however. Twenty years of sin to be confessed might tax even a lenient Franciscan. I got up instead and left the church and went across a pathway into a museum. This museum is famous as the smallest in Ireland. Its greatest treasure is a copy of the *Annals of the Four Masters*, which lies in a glass case inside the door. John O'Donoghue, a famous folklore collector, had translated this particular book. He was a very interesting man who among other things had walked the length and breath of Ireland collecting materials such as place names, etc. Now he was a real walker! This meant he was the ideal person to translate the book. He added a lot of footnotes from his own knowledge which add to the relevance of the text.

There is an assortment of weapons in the museum, in various levels of disrepair. These made little or no impact on me. I doubted very much from the look of them whether they at any time made any great impact on anyone else either.

I went outside and had a further look around. During my wanderings, I came to a lump of rocks situated on a beautiful spot overlooking the beach on Rossnowlagh. This was no ordinary heap of rocks, as many of the rocks had writing on them about people now dead. There were all sorts of rocks from big to small, all constituting a memorial to the grief that some people felt. Some had just plain writing on them, some had ornate artwork, but no matter how big, small or ornate they all held a memory of a person. These rocks were a collective memory, a sharing of sorrows, a celebration of lives and living, a search for healing, a connection with the living and the dead. The simplicity of a rock pile is a powerful message on the need for people to connect, to realise that we are part of something greater than ourselves. It is also a cry in the wilderness, a hope that someone will hear us in our pain and sorrow. Is there anyone out there? Whoever had chosen this spot for such a memorial had chosen well. It is a place of beauty but also a place of peace and quiet. It is a spot where people can come and reflect.

I found out afterwards that this memorial had been started as a reaction to an IRA bombing in Warrington in England where two young children lost their lives. The initiator was a local teacher who, out of despair for the futility of violence, decided that a site should be provided where people could make a gesture calling for the end of violence in this country and to promote reconciliation. The first stone was laid in 1993 in memory of the children in Warrington. Other people put their stones on top of this one, either in relation to Warrington or for their own personal reasons.

It is fascinating to see how the fortunes of the Franciscan involvement in Donegal have ebbed and flowed over a span of six hundred years. I personally welcome the fact that they are here, as their religion is not strident and not about the exercise of power. Though I am sure power plays some part in their lives, as they are human after all, their purpose is primarily about healing and supporting the inward journey. Given the discredited state of the Catholic religion in Ireland I think the wider Church would have more success if they followed this more gentle, though ultimately more difficult route. Their philosophy is encapsulated in the Prayer of St Francis and in the *Charter of Minority*. The prayer of St Francis goes as follows:

*Lord make me an instrument of your peace.*
*Where there is hatred, let me sow love.*
*Where there is injury, pardon.*
*Where there is doubt, faith.*
*Where there is despair, hope.*
*Where there is darkness, light.*
*And where there is sadness, joy.*

*O Divine Master, grant that I may not so much seek –*
*To be consoled as to console;*
*To be understood, as to understand;*
*To be loved, as to love;*
*For it is in giving that we receive –*
*It is in pardoning that we are pardoned;*
*And it is in dying that we are born to eternal life.*

However the slogans contained in the *Charter of Minority* pose a real challenge for all religions. Some of them go as follows:

"*Let them rejoice when they live among people of little note and despised, among the poor and weak, among the sick and lepers and among the beggars of the roads.*"
"*Not to be served, but to serve.*"
"*Let them wield no power or control.*"
"*Let no one be called 'Prior'.*"
"*Let them not be too concerned for temporal things.*"
"*Let them serve and be subject to every human creature for the love of God.*"

That night in order to continue the religious theme I decided to go to a pub in Donegal town and it was here that I met Ivan from Moldova. I had seen him around the town a few times previously, as he was a resident in the asylum seeker hostel there. He was standing beside a pillar in the pub on his own with a glass of beer in his hands. When he saw me a great big smile lit up his face and he came over to say hello. Ivan is a tall, swarthy, healthy-looking man in his mid-thirties. His English however was very poor, and he was very difficult to understand. During the course of our conversation he chain-smoked.

I pieced together his story the best way that I could. Ivan was from Moldova and has a wife there and four children. He had been involved in the military for a number of years before the revolution. After the revolution he fled from Moldova in fear for his life as the power structure had changed there. He talked in an animated manner as if it were important that someone understood him and engaged with him. His eyes filled with pain as he mentioned his family. With much difficulty he stated that he wanted to get a job here and take his family over to live with him. This was his hope but the odds on achieving this were stacked against him. Firstly one could wait years for the asylum process to run its course, and at the end of it the likelihood was that he would not succeed. Asylum seekers are not allowed to work or earn any money while their asylum claim is pending. He gets €19 a week to keep him going, and on that he is unlikely ever to be able to take his children over. Some asylum seekers manage to get work unofficially. I think Ivan got some short-term casual labouring work, so he was able to afford a drink. He insisted that he bought me a drink, I think grateful that someone was listening to his story.

All his communication was tinged with a feeling of helplessness, of a dream that was fast disappearing over the horizon. He told me that Ireland was his last hope. His journey since Moldova had brought him to Germany, Holland, France, Spain, Portugal and now Ireland. He kept saying that it was "impossible, impossible" when I asked him could he not get asylum status in any of these countries.

"Ireland, last chance, last chance," he said.

You could sense his feeling of failure in being unable to support his family. If you were to hazard a guess, the weight of this failure will lead eventually to Ivan losing contact with his family. He will become another wanderer on the earth.

I bought him a drink and after that we both left the pub. My head was throbbing with the effort made in understanding him, or then again it might have been the Guinness. He walked erectly down the street and over the bridge to the hostel. On enquiring about him afterwards I found out that he had been issued with a deportation order, and had disappeared before it could be executed. Somewhere in this world he still wanders, seeking a place, seeking a purpose, seeking a home, trying to make sense of it all. He is displaced from all he knows, from his language and culture and from anyone who meant anything to him. The echoes of many Irishmen who wandered parts of the world resonated in him, many of them victims, very few of them achieving the sweet smell of success.

Our rules and regulations about who has a valid claim for asylum cause much suffering among people who may have to wait for years in order to know whether they are successful or not. Their life is filled with days and days of waiting. Having nothing to do, nowhere to go is soul-destroying for everyone. If they were allowed even to do some work it would make it easier on everyone and ironically less expensive for the State. The Western world is comfortable but a lot of the rest of the world is in flux and experiences profound poverty. These two conditions are interlinked, in that a lot of our wealth is based on their poverty. We utilise their countries' labour and resources for our benefit and then try to protect ourselves from the consequences of our own actions by keeping people out of our country. Looking at the globe generally asylum seekers are likely to be an increasing part of our experience. If we embrace this change we have a chance of helping to enrich our own country, culturally, spiritually and economically. It is a process, which needs to be thought out and planned. If we treat the whole process suspiciously then we are likely to end up with entrenched and divided societies.

## Rossnowlagh to Bundoran

If there is such a thing as 'more peaceful than peaceful', it was the Friary in Rossnowlagh in the early morning. I stood outside the church listening to the birds chirruping in the surrounding trees. Even at this time there were a few people arriving to pray, or to search for some other connection in life. One sprightly elderly woman parked her blue Nissan car and said a cheery hello to me as she went into the already-opened, waiting Church. I decided to head in a different direction, taking a small road to Ballyshannon, which went over undulating countryside, and looked to be more interesting and quieter than the other bigger road to Ballyshannon.

There were three things that stood out for me on this road. The first was trying to avoid the menace of numerous tractors, which with hay balers attached filled up the whole road and seemed to be intent on running me over at every corner. When I heard the tractors coming I would have to scramble onto the ditch to avoid them. Being a good day it seemed that everyone was interested in getting their hay baled and they were not going to waste time slowing down for some inconsequential walker on the road. The second thing I noticed was that a large flock of starlings swooped in and landed on the roof of an old house and on the surrounding electricity wires. Their chattering filled the air with the sound of urgency. There seemed to be something dark and oppressive in their presence. My father always said that when starlings behaved like this, it was a sign of rain coming. He was bound to be right in making that particular statement – the only thing in doubt was the timing. I thought it would probably rain tomorrow which meant of course I had a good chance of keeping dry today. No wonder everyone was anxious to get the hay baled and taken care of. The final point I noted in that morning's walk was that I saw a hare, with three white legs silhouetted on a small hill, feeding warily. I have always thought of hares as somehow magical and have experienced a thrill of excitement every time I see one. Even when they would chop down my newly planted trees I would always forgive them. I remember one early spring morning; I was walking on the lane near my house, when I met a hare face-to-face only a few yards away from me. He sort of looked at me for a few moments, before turning and unhurriedly sauntering across my lawn leaving a dark trail in the glistening, early morning dew.

A feeling of melancholia swept over me – maybe it was the starlings – but I found it hard to get enthused by the countryside, the wildlife or the people I encountered along the way. A sense of 'what is the point of all this' descended on my head and got stuck underneath my scalp. There seemed to be no way in the world to get rid of this feeling. Did my walking here have any meaning at all outside of my own head, or for that matter even within it? The enormity of the universe was on my shoulders; its scale oppressed me, intimidated me and made me feel worthless. I had no real meaning. Nature itself seemed heavy and oppressive, offering no consolation. Did the universe have any purpose other than just some chance explosion at the beginning of known time? Billions of years later, and after countless mass extinctions on the Earth, here I was walking this little road between Rossnowlagh and Ballyshannon. It was all plainly ridiculous. What quirk of fate had put me here? I was but a grain of consciousness that had flickered forth for a while and which will fade away again. I felt like a cosmic spark – no more or no less. You should live for the moment I heard that mantra call; enjoy that spark whilst you still can. On reflection maybe I was just being bothered by the fact of ageing on this day. How could I accept the aches in my legs, when I could remember the way I once so effortlessly ran?

I looked back from the top of a hill over the sea at Rossnowlagh and watched the massive waves crashing and foaming upon the shore. My mind seemed full of incessant thoughts all pounding across my brow like the waves and more thoughts of transience and loss filled my head. Was my only role in life to pass on DNA in what we know to be a futile bid to preserve the species? Was there anything permanent that will last through eternity: a love, a friendship, a laugh, a connection? Will our atoms smash free and start off again, performing a new dance of meaning with no connection to the past existence? What will my atoms turn into: a firefly, a dragon, a blade of grass, a grain of sand or a cosmic quirk?

'What easy comfort religion is,' I thought. 'It is an easy way of not thinking about things. Is it just a set, meaningless rota in life? Why do I have these thoughts, why can I not be calm and peaceful?'

With all these thoughts thundering through my head and of course no resolution in sight, I suddenly found myself near the town of Ballyshannon.

Ballyshannon is situated on the Erne River, with a dam located on it about a mile from the town. This is now the main source of electricity for Co. Donegal. Ballyshannon was once, about a hundred years ago, the biggest town and sea port in the region but then the port silted up and Ballyshannon has been in decline ever since. It has now settled into a rather faded grandeur, which struggles to break out every so often.

On the road in front of me there was a commotion. A young man was trying, in vain, to push a car with two large women inside it, who as it transpired were holidaymakers from Northern Ireland. As a gentleman, I inquired of the man if there was anything I could help with. He looked at me with a modicum of relief in his face and asked if I could help push the car, to see if it would start. One of the passengers was obviously the navigator, for the other helpfully remained inside as myself and the young man started pushing! We strained our sinews against the resistance of the car and finally succeeded in building a bit of speed. It was all to no avail – when the driver let out the clutch, there was no sign of life in the engine. Not too easily daunted we tried again, but after about five more efforts at starting the car the woman behind the wheel said she would park it in a small lay-by. I think she belatedly recognised that we were knackered, which she probably deduced from my red face and wobbly walk. Relieved, we pushed the car into the lay-by. The woman then said she thought that the car was in fact out of petrol. With a smile she said she would phone her husband to go to the garage and get some. Seemingly he was in a pub down the road. Sensible man – getting others to do the donkey-work for him while he was sitting back relaxing himself.

Still in this mood I entered a road called the Mall, which takes one into the heart of the town of Ballyshannon, skirting the estuary and the bay. The most interesting thing that happened to me there was that I met a shrew walking along this track towards me. I stopped. He came bustling along and nearly banged into my toe. At the last moment he realised that there was potential trouble, so he turned and scurried in the other direction. I followed for about twenty metres as he looked for an escape route through a wall. He finally found a crevice into which he headed. As I passed I looked down and saw the two brightest, blackest, shiniest, alert eyes I ever have seen staring out at me. It was an electric moment. When I passed he re-emerged and headed in his original direction. If I were a shaman I would be claiming this as my power animal – just my luck to get a shrew when I always fancied a wolf or a dolphin. Ah well! It was one of those days, and wisdom is as likely to come from a shrew as a dolphin.

Further along the Mall a young woman with a baby in a buggy and two other children (a boy of about seven and a girl of about nine) were coming towards me. An old baseball cap was hanging on the branch of a small tree that was overhanging the footpath. The boy spotted the cap and ran to get it. The little girl suddenly became animated.

"Don't touch that cap. It is full of germs!" she shouted.

I wondered to myself where she had heard that statement before. Amazingly the young boy stopped and turned his back on the baseball cap and returned to the phalanx advancing along the footpath. I stood aside and as they passed I briefly contemplated taking the baseball cap myself. Seeing however that I already had a baseball cap on my head I decided it might be a bit too greedy, and it might be traumatic for the boy. God knows how he might turn out if he saw an adult taking the cap that he thought was his. I then rather graciously decided to leave it to the next child who would come along, or maybe this little boy might come back for it when not watched so closely.

I stood for a while and looked over the Erne estuary. A few small pleasure craft were moored on a small island in the middle of the estuary. It was here that Colmcille came to the rescue of Ballyshannon. The early Columban writers from Adamnan to Manus O'Donnell were keen to show that Colmcille was a superior saint to St Patrick. This is never stated baldly in the text but is left for you to assume through the actions described. The story goes something like this. When Patrick was converting Ireland he came to the Erne River which today flows into the Atlantic Ocean at Ballyshannon. Patrick got a good reception on the northern bank of the river where the people converted to Christianity and lands were donated for Churches etc. On the southern side of the river Cairbre, son of Niall of the Nine Hostages, refused to have anything to do with the new faith and he even had the temerity to refuse the saint land for churches and dwellings. In a fit of pique Patrick put a curse on them. The result of this curse was that from then on no fish would be caught on the southern side of the river and only a very small number would be caught on the northern side. This seems a bit harsh on the people who cooperated with him and were respectful of him. It just goes to show you that it does not always pay to be nice to people and that vengeance is a juicier fruit than loyalty rewarded.

However in the time of need a champion usually arrives. In this instance it was Colmcille, no matter if he were but seventy or eighty years late. Colmcille was fresh from sorting out the demons in Glencolmcille. No doubt he thought being on a roll he may as well sort out Ballyshannon as well. Just north of the town he met the local holy man Barrann mac Muiredhaigh who had helped him cast out the demons in Glencolmcille and who was lamenting that he had lost his holly staff in the conflict there. On hearing this Colmcille – in true epic Arthurian style – raised his own staff, also made from holly and stretched it out towards the sea. Wonder of wonders! Up popped Barrann's staff out of a rock in front of them. A stream of water gushed forth upon the track created by the staff so that there is a well of water in that place until this time. This well was called 'the trough of Barrann' as Colmcille said that the well should be called after Barrann.

Colmcille had restored Barrann's staff to its rightful owner and created a new holy well; he then proceeded to deal with St Patrick's curse. He lifted the curse so that the fish came in abundance to the river. He also called on the rocks in the waterfall to 'abase' themselves so that the fish could get up the waterfall more easily. One side of the waterfall lowered itself in obeisance to Colmcille, and the river Erne became the best fishing river in Ireland. In this way Colmcille was shown to be a more powerful saint than Patrick. We may laugh at such goings-on, but one of the great driving forces of humanity is the need to be seen to be better than some rival. He must have had some power though because the river up until recent times was one of the great fishing rivers of Ireland. No power lasts forever because the river has now reverted to a very minor fishing river again because of the construction of the aforementioned hydroelectric dam on the river upstream from Ballyshannon in the 1950s. I think we need someone like Colmcille to come again and weave some modern magic.

Despite Colmcille's intervention the river forms a divide to the people living in the town. The two sides of the river are in different parishes but not only that they are in different dioceses as well. These lines have left a mark on the town with a degree of suspicion between both sides. So maybe the legacy of Patrick was significant after all, and he might be happy to know that the division he fostered when he first came here is still in operation today. It may seem that these stories are 'fantastical' but they have to be seen in the context of the times in which they were written. In Ireland at that time Christianity had divided into two competing sects, the followers of Patrick and the followers of Colmcille. Each side was trying to gain influence over the people, and story is the most powerful medium there is. In a sense these stories are no different to the stories that politicians tell us today in order to get elected. They also have a similar relationship to the truth.

I wandered around Ballyshannon for a while and sat for a while on the footbridge across the Erne. From here one could see up the river with a good views of the dam. If one looked the other way it was possible to look out the estuary. A young man in army uniform passed followed by a group of teenagers talking on mobile phones.

I left Ballyshannon going up past the Rock Hospital. This is the spot where I was born. I pause a moment and look in as if trying to catch a memory. All I see now is a large slightly depressing looking stone building; there is no moment of magic in the air, no spiritual connection with this spot. I think about my brother who died stillborn, and how life might have been different if he had lived. If he had lived perhaps I would not have been born. A different mark would have been made on the annals of time. I feel that he is an entity out there sometimes inhabiting a world I cannot reach and to which I have no apparent connection. It should always be an honour to pass by the spot in which you were born. The fact that I cannot make a connection with the place may have to do with the troubled history of the building.

Early-nineteenth century Ireland saw a lot of poverty and destitution in the country. This was catered for on a charitable basis by a number of local committees comprised of the clergy and landed aristocracy. In Ballyshannon in 1840 a committee was established calling itself 'The Board of Guardians of Ballyshannon Union'. This was formed from the landed elite of the area as well as the local M.P. Colonel Connolly who chaired the committee. They were responsible for erecting the building in which I happened to come into the world so much later. This building was completed in 1841 and comprised of a master's room, dormitories, male and female 'idiot' wards, boys and girls schoolrooms, laundry, kitchen etc. The whole front of the building was kept as a meeting place for the 'Board of Guardians'. This place became home for the destitute and the 'idiots' of the area. The men worked at stone breaking and the women worked at knitting and laundry work. With the arrival of the Famine in the years 1845-49 the numbers seeking refuge of any kind increased alarmingly, from just over 100 people staying there the numbers increased to 900 inside the building and over 1,000 outside, all looking for relief. Many of these people died from the effects of starvation and disease.

A fever ward was added on to the building to try to cope with disease in the building. There were stories of unburied bodies piling up in the room for the dead. No wonder the building does not resonate with goodwill; there are too many unhappy memories enclosed within its walls.

John Mitchell the famous Irish Nationalist and writer described one of these places of local bureaucracy and suffering as follows, in his *Jail Journal*:

*"Rearing its accursed gables and pinnacles of Tudor barbarism, and staring boldly with its detestable mullioned windows, as if to mock those wretches who still cling to liberty and mud cabins – seeming to them in their perennial half-starvation, like a Temple erected to the Fates, or like the fortress of Giant Despair, whereinto he draws them one by one, and devours them there:- the Poor-house."*

The workhouse continued up until the 1920s and has been used for a number of things since including hospital, library and school. It is now a welfare home for older people. It may be that some of those older people are 'today's paupers' who are locked away from society when no longer wanted in their families and communities. After I was born there, my mother did not stay long after the birth – I think she must have felt the strange vibes of the place.

After leaving Ballyshannon the countryside was relatively flat, as I headed towards the hills and mountains of Sligo and Leitrim, which rise steeply from the plain. There was now the definite feel that I was headed into a different land, though I had to pass Bundoran in order to leave the county of Donegal. I passed a house with rows of teddy bears in the window. A small songbird fluttered on to a branch right beside my head. He showed no fear whatsoever; he then flew over to the teddy bear house at the other side of the road. I reckoned they must feed him, he was so tame. This looked like a child-friendly house, at least looking outwards to the world. If one was a child inside, I wonder what the view would be.

Growing up I had two teddies. One was a traditional teddy and the other was a long-limbed, rather wobbly creature that someone had made for me. For years and years they shared the bed with me. These teddies got lots of rough and affectionate treatment. Time went on and my consciousness of the teddy bears disappeared. Then I had children. With great ceremony and with full awareness of the importance of the occasion I presented my teddy bear to my son.

I passed this evocative 'teddy bear' house and came across a man in his stocking feet in the middle of the road. He was gazing at a white van, which was parked in a lay-by up the road. When he saw me coming he got embarrassed, and shuffled off with one sock half coming off. This was despite my best efforts to engage him in conversation. Even a stock phrase such as "Do you think the weather will hold up" failed to detain him. He disappeared into the house banging the door behind him. When I reached the lay-by I looked around the van that was parked there. I wondered what engaged the man's curiosity about the van. On the surface it was similar to countless other white vans that roamed the countryside.

I walked into Bundoran along a back street and past a small county council housing estate. Children were playing on skateboards on broken tarmac. Some other boys were kicking a football against a wall. Bundoran is one of the traditional seaside resorts of Ireland. It's a town full of caravan parks, bed and breakfast houses, guesthouses, hotels, amusement arcades and cheap restaurants. In the last number of years it received a tax exemption, which has resulted in a proliferation of apartments in the town bought by rich investors. Bundoran, during the summer months has depended for years on the tourist trade from Northern Ireland. There was always a strong connection between Bundoran and the 'North' but this however became very pronounced during the years of the 'Troubles', from 1969 on. Entire families from babies to grandparents to uncles, aunts and cousins all moved *en bloc* during the Marching Season to the refuge of Bundoran. In recent times a new breed of tourist has moved into the place. These tourists wear long hair, baggy shorts, drive old colourful vans and antique cars. Bundoran has become one of the principal European centres for surfing. Look out to sea on a day with rough seas and one will see the black wetsuits of the surfers mingling in the white surf.

Most Donegal people you talk to look at Bundoran with disdain. There is an immediate attempt to deny any ownership of the place at all. They all say (and I generalise) 'I would hate to live there'. Bundoran is like a part of themselves that they don't like and will go to any lengths to disown. The only people who disagree with this of course are from Bundoran itself, especially local politicians and business people. They are afraid that any bad publicity will hit profits and influence.

The street of Bundoran on this August day was full of holidaymakers, most with Northern Ireland accents. Families, some with push chairs, were wandering around the streets going from cheap restaurants to ice cream parlours, to amusement arcades. Lots of children were laughing, dancing about and giving out. Many of the pubs were full with people overflowing onto the street, pints in hand: men in shirt sleeves with waists pouring over trousers and young women wearing jeans and short tops. There was no sense of malice in the air, just people enjoying themselves in their own way; banter filled the air. A girl in her early twenties with probably a bit too much drink on her hailed me. Secretly pleased, I smiled and walked on.

I decided to go in to one of the bigger amusement arcades to see what fortune fate had in store for me. Most of the amusement 'palaces' were set up in the same manner – the front to cater for children and adolescents, lots of arcade games involving shooting, football and driving, dancing machines, lucky dips, fluffy toys, photographs etc. and in behind where the real action takes place. This 'in-behind' spot was the world of gambling and slot machines where real money can be made. I walked around the arcade and the place was full of middle-aged and older women who were intensely focusing their attention on one or more slot machines. Their hands moved to the rhythm of the machine, inserting coins, pressing buttons, pulling handles. Each of these actions produced a distinctive noise, be it whirring, buzzing, and clanging. Then a hush, as ears are perked for any prospect of winning, the noisy clamour of coins rushing out of the machine. Most of these wins were small, just enough to keep you involved for another while. Just occasionally there was a sound of a jackpot being won, usually in some other part of the building. This was a solitary, preoccupied world in the midst of addictive hubbub.

I decided to join in the fun so I went up to a cash kiosk, bought a box of coins and plonked myself down beside a small thin woman of about forty with peroxide-blonde hair, busily playing three machines with cigarette in hand. She alternated between the machines, playing each one twice before moving to the next one. She certainly had no time for a chat: gambling was a very serious business indeed. The fates must have been with me however for lo and behold, after putting my third coin into the machine it suddenly shuddered and dispensed a clatter of coins into the holder and then with a final shake it reluctantly let go of its final coin. I could feel the resentment from the woman beside me; I could nearly hear her thinking 'If only I had played that machine...' In her head my winnings were her loss.

At this stage I had a dilemma. Should I take my winnings and go or stay and see if I could win some more? I thought to myself that I would be cute and play a different machine, as this one would not be paying out any time soon. On this other machine I proceeded over the next thirty minutes to lose all my winnings. The house won again. As I left the arcade the blonde woman, yet another cigarette in hand, was still playing. Maybe she knew more about this than I did? There must be a way to beat the system!

Did Bundoran conform to the journalist's opinion? Every experience is a snapshot in time; my experience of Bundoran on this day was not like the journalist's, but then again I wasn't there at night when things get more fraught. Bundoran is not a place I personally would like to spend a few weeks. I think that every region needs a place like Bundoran, where people can go every so often to give expression to that part of themselves which panders to the senses.

I finished the day by taking the path to the top of the cliffs, which forms part of the attraction of Bundoran. I sat there and gazed out across an unusually calm sea. I knew that tomorrow the waves would come pounding in again. Why think about the future when I could appreciate the present – that famous 'now' moment.

## Inishmór – The Island

The literature documents that Colmcille went to many of the islands of the Irish and Scottish coasts in order to spread his influence. The most famous island associated with Colmcille is Iona, which lies off the Scottish coast, and it was from here that he carried out most of his missionary work on the British mainland. The islands he is most associated with in Ireland are Tory and Arranmore off the coast of Donegal and Inishmór off the Galway coast. A walk tracing Colmcille's footsteps without visiting an island would (in a sense) be incomplete because of the importance of islands in Colmcille's day-to-day consciousness. After some deliberation I decided to visit Inishmór in the famous Aran Islands. I had never been there before – Colmcille was more purposeful, in that he went ostensibly to pay a courteous visit to St Enda, the local 'head honcho'. In reality he was planning a religious coup.

Inishmór is the largest of the three Aran Islands situated off the Galway coast. The Aran Islands may be close to the coast of Galway, but geologically speaking they are part of the famous limestone Burren in Co. Clare. Limestone rock in all its forms is the dominant feature of the islands and has provided inspiration for artists over the ages. It is a soft rock with sharp edges, which some people say is also a feature of the people living on the island. One thing is sure – Inishmór is a place that has been immersed in spirituality over the millennia, possessing a multitude of fascinating archaeological sites dating back thousands of years.

When we think of islands of the west coast of Ireland we now think of isolation and marginalisation. In reality however islands have been some of the main centres of power, religion and trade in our history. This trend developed from the earliest times of habitation. Some of the first settlers in this country built islands called crannogs in the middle of rivers and lakes as a means of defending themselves from unwanted human and animal intruders. It was logical therefore that islands such as the Aran Islands developed into natural centres of power, as they were more easily defended. On the other hand the interior of the country, being heavily forested, was a lot more threatening, full of human and animal threat. So it was very strategic for Colmcille to try and spread his influence on to as many islands as he could.

Before Inishmór, Colmcille went to Tory Island off the coast of Donegal. It is important to tell of his visit to Tory in order to put visits to other islands in context. In the literature it is stated that an angel told him to go to Tory. I am sure one excuse is as good as another. It is certainly advantageous to get divine approval for your actions, a lesson well learned by countless religious and political leaders since. When Colmcille reached Tory he was not well received by Oilill, the King of the Island. Despite divine approval Oilill trenchantly refused to give Colmcille any land for his church and monastic dwellings, as he quite rightly saw him as a danger to his rule of the island. Colmcille then seemed to back down and asked if he would at least consider giving him a piece of land the width of his cloak. Oilill said he would, for he could see no harm in giving him that much. Colmcille took off his cloak, laid it out on the ground. To the surprise of all assembled it spread out to cover the whole island. Perhaps this is where the saying 'give an inch and take a mile' comes from?

As you can see Colmcille would stop at nothing to get his own way especially, when it concerned furthering his religious cause. Oilill flew into a rage at this chicanery and set his most venomous hound on Colmcille so as to kill him. Colmcille said a prayer and the hound dropped down dead. Oilill on then gave the whole island to Colmcille for his use and asked to be baptised into the Church. Coward! But I suppose the wise thing to do when confronted with superior power, is to submit and hang on to what influence one can.

When Colmcille went to Inishmór he tried the same trick on Enda. This time he didn't have the excuse that the ruler was a pagan. Enda is recognised as one of the most learned of Irish saints, but Colmcille thought that he should have land for his monastery on the island as well. In fact he thought that he should have the whole island. Colmcille made the same request, asking for only the ground that his cloak would cover. Enda acceded to this request graciously enough. When Colmcille laid the cloak on the ground, Enda recognised what was happening – he lifted the cloak when it had only covered one field. He then refused to give Colmcille any land whatsoever. Quite right he was too! Colmcille did not exactly curse the island but he did the next best thing – Inishmór would not prosper because it would lack his blessing. Many ills are reputed to have fallen on Inishmór, one of which is that it would have no turf or wood for fires from that day on.

Like any politician Colmcille was a master of spin. He was only stating the obvious because even at that time Inishmór was a windswept barren place that was not conducive to the growth of trees or bog. He was putting the blame for the lack of prosperity squarely on to the shoulders of Enda.

My friend Martin decided to accompany me on the visit to Inishmór to see for ourselves the 'effects' of Colmcille's curse. We have made a lot of journeys together, usually on a bicycle, and share an ability to not annoy each other too much. This may be due to his job as a human resources manager for a multinational company. His planning skills are not so good however, as a storm blew up on the day we decided to visit Inishmór; this was entirely his fault, and I kept on reminding him of this fact all morning. He told me that I had brought the weather with me from Donegal. During the day the winds reached 75 mph and the rain was driving across the rocky landscape of Connemara out of dark, angry, grey skies.

"There is not a hope in hell that we will get a sailing to Inishmór today," said Martin once more, as we sat in the lounge of a pub in Connemara overlooking the harbour.

"You would be lucky to get a sailing today, right enough," said a rather rotund gentleman who was the only other occupant of the lounge bar.

He had been sitting quietly at a table near us, supping a pint and apparently minding his own business. To mind one's own business is never a good idea in a bar, because one of the main reasons for going into a bar is to hear all that is going on in the locality. It should have been no surprise that he thought it would be worthwhile to join into our riveting conversation. He had an easy friendly manner and conversation in a bar is never meant to be private, especially if there is the prospect of a good argument, discussion or the sharing of a juicy piece of gossip. We found out that our friend was a former gaelic footballer turned salesman. We had an extensive discussion about the state of football and politics. This man exuded the aura of someone tired of the salesman's life, but who is trapped into that way of life. However football touched his soul, and as he talked about it, enthusiasm came back into his eyes. Everyone needs a passion in life, especially in a bar.

We ordered soup and sandwiches from the barmaid and Martin, in need of a shot of adrenaline ordered a white coffee. A look of puzzlement spread across the barmaid's face.

"A white coffee," she repeated, in a questioning tone.

"That's right," said Martin.

A few minutes later she came back with a black instant coffee and a small jug of milk. Martin had expected a coffee made on hot milk. He looked bemused.

"Is the coffee OK?" asked the barmaid.

"It's fine," said Martin, practising his human relations assertiveness skills.

It always pays when you know to cut your losses. Replenished if not fulfilled we said goodbye to our football/salesman colleague and headed, more in hope than expectation, to the harbour. The wind was howling and the rain was driving nearly horizontal across the pier. Much to our surprise we found that the ferry was indeed going out to the island.

Rather dubiously we boarded the ferry along with a gregarious gathering of people, a wedding party heading out to the island. Apparently it is now popular for people to go and get married on the island, as it somehow seems more authentic to them to wed on a mysterious island like Inishmór than in the church down the road. Safely ensconced on board the ferry we got talking to the soon-to-be-wed couple who were sitting just in front of us. They told us the wedding was going to be in an old historic church on the island called Teampall Ciarán, the main feature of which was that it had no roof. How optimistic can you get in Ireland? Is this what love does to you? I suppose at times we need something that blinds us to the reality all around; looking out the window at the black grey sky we wished them luck!

The ominous clouds did not seem to be bothering anybody too much, as there was much joviality amongst the wedding party; people were talking, taking photographs and pointing video cameras indiscriminately in every direction. How do people ever edit videotapes – do they spend the whole winter watching their outings all over again?

I remember once reading about a man who has the perfect memory. He has the capacity to remember every detail of a whole day. The only trouble is it takes him a whole day to do it. It strikes me that video camera tapes are a bit like that, full of tedious detail. Anyway we featured prominently in the footage, so much so that in the future when the happy couple review the tapes they might wonder who invited that pair of idiots to the party.

The ferry then took off and started to sway violently from side to side. There was no one daring to stand now. Everyone remained rooted to his or her seat as a worried tension filled the cabin. In fact – let us call a spade a spade – it was downright fear. However the ferry progressed at a remarkable speed. What sort of foolhardy captain have we in charge here? I thought to myself. It could be that we were all like lambs to the slaughter, so easily did we put our lives into the hands of someone else. For all we knew the captain of the ferry could have a bottle of whiskey in each hand and a manic look on his face as he brought us all for a personal introduction to King Neptune. On occasions (reassuringly!) the captain would cut the engines as a bigger than usual wave approached. Looking out the windows of the ferry one could see oncoming walls of water. When they were close they would blot out the view of the sky as they rumbled through us. On one occasion the boat went over so far that I thought it would never come back up again. I looked at one crewman's face to see if he was in any way worried. If he was it did not register on his thin aquiline face. Probably a good poker player, I thought suspiciously. He spent the entire crossing assisting people who were getting sick or who were about to get sick. I am sure this is one of the high points of his job!

A deathly pale young woman struggled up to him and asked him if she could go outside (to be sick). He looked at her with a kind amusement in his eyes.

"If you go out," he said, "make sure and you don't fall overboard because the paperwork is horrendous!"

He then helped her to go somewhere more appropriate for her physical state.

Everyone was quiet; there were a lot of nervous glances at each other as people non-verbally shared their concern with each other. Sometimes the silence would get too much for somebody and they would try to puncture it with black humour. If one could put in a bag all the thoughts that were running around the ferry on that crossing I have a feeling that it would be so heavy that it would sink quicker than the ferry. Eventually after what seemed an eternity the waves started to get smaller as we approached shelter of Inishmór. The tension eased, people got up from seats that they were previously glued into, and the noise of human interaction rose like the chant of bees in a hive. Looking out the window we could see one of the naval ships sheltering from the storm – softies!

Cameras started flashing again, the woman sitting in front of us took out her video camera, on which we again featured. She asked us what we thought of the crossing. We told her we didn't think it was too bad, hoping to give the impression of seasoned travellers and hoping she didn't notice how pale we were. If she had noticed or commented on our pallor, I had an ingenious excuse already prepared; we could have told her that we had just been released from prison. This excuse is the product of reading too many cowboy books in my boyhood, in which the escaped convict could always be recognised by his pale complexion. I suppose though, that the sunny Wild West of America has a slightly different climate to the wild west of Ireland. In this country it is probably the convicts who have the tan!

We disembarked from the boat with tremulous legs amidst a spreading assortment of bags, cases and musical instruments of the wedding party. It looked like it might be one great party as they had enough stuff with them to last at least for a month. There was now an infectious, manic excitement rolling through the guests accompanied by an aimless energy, which in all likelihood would be dissipated later in a pub. We went off in a different direction and struggled to our bed and breakfast, only to find that our booking had not been confirmed – another example of Martin's bad planning. However given the bad weather and the fact that her other guests had 'chickened out' the woman was able to put us up.

Satisfied that we now had a bed we decided to go into Kilronan village, which was about 2 miles away for something to eat. We hailed the first minibus we saw and surprisingly it stopped for us. We climbed aboard to find the bus full, with twenty young women from Castlebar (a nearby town on the mainland) all in gregarious mood and high spirits. We looked at each other and thought that it must be true that the island was a centre of the spiritual life after all. Why else would so many young women be coming to Inishmór?

"All these quiet women must be here for the religion," I rather loudly opined to Martin.

"They are a holy looking bunch of people all right," he replied.

We were absolutely shocked that such an obvious truth would be greeted with absolute mirth and uncontrollable laughter. Our illusion was totally shattered by a maelstrom of protest and insults.

"No island man is going to be safe this weekend!" announced one of the seemingly demure women.

This proclamation was followed by many hurrahs and cheers. We told the driver he was lucky that we had come along to save him. He didn't seem too daunted by the prospect, however. After all, he was getting €2 a head for a 2-mile journey. It was no wonder he had a resigned look on his face!

The next morning we got up early, as we planned to walk across the island to Dun Aenghus. The fort is one of the most famous sites on the Aran Islands. We looked out the window but the sky was ominously black. Over breakfast curiosity got the better of us and we decided that we would have a look at the old church where the wedding was going to take place. Who knows, we reckoned, if we play our cards right we might even get an invite. Miracle of miracles, it was dry when we left the bed and breakfast, but the sky was still threatening. Teampall Ciarán was about a mile away, and we approached the old church by overgrown paths between the stone walls. Cattle were grazing along the paths and they remained more or less oblivious to us as we passed. We clambered over a number of stone walls on the final approach to the church; we didn't know it then but we had chosen the most awkward route possible, as there was a main path that went right to the front of the church. But sure, what else would you expect when Martin assumed the job of navigator! As we crossed the walls we noticed that there were no gates on view in this part of the island; the gaps between fields are built up with stone, which can be easily dismantled or assembled when needed. When we got to the church we found that Teampall Ciarán still had four solid, well-preserved walls but as everyone had previously informed us, the roof has long disappeared. Gravel had been spread to act as a floor. There was a stone altar under a long window opening with an incredible view to the sea below. One can see why it would appeal to hold a special event such as a wedding here, especially if viewed on a sunny day. Like lots of churches it is located in one of those magic spots our religious ancestors were so good at locating.

Teampall Ciarán itself is built upon the ruin of a previous church called Mainistir Chonnacht. It is dedicated to St Ciarán who founded Clonmacnoise and spent seven years on Inishmór as a pupil of St Enda. The original Teampall Ciarán was probably built in the eighth century. This church thus gives us a connection with the ultimate goal of the walk, unifying the 'gold' and 'silver' strands of the dream. Outside the church there were a number of stone slabs inscribed with crosses upon them. In one of these was a circular hole. I proceeded to try and take a photo of the sea below through it. Martin looking at my contortions laughed.

"I always knew you were a bit strange," he said.

"This photograph will make me famous and then the laugh will be on the other side of your face," I said, as I waved my disposable camera in his face.

"You got that right," he said. "That photograph will certainly give us a good laugh."

We then spotted a middle-aged couple dressed in snazzy hiking gear coming up the grassy path towards the church, passing a cow and calf on their way. Being the curious sort we said hello to them, because really, you could not ignore anybody in a place like this without being thought of as strange. They told us that they were going to the wedding and they had come to check out the place. Ominously, just at that moment a light drizzle of rain started to fall.

"I think I will come in my waterproofs," said the husband.

"The bride is coming dressed in white!" his wife announced, laughing.

"Well you are lucky in that you have the sky as a roof today," said Martin helpfully.

"And even luckier to have the clouds as insulation," I added.

They dutifully laughed at these observations.

"Do not despair, at least the lawnmower is working," I said, pointing at the cow and calf working away, assiduously cropping the grass on the path to the church.

"They are spreading some welcoming petals along the way as well," added Martin.

"I suppose that wearing wellingtons to the wedding would be out of the question?" said the woman to her husband.

We all laughed at the prospect of a great day's entertainment. At this stage the wind picked up and it started to rain more heavily. The couple made a dignified retreat in order, I am sure, to ponder future tactics. We made for the road that would take us to Dun Aenghus.

This part of the island is a maze of stone walls that carve their hodge-podge designs into the landscape. These walls are a living testament to the people who cleared the land in order to make small fields. When they had cleared the fields they then had to carry seaweed and sand and spread it on the surface of broken rock in order, over time, to make a surprisingly fertile soil. The walls, which are in the main from five to six feet tall, provide shelter for the animals from the strong winter winds, hail, and rain. The walls also shelter the soil and help preserve it against erosion. These walls also gave us some protection against the driving rain, which was getting heavier as the minutes went on.

As we walked along Martin continued the theme of matrimony by telling me about a wedding he had attended some twenty years previously. One of his friends was marrying a woman from Munster, which is as far away as you can get on the island, meaning that both the bride and groom's invitees would be total strangers to each other. The officiating priest was a man well known for his passionate beliefs, especially those that had a Republican flavour. All went well up to the end of the meal when the priest was asked to make a speech, which the custom has it, is usually to extol the virtues of the bride and groom and praise both families. The priest ignored the usual protocol and went directly into delivering a deeply republican speech. He announced that the couple were a credit to the country that had produced them. (Parents have a very minor role in this process it seems). He continued by emphasising how this was now a fine, free, independent country, but it should be remembered that it had not always been free. He extolled the virtues of the many fine people who had given up their lives to produce a country where people like the bride and groom could grow up happily. At this stage, Martin said, he got so wrapped up in his subject that he forgot all about the bride and groom and continued to talk passionately about Ireland. During this his voice got deeper, his face redder, his eyes larger as he went into detail on the numerous ways in which this was such a great country. Then, aroused to a deep fervour, he urged everyone to stand up. When everyone stands the usual ritual is that toasts are made to the bride and groom. But to the utter bemusement of the happy couple and their guests he ignored the convention and urged everyone to sing 'A Nation Once Again', a well-known republican anthem. This he began with a bellowing voice, which was well accustomed to being obeyed. It is no wonder the Catholic Church compares the people to the lambs of God! Of course the priest regards himself not so much an extension of the people but as an extension of God himself, which is a typical approach to management!

This song ('A Nation Once Again') believe it or not was voted the planet's favourite song in a 2002 poll organised by the BBC World Service. This poll attracted votes from 155 countries and for about 7,000 songs. John Lennon's 'Imagine' was nowhere close in the poll. Queen's 'Bohemian Rhapsody' finished in tenth place and was the highest-ranked British song. A close runner up was a Hindi song and another high finisher was that well-known song called 'Poovum Nadakkathu Pinchum Nadakkathu', which was sung by Tamil vocalist Thirumalai Chandran. This really demonstrates why we should take phone-in polls seriously! The online canvassers may have been related to this priest because they were urging people to register '800 years of British oppression' as their reason for nominating the song.

There was now some activity on the road behind us. A horse and trap came trotting by. It was piloted by a weather-beaten man well used to the vagaries of the climate on the island. On the back of the trap a miserable-looking couple were getting more sodden by the moment. They probably wondered why they had bothered taking such a conveyance on a day like that. They certainly did not acknowledge our existence with any look or gesture. They were followed immediately afterwards by a large group of cyclists of mixed abilities and ages. However in contrast there was much laughter as they passed by. (The island does a big business in hiring out bicycles, as it is the ideal way of exploring the island). We gave them as much encouragement as we could, by shouting to them that they had a puncture in their back wheel. Sure what else would be slowing them up? Mutual pleasantries delivered, we followed them as fast as we could. The landscape became rockier and the fields disappeared, as it had been impossible to clear the land in this area of the rocks to form fields. We passed a lake and now we could see Dun Aenghus on a hilltop to the left of us.

A pick-up truck with a load of boxes on board passed us and of course splashed us. Shortly afterwards we came to a cluster of tourist shops. Outside one of the shops, all the boxes, which had been on the truck, were stacked and two elderly women were struggling in the rain to take them into the shop. We offered our services, which were accepted without demur. We carried the boxes inside and stacked them all, as ordered at the back of the shop. When we were finished we tried to engage the two women in conversation, but it seemed that these two shopkeepers were too busy to do that. The impression given was that they were too canny to fall for the wiles of two con men like us. They appeared to think that we were up to no good, trying to do them out of something, like looking for money or maybe even that we were trying to chat them up. We did ask where we could get a cup of coffee. They assured us with scarcely concealed relief that they had no coffee in the shop but that there was a coffee shop nearby which might serve us.

Seeing that they had no more work for us to do, we ran to the coffee shop through the belting rain feeling very chastened, as if we were small boys who had done something wrong. As we tumbled puffing and red-faced through the door, we were greeted by shouts of derision and merriment. The cycling group who had passed us earlier were all there. Suffice to say that we suffered for our earlier comments about punctures. Martin went up to the counter and asked yet again for a white coffee. Getting a bemused look he quickly changed his order.

"Ahh, make that a tea instead," he said.

The waitress was a sullen, pretty girl who obviously was not enamoured about being in this particular spot at this moment in time – she did not give a damn. We were just more tiresome tourists who had to be barely endured. However the cyclists (God bless them) had homemade cake and sweets; despite the earlier good-natured insults they had no difficulty in sharing with us. This big gang of over twenty people were all from the same extended family, and they regularly went away together as a unit; what a great achievement. I am sure it is great for all of them to belong to a large gathering of people who seemingly get on so well together.

Miracle of miracles, the rain suddenly stopped. Looking at the sky we reckoned that the dry spell would not last too long, so we made a dash for Dun Aenghus. There is a recently built interpretative centre at the foot of Dun Aenghus, which tells its known history. A small entrance fee of about €2 is charged for the pleasure of visiting the fort. Having joined the queue we found after a period that it was not moving. On investigation we saw that a tall German man laden down with cameras and video recorders was arguing with the ticket receptionist. He was protesting in a loud voice, saying that it was a scandal that he had to pay into a public site. (I presume from this that no one pays into anything in Germany). The receptionist eventually called for the supervisor, who remained firm about the entrance fee, though she gave him the address of Dúchas, the heritage body who manage this site. He eventually bought a ticket, stating that he was going to write to Dúchas to complain. The letter would probably cost him more than the entrance fee.

Dun Aenghus is one of the most dramatic Iron Age stone forts of Western Europe, perilously perched on the edge of a 300-foot sheer cliff that drops straight down to the sea below. It has three rows of defences forming roughly concentric semicircles. The innermost has wall-walks and wall-chambers, and a large entrance passage, which has been restored. Outside this is a second and third wall each about ten feet high and thirteen feet thick. Beyond these walls stand thousands of lance-like stones, placed close together in the ground, to prevent easy access to armies wishing to attack this place. This type of defence is still useful today. The term for these stone stakes is *chevaux-de-frise*, originally soldiers who used a wall of lances and spears to stop cavalry. It is remarkable to think that thousands of years ago people lived here on the top of these sheer vertical cliffs above the swell and roar of the Atlantic Ocean. I wondered how they managed to care for their children in such a spot. Did they give them wings? Well I hope not prematurely anyway! Any time I take any of my children near a cliff face, I get paroxysms of fear, and I don't rest easily until they are far away from it. It must have had some benefits for child rearing in that time. I am sure they had no need for the threat of the big stick!

A group of teenagers were gambolling about at the edge of the cliffs. A red-faced middle-aged man shouted at them to be careful with no discernible impact. He then went up to them and persuaded them to lie down and look over the edge of the cliff. A few more teenage boys came up and of course caught the feet of the boys who were lying down and mockingly threatened to dump them over the side. The man again had to bark an order. He was obviously a youth leader or a teacher who was taking this group on an educational tour. I pitied him. They all rose as one mass of restless energy and proceeded in an edgy, agitated flow along the cliff face, jostling each other as they went. Some of them stopped, got stones, threw them over the edge and then rather fruitlessly strove to see them hit the sea below. These were young men trying to make an impact, striving for recognition. Our society usually avoids groups of boys like this, as they are seen to be a threat rather than a group of people with whom to make a connection. It is not easy for us to engage with the jumbled up energy that is adolescence. Herman Hesse described this period as being the time of 'the child who is no longer a child', people who in our modern society are stuck in a time of waiting with no specific role to fulfil. It is often a time of aimlessness and loneliness with no affirmation from the wider society, which is in fact the thing they need the most. Fair dues then to the youth leader who brought them here, probably for little or no reward. God help him if anything happened to any of them. Individuals, the bureaucratic organs of state and the media would pillory him. He would be sued for every penny he was worth by people who generally do not give a damn. He would be told that he had acted irresponsibly in bringing young people to a dangerous spot like this. We give awards to celebrities and ignore people who give of themselves to others. We get the type of society we deserve.

On all the circular walls of Dun Aenghus there are signs forbidding people from climbing or walking on them. We got talking to the woman whose job it was to enforce these rules. She told us that there had been a real falloff in the number of tourists since '9/11' in the States. She was a red-faced, middle-aged woman with a rather severe expression, the type of person who does not easily see another person's point of view. I judged she would be excellent to have around in a crisis, as she seemed to have a very practical nature. She is probably none of these things, and these are obviously my own judgements. We talked about the wedding party we had met coming onto the island. Of course I should not have been surprised that she knew all about it. She then informed us that there has been on average three weddings a week coming onto the island from the mainland. On impulse I asked her where the island people got married. She immediately said Galway, which if you don't know is the nearest city on the mainland to Inishmór Island. Typical, I thought. Mainland people were searching for the romanticism, spirituality and the nature of an island whilst the island people were looking the other direction to the lure and excitement of the city. I suppose this is fairly typical of the human condition, as we are never satisfied with what we are.

Suddenly something grabbed the attention of the warden.

"Come off that wall immediately!" she shouted.

Our eagle-eyed conversationalist had now turned into a spiral of fiery energy. Official business called. She left us in an abrupt manner and strode towards the unfortunate subject of her ire. This was a woman with three young children all probably under six years of age. This young mother had placed her children on the steps leading up to the walls of the fort with a view to taking a photograph of them. She pretended for a moment not to hear the guardian of the walls, and endeavoured to take the photograph before the swirl of energy arrived. This was to no avail because a new command that could not be ignored filled the air.

"Did you not hear me? Get those children off the walls immediately!"

Everyone else certainly heard her. The woman reluctantly abandoned her photo in obvious embarrassment. Without ever glancing at her tormentor she took the three children off the steps, arranged them in a permitted position underneath the walls and proceeded to take her photograph. The children and the eldest girl in particular kept a wary eye out for any further possible humiliation. The expressions on the children's faces should make for a very interesting photograph indeed. Having accomplished her task, the warden went on a tour of inspection to see if there were any other miscreants.

Looking over the part of the island visible from Dun Aenghus one could see the wet, grey sheets of rock glistening and shining like mirrors in the watery sun. Interspersed amongst the rocks there were small patches of brown grass. This particular area of the island had been too rocky for even the people of Inishmór to make fields out of. Looking the other way across the ocean we could see the next sweep of rain heading across the ocean. The sky had joined forces with the sea in threatening colours of black and grey, swirling towards us. The view and the light disappeared as the fluid wall approached and then effortlessly engulfed the land. Rather than stay and experience what life would have been like in a rain storm if living on Dun Aenghus we beat a cowardly retreat from the fortress.

The rain caught up with us as we left the site. We looked at each other and neither of us fancied walking back to Kilronan in the downpour. We spotted a minibus and asked if we could have a lift. The minibus driver apologised and said that he had a full load already. We considered hiring a horse and trap, one of which was tied to a gate just outside the centre, waiting on lazy tourists like us. We took a look at the bowed head of the bedraggled horse who studiously avoided eye contact. Recognising defeat we took pity on him and headed off walking instead.

Heads down we walked into the pelting rain. We went for a mile or so when another minibus pulled up beside us and the friendly-faced driver offered us a lift. We thankfully climbed on board. The minibus driver put a different complexion on the storm we had encountered on the way over to the island. He told us that all the lobster fishermen spent the morning looking for pots that might have been blown ashore during the storm. For these men he said the storm was a disaster, as it wiped out a significant proportion of their yearly earnings. To us it had been a rather 'safe' experience that we could later talk to our friends about; to these fishermen the storm had brought real troubles and hardship.

The driver knew a lot of the fishermen in Donegal, and Killybegs in particular. He had owned a boat for a while but was forced to give it up as he found difficulty in meeting the repayments. He put the reason for this fairly and squarely down to the excessive amount of fish quota that the bigger boats were allowed to catch as opposed to the smaller fishermen. As in many businesses the smaller operator was being forced out. For an island people who have made their living from the sea for generations upon generations it is a fairly grim prospect. This situation is being felt in various other small coastal communities around the country. Because these small-time operators are a powerless segment in our society their wishes are always overlooked. The focus for developing an industry should start with the indigenous fishing families. These people however are not listened to, and are excluded from licensing and grant aid. The driver had a sympathetic audience when he talked about the difficulties facing smaller operators.

As we arrived in Kilronan, the mini bus driver asked us where we wanted to be left off, whilst informing us that based on his experience of the sea there was going to be no let up in the rain. After due consideration, lasting at least two seconds, we asked him to drop us at the nearest pub. I can truthfully say that I have very little memory of events thereafter. I have some hazy memory of an important football match on the television, of a group of students from Trinity, of people from Italy and Glasgow, of a musician vainly attempting to play the tin whistle, and of other wet tourists coming into the place not to drink but to avoid the rain.

Afterwards in the nearby restaurant Martin and I had a discussion on the role of the Church in Ireland. The conversation was well lubricated from the early evening's drinking. I talked about our parish at home which has four priests in four big houses. I was expounding on the need for the Church to develop a new vision, because the traditional model based on power and separateness was not healthy, and it was not working. Martin thought that the old model was a large contributor to the mental ill-health of a lot of priests. This came out in different forms such as high rates of alcoholism, and unfortunately as we have seen in the abuse of children. I think that most of the priests joined with the highest of motives but idealism can only sustain you for so long. The combined forces of power, loneliness and celibacy can corrupt these ideals. Thus we reckoned having four priests in four separate houses is not a model for the future unless priests are allowed to marry. In the course of the meal we designed how the Church should look on the macro level and the micro level of the parish in question.

On the macro scale we decided that the Church needed more humility: priests have to become facilitators of spirituality rather than directors of religion. Priests should be allowed to marry and have relationships, and of course women should be allowed to become priests. It is patently ridiculous that half the human race is excluded from participation. We had a debate on whether the Church should renounce all wealth but did not come to an agreement about this. We did agree however that religious services should be designed and performed by people themselves, using their unique and special skills. We thought that participation was the key.

On the local parish level our recommendation was that one of the four houses should be turned into four flats for each of the priests. The house would have a common kitchen. We recommended that one of the other houses should be turned into a performing arts centre for young people from rock music to games centre. One of the other houses should be turned into a spiritual/healing centre where people could come for re-energising in the personal, physical, social and spiritual journey. The other house should be sold in order to help finance these developments.

When I got home I shared my views with my children that religious service should be a participative rather than a passive exercise. My children vehemently gave this idea the thumbs down. They have a memory of a priest who tried to involve young people in the Mass through creative dance and music etc. Their view was that it made the whole show far too long. Their definition of the ideal service is the shortest possible Mass with the least possible input! In essence this is the spiritual challenge for the Church, how to engage young people in the life of the Church that is more meaningful than performing empty rituals.

The Aran Islands have a spiritual connection for people. It has been a place where for thousands of years people have come in order to make some special connections. From Enda to Colmcille to the present day it has been a place of searching and worship. Perhaps being so close to the sea and the sky is the thing that gives islands like Inishmór their special meaning. Perhaps it is here and in places like this that people will come searching once again for meaning and connection.

Exhausted after such an intellectual conversation we retired yet again to a local pub. It so happened that the new football pitch had been opened on the island that day. People had come from all the other islands and from the mainland to help the local people celebrate. Like stout warriors of yore the bad weather seemed to have no negative impact on their commitment, as the pub was heaving with people. I have never in all my life seen a pub so jam-packed with people. It was virtually impossible to move in the place and of course the music was so loud that we could hear nothing anyone said either. It took us about ten minutes to struggle our way through the throng to the door. On the way home, again taking our lives into our hands, we called into another pub. We found the survivors of the wedding party firmly ensconced there. We renewed old acquaintances that we had met earlier and found out that the wedding in the roofless church had to be transferred to a hall. That inconvenience however seemed to have had no impact on the level of celebrations, which were still in full, good-humoured flow. One of the older men we met informed us that he had worked in Guinness brewery. He kept on telling us that the Guinness served nowadays in no way compared with the Guinness of yore. "The lowest common denominator," he kept repeating. From his red face and portly demeanour we could tell he was a true expert in the field.

The next day the sun was shining bright on the Inishmór landscape. We said "to heck with the walking" and hired bicycles for the day. The highlight of the day and indeed of the trip to Inishmór was going to the Black Fort, which we ironically had to walk to over rocky terrain. This is now a smaller less commercialised version of Dun Aenghus. Historically however it is claimed that it was a bigger and more significant fort than Dun Aenghus in its heyday. It is similarly perched on a sheer, vertical cliff face and has the same design. Unlike Dun Aenghus there are no crowds here, just a few stragglers like ourselves who were not put off by the inconvenience of walking over rocks. This solitude allowed me an opportunity to appreciate the fort, to savour the elements and wonder yet again at the lifestyle of the people who perched like the sea birds on the top of a cliff. There were no signs here warning people against standing on the walls of the fort. I sat on the top of these walls watching the waves come in far below on the cliff face opposite us. They came in with their own particular rhythm; every so often a series of large waves would strike and send mountains of spray flying over the top of the cliffs, which are hundreds of feet high. For a while afterwards the sea subsided, became relatively calm and you would think that no more big waves were going to come, pounding in.

I would often be on the verge of giving up when another flurry of big waves would strike. When you sat quietly for a while the sea hummed in your being and the boom of the big waves acted like a jolt to the system producing exhilaration and awe. It is of course nice to observe all of this from a safe distance, where you are not exposed to the full power of the sea. The rhythmical hum and clash of the sea was hypnotic and I sat there a long time feeling it vibrate within me, washing tensions away. Down below the seagulls and kittiwakes nested on a sheltered part of the cliff face. Some of them were circling in the air rising and falling as if in harmony with the waves. When a big wave came in they rose with the spray as it surged from the rocks below. After each surge of energy everything would calm and settle for a while, and the birds would subside to a lower level of circling and banking. How do these birds know that a big wave is coming, what clues can they perceive and are they ever caught out?

Three Germans came along, two women and a man. We exchanged pleasantries. They pondered the scene for a while and moved on. A short time later we followed them.

On the way back to our bikes we heard a riotous clamour coming from land cliffs to our left. Two herons were fighting, wings flapping awkwardly, accompanied by raucous guttural sounds. Finally one gave up and flew away. The other returned to the perch and roosted there, looking as if nothing has happened.

"That must be the wife," said Martin.

I laughed and then it struck me that love and war are the opposite sides of the same coin. The sounds of both are similar, followed by the same type of exhilaration – at least in the short term. Maybe that is the answer to the problems of the world – let us do away with love and we will end war as well. This sounds like the images we had of heaven when we were children, all full of serenity, divine music, prayer and utter boredom. As we walked over the limestone fields and looked at the ground we saw that little flowers were growing in through the holes in the rock. Each is encased in its own microclimate sheltered from the salt winds.

We had planned to see one more place before we caught the ferry back to Connemara. St Binnan's church is reputed to be the smallest temple in the world – so how could we come to Inishmór and not see it. This proved elusive however, as even though it was marked clearly on our map, we could not find it. The quality of maps being made leave a lot to be desired – it certainly had nothing to do with our eyesight! We stopped and asked a man the directions to St Binnan's. He was a man probably in his mid-sixties, dressed all in black with a cap. In his youth he would have been a powerful man. Now he looked as if too much physical toil had left its mark. He stood thinking for a few moments and then became upset. He told us he couldn't remember where it was.

"My memory isn't what it used to be," he said.

As we turned to go back the way we had come he was talking to himself in an agitated manner about St Binnan's, trying to reach into the depths of his mind for a piece of relevant information. Later on we saw him going into a pub. Well at least some landmarks remained familiar to him, or maybe he was going in to forget what he had forgotten. We finally found St Binnan's church, the only trouble was that it was at the top of a big hill and we would have to climb back up to it. As it was getting near ferry time (that's our excuse and we are sticking to it) we decided that we would abandon St Binnan and get a cup of coffee instead at the harbour. As we cycled back the small aeroplane of Arran Aer was taking off. It probably was taking with it some of the dignitaries who had opened the football field on the previous day. On the way back we started racing as we used to do on the bicycles *yahoo*ing as we went along the narrow roads.

We got our cup of coffee in the only café we could find. It was like the Riviera because we could sit outside on specially arranged tables and chairs to drink it. The only thing we had to do was to wrap up to protect ourselves from the cold wind and by the time we got settled to drink it our coffee had got cold. It served us right for rather pretentiously posing as southern Europeans. There was a pub opposite us called the American Bar. Why would anyone on Inishmór Island, lying in the Atlantic Ocean, off the West Coast of Ireland call a pub 'The American Bar'?

Was it because tourists who in looking for new experiences always seek out the familiar for security and a sense of connection to what they have left behind? Or is that they are so locked in their own routine and culture that they cannot step outside it? I suppose it is similar to the phenomenon of Westerners eating in McDonald's in Beijing. Alternatively it might reflect the aspirations of the owner who may be looking for inspiration at that much bigger lump of rock next stop across the Atlantic.

# Out of Donegal: Bundoran to Sligo

Bundoran was cool in the early dawn, a brisk wind blowing up the long main street swept bits of rubbish into swirling dances on the pavements. In comparison to the hubbub of the previous day the town was quiet, though not completely empty. A few young men were wandering down the other side of the street; they looked like they were finishing yesterday rather than beginning today. Two other men were standing on the footpath with lunch boxes under their arms, presumably waiting for lifts to go to work. I left Bundoran and Co. Donegal sleeping behind me as I headed in the direction of Kinlough, five miles away.

About half way between Bundoran and Kinlough I sat on a wall beside an old house, to rest for a while and to have a drink of water. Birdsong floated all around, filling the air. A little wren alighted on an old untended flowerbed in front of me, his body a quiver of perpetual motion. He hopped from one stone to another and then onto a swaying leaf; all the time his head was bobbing in different directions, in search of seeds and danger in equal measure. He then flittered down into the shrubbery of wild rose, catmint and dock leaves, which shook in response to his every movement. A moment later he hopped out again, his head still bobbing and fluttered away.

Kinlough is typical of most Irish villages in that it contains a shop, Post Office and any number of pubs. In the morning this Co. Leitrim village was stirring into life and the sun had come out, burning away the mist. There was activity outside one house where a man was instructing a young person on how to clip a hedge with an electric hedge cutter. He gesticulated animatedly to the young person, to make sure and avoid cutting the electric cable. Another youth was driving a quad bike, going around picking up the clippings. The man interrupted his supervision of all this mechanical activity to shout a greeting.

Farther on up the street an older man was working in his garden, which had as its main attraction a life-size wooden donkey and cart. The postman drove into this street, got out of the van and started talking to the man. They both wandered over to have a look at the carving and engaged in an animated discussion, which featured much pointing at the wooden donkey's head. The finer details pertaining to the quality of the design must have been discussed. They then wandered off around the garden, laughing and talking as they went. Obviously here the postman still performed a social service as well as delivering mail – and was apparently an art critic to boot. Sadly this idea of the postman having a social dimension to his/her role is fast dying, as it is not allowed within the current 'efficiency' mantra. These considerations did not weigh too heavily on this postman however, as every time I met him on the road after that he gave me a big friendly greeting.

I left Kinlough via a small road. The hills in front of me were not particularly high, but they were spectacular in their own right. They cover an extensive area of Sligo and Leitrim and the best known of these mountains is the table-topped Ben Bulben. The mountains/hills rise into a limestone plateau, the edges of which have been formed by erosion into sheer cliffs that sweep down 1,000 to 1,500 feet to the plains below, providing a magnificent backdrop. In the sunshine a bare-chested man was cycling up the hill into the village. (Some Irish people go mad once they feel a bit of warm sun). The sweat was rolling off him as he passed by, straining against the hill. Beyond the village people were out mowing their lawns, many of which were overgrown after all the previous bad weather. I passed a small house on my left-hand side. In front of the house two small boys, possibly twins, were playing with gusto on a tractor-trailer, building some elaborate structure with bits of wood. They looked up as I passed and shouted hello. The younger of the boys hopped up and asked me if I knew John McIntyre. I shook my head.

"No I never met him," I replied.

The older boy turned to the first boy.

"Don't be silly, he doesn't know him. That man is a camper."

They then asked me where I was from. As I told them, a lithe girl hopped out through a window on to the windowsill to see what was going on. She waved at me and disappeared back in the window like a jack-in-the-box.

There was a lot of activity on this road. Three people who were walking in front of me disappeared into a house. A hardy looking woman went past on a bicycle. She was about fifty years old and wore an anorak and a scarf (no chance of sunburn here). She did not acknowledge my greeting. She had a troubled look, a face that had not experienced too much joy. A writer once said that you have the face you deserve at fifty, however this is far too harsh as some people are dealt poor hands (and faces) in the first case.

I turned on to a smaller road that passed alongside a collection of farmyards. Out of one of these farmyards a woman appeared and said hello. A car halted behind me in the middle of this small road and the male driver started talking to the woman. They sounded happy to see each other. The buzz of their conversation accompanied me for a short while until it faded into the landscape. The small road rose higher and underneath me to my right a plain stretched for miles, all the way to the sea and Mullaghmore where Mountbatten's castle stands out like a sentinel at the edge of the ocean. Earl Mountbatten was the grand-uncle of Prince Charles who died in a bomb explosion in a boat, detonated by the I.R.A. in the distant bay. Today the bay looks so serene that it is hard to believe that such violence erupted there. However if we look closer at any landscape there is always evidence of violence to be seen. Things only look serene at a distance.

The entire universe as we understand it was born out of the most violent explosion imaginable, and this violence is part of us whether we like it or not. Out of that first explosion all the forming forces of the universe appeared, weaving their patterns and designs upon living matter. Time and space were created, so without that violence there would be no opportunity for us to exist in any form that we know about. In fact many of our greatest achievements and expressions of creativity have their origins in experiences of violence and conflict. Humans however have a penchant for stupid, irrational violence that seems to be unique in Nature. Perhaps Arthur Koestler was correct in saying that this was because the human brain evolved too quickly and that there are insufficient connections between the right side and the left side of the brain.

As I walked along this narrow road of lush verdant hedgerows a butterfly crossed in front of my eye. It fluttered up the road in front of me seeming to keep pace with my stride. Luxuriant vegetation is ideal territory for butterflies; they do not like things too neat and tidy. Another butterfly joined the first and, as if attached through an invisible cord of light they performed a choreographed dance of love or war in the sky in front of me. I never thought that butterfly flight was precise, but this dance was perfectly sequenced. Seemingly satisfied after the flurry, they separated. Each went their own way, their speckled design disappearing into the distance.

Did you know that butterflies see a world totally different to ours? They see in ultraviolet light, the ingenuity of which is that they send one set of signals to us and a completely different set to one another. All those patterns on their backs are really signs to predators that they are poisonous and dangerous to touch or eat. Humans however do not view them as dangerous, either because we have forgotten the signals of Nature or because we have no interest in eating them in the first place. We regard their patterns as beautiful. One author memorably described them as the 'stained glass windows of the outdoor cathedral'. Butterflies have captured the imagination of people down through the ages perhaps because they embody transformation. How something as beautiful as a butterfly transforms itself from a chrysalis is one of the wonders of Nature. They give us hope that we can always change, become more wonderful, and in some instances help us form a connection to our supernatural side. However butterflies reserve the real show for other butterflies. We only get a glimpse of their magic because they communicate in ways that are only visible in the ultraviolet light range. This is a spectacular show, each butterfly having an aura of 'flashing lights' in various patterns as they move their wings. The more vivid the display the more attractive the individual butterfly.

Nature is amazing too in that those plants like the Buddleia recognise what type of environment the butterfly likes. It emits a wave vibration similar to ultraviolet light and consequently strikes butterflies as a nice place to hang out. In return the butterfly helps the Buddleia to propagate. Nature strikes its own deals: and we sometimes wonder where the entrepreneurial spirit comes from?

Of course as a country we have produced folklore that features butterflies. Consider the story of Etáin, a beautiful princess who had an affair with a supernatural being called Midhir the Proud. This of course aroused the ire of Midhir's wife Fuamnach, who cast a spell and turned Etáin into a butterfly. (I do not know what she did to Midhir!) It was Etáin's lot that she was blown around the wastelands of Ireland for a thousand years. At the end of that time Etáin arrived at the banqueting hall of Etar, who was the King of Leinster. Being tired after all her journeys she fell asleep in the roof of the hall. It so happened that there was a banquet in the hall that night. During the banquet Etáin drifted down into the wine glass of the queen of Leinster who promptly drank her. Nine months later the queen gave birth to a beautiful princess, whom she called Etáin. I wonder though what would have happened if the butterfly had fluttered into the king's wine glass instead of the queen's?

Descending a hill I arrived at a crossroads with an old two-storey pub and shop, which was closed and showed no evidence of recent activity. It was there that I met two men sitting on a ditch. One was young, probably in his mid-twenties; the other was older, probably in his seventies. The younger man was very friendly and talkative. Initially the older man seemed the exact opposite – uncommunicative and unfriendly. We initially talked about the weather and farming. The younger man told me that the pub has been closed since the owner died. He then filled me in with the real news, which was that the owner had left £3.5 million in his will. Obviously there was a bit of ill feeling locally about this publican.

"He wouldn't give you tuppence, he was so mean," he said caustically.

This probably meant that my friend had not been remembered in the will and that some long lost relative had claimed the lot.

"No wonder he gathered in all that money then?" I offered.

"Much good it did him," he replied.

"I suppose you were good customers of his?" I asked.

"Ahh, we stopped going in there at the end. The craic went out of it."

"Well I am sure someone benefited from it all," I probed.

"Aye, a nephew got most of it," he informed me.

We agreed it was a pity that so many small pubs were closing down in rural areas. I conjectured if the clampdown on drink-driving might encourage some of these pubs to stay open. He shook his head.

"No, young people now use taxis all the time," he said. "They all head into Sligo and Bundoran."

The use of taxis in rural Ireland is surely one of the big changes in habit that has occurred in recent years, and they are more likely to be used by younger people. The older generations are more likely to take a chance and drive after drinking.

As I was about to leave the old man, who had said nothing up to this, became talkative. My impression of him as being unfriendly was completely wrong. He talked about the lack of tourists in the area, and how a local man had banned all the hikers from walking across his lands to the mountains.

"How could you have tourists and have people like that about?" he exclaimed.

He told me how local people had built a hostel at Ben Whiskin with a view to catering for hiking tours. This was all rendered useless by the actions of this man.

"The hostel is lying there useless now," he said.

At a house further down the road from the old pub, a pleasant-faced teenage girl was leaning on a wall, face cupped in her hands, lost in her own thoughts as she gazed across the fields. She dreamily said hello as I passed. Above me soared the magnificent mountain of Ben Whiskin, which rises like a gigantic surfing wave, frozen in time and motion above a flat plain stretching to the sea. At the next house a lean, friendly man was out working in his lawn. He informed me that he had just bought the house and was getting stuck into sorting out the lawn. He asked me if I recognised what sort of small trees were growing there. I prided myself on some knowledge of trees, so I helped him as much as I could. He gave me a glass of water and I asked him how far it was to Lissadell, the next stop on my journey. He assured me with a steady gaze that it was not too far. All I will say, with the benefit of hindsight, as advice to anyone who is walking on the back roads: Don't bother asking how far it is to anywhere, because no one has a notion of the real distance. They will tell you with conviction of the distance as if they had measured every last inch of it themselves on foot; if you have a map, work it out yourself.

I met a fine example of this self-sufficiency later at a crossroads in the form of a German cyclist. He had hired a bike out for the day and he was heading to the beach at Mullaghmore for a swim. He told me he was touring all around Ireland. Like a lot of Germans he had researched his journey thoroughly and knew where he wanted to go and why. Some people might laugh at such an approach to travelling, preferring a more *ad hoc* approach. All in all I think people get more out of travelling if they prepare. Instead of cycling along some main road with incessant traffic he was able to cycle comfortably along quiet back roads. He had a good map that ensured he did not get too lost, and to top it all he could go for a swim on one of the best beaches in the north west: not bad.

At the angle I viewed Ben Bulben, the vertical ridges on the top third of the mountain looked like a series of columns stretching from one end of the rectangular mountain to the other. In my imagination they looked like the profiles of Egyptian pharaohs carved into the soft limestone mountain. Ben Bulben is certainly one of the most striking mountains in Ireland; not so much for its height but for the way it dominates the surrounding plains. The road now took me higher up above the plain, with panoramas of sea and mountain all around. This day seemed to be 'butterfly day', as yet more butterflies accompanied me on the way.

I descended onto the main Sligo/Bundoran road. Here the traffic was streaming past in a near continuous flow. There were even people on bicycles in single file in the traffic.

'Go on the back roads,' I thought about shouting to them.

I eventually managed to cross the road and headed down a narrow road to Lissadell House. I passed a holistic healing centre, which was in essence a converted bungalow. The growing interest in alternative therapies and healing is a feature of our time. I think part of us realises that conventional medicine is incomplete in its approach – we strive to obtain more care, love and attention in times of illness. However there is a part of our society that is preoccupied with health, because we can no longer stand the thought of death. Yeats in one of his poems said:

*Many times man lives and dies,*
*Between his two eternities.*
WB Yeats – 'Under Ben Bulben'

We can only enjoy living if we accept death and endings as a necessary part of our existence. We have to let things go in order to live to the full. The child has to let go in order to move to adolescenthood; the adolescent has to go in order for the adult to emerge and so on until the final departure from this life. The two eternities stretch out there at the extremes, before birth and after death. On my more optimistic days I reckon that as I have emerged out of the primordial soup at least once there is no reason why I should not do so again.

In front of me a family of husband, wife and three children were herding cattle along the road. The father was in front of the herd and he opened a gate and capped the cattle into the field. He then raced into the field after them. I got talking to the woman. She informed me that they were going on holidays to Portugal the following day, and that they had to change the cattle into fields which had an ample supply of water. She told me that they had been in Portugal before they had children, and that they had enjoyed it a lot. Seeking some reciprocal information, she asked me what I was doing. When I told her she started telling me the history of the Lissadell estate but before she could finish there was a loud impatient shout from the field.

"He's roaring. I had better go," she said.

With a laugh and a wave she was gone.

As I came to the avenue leading up to Lissadell House, a few cars passed me on the way up. Lissadell House is a big grey Grecian Revival house owned by the Gore-Booths, descendants of Elizabethan soldier Sir Paul Gore, who was granted a large tract of 4,000 acres in Co. Sligo for his contribution to the British forces in the early seventeenth century. London architect Francis Goodwin designed this house in 1833 for the Gore-Booth family. The house is most famous however as the home of Constance Markievicz (née Gore-Booth), the Irish revolutionary leader who was sentenced to death for her part in the 1916 rising. The death sentence was later commuted, primarily because of her connections to the English aristocracy, and she was set free. She then went on to become the first woman elected to Westminster as a Member of Parliament. As she stood as a Sinn Fein candidate she never took her seat there. After Independence she was elected to the Irish parliament and became a cabinet minister in that government. How this woman from a privileged Anglo-Irish background ended up as a revolutionary leader is a fascinating story, the subject of many books. She always had an independent spirit, and loved to ride her horse over the thousands of acres. In doing so she came into close contact with the tenant farmers who worked on their estate and with whom she developed good friendships. She was struck by the poverty endured by these people, and became uneasy at the part that her family played in this. She argued regularly with her father about this and the obvious injustice seems to have left an indelible print on her consciousness. After leaving home she travelled, met and married a Polish Count and returned to Ireland to live. It was a seeming natural step for her to join the burgeoning late-nineteenth- and early-twentieth century movement towards Irish national self-determination. This movement that became increasingly trendy and encompassed literature, poetry, Irish mythology, workers' rights and socialism, also incorporating the physical force revolutionary movement. One blended into the other and when the opportunity for revolution presented itself during the First World War, Yeats' 'terrible beauty' was born. Countess Constance Markievicz passed into legend.

The last time I had been at the House it had been closed. This time there were people walking around the grounds and sitting on the lawn so things looked more promising. I went up to the big double doors of the building, and as they were slightly ajar I pushed them open. There was nobody inside. The entrance lobby had a large staircase, in the middle of which rather incongruously stood a stuffed bear. In one corner there was a desk with literature, leaflets, entrance tickets etc. I presumed the person who was supposed to be there would be back shortly. I went over to look more closely at the bear when somebody shouted in an irritated manner.

"Oi, you in there!"

In through the door came a tall skinny man, who looked like John Cleese in *Fawlty Towers*, without the moustache.

"We are closed," he said, in an aristocratic precise English accent. "Did you not read the sign?"

"No," I replied in all honesty.

"Which way did you come in then?" he demanded.

When I pointed out the door I had come in, it mollified him somewhat, as it seemed I had come in the side that had no 'Closed' sign displayed.

"We have to close sometime," said he, pointing to his watch.

It was exactly 5.00 pm – the closing time. I then decided I would chance my arm.

"I walked all the way from Bundoran to get here," I said. "Is there any chance of having a quick look around the house?"

This approach cut no ice with him, and he abruptly shepherded me out the door. His look said, 'Sorry for your trouble: what do you expect me to do about it? Can't have people wandering around the house at all hours of the day or night!'

He probably had a point. I felt a small bit like Manuel in *Fawlty Towers* though, a bit of a nuisance that had to be tolerated. On the doorstep I asked him if he knew of any bed and breakfasts in the area. He said that there were probably ones in Carney, which was the nearest village. On reflection he thought that he might have the phone number of a closer bed and breakfast, so we stepped back into the hallway whilst he went off to get it. He must have thought that I was going to follow into the main part of the house, because he pointed to the vicinity of the desk in the hallway and told me to "stay there". A young woman appeared out of one of the doorways in the hallway and bounded lithely up the stairs past the inert bear. He then came back with the phone number and gave it to me. The bed and breakfast was three miles in the wrong direction but he said it might be closer than Carney. As we left he pointed to an A4 sheet of paper, which was stuck to the door.

"Did you not read that?"

"No," I said, shaking my head.

This notice gave a brief history of the Gore-Booth family from the 1830s to the present day. It contained a picture of the house and of course the opening and closing times. It was obviously still annoying him that I had entered the house in or around closing time. Obviously my charms had not worked in convincing him that I was not a chancer of some sort. I thanked him for his help and he strode off at a brisk walk back into the house, locking the door behind him.

It must be difficult having to share your house with the public. How do you preserve your privacy when you have created a public space which unknown people share with you? Some people will always take advantage and push boundaries. I presume he keeps part of the house private. However people do it all the time in the tourist season: bed and breakfasts are a prime example. They have to share their house with whoever walks in. It takes a lot of trust and goodwill. Outside the house I talked to a man with a Scottish accent who was washing a car. He worked on the estate, although he didn't have much local knowledge, especially where there might be bed and breakfasts. I walked out the other entrance of Lissadell in the general direction of Carney.

There was a nice beach just outside the estate. It was packed with people, probably for the first time this summer, as this was the first sunny day in a long time. A few miles further on I reached Carney village, which is neat and pretty – probably a bit too manicured for my taste but certainly a lot better than most of the small villages on the road. The first bed and breakfast I called into had no rooms available. The friendly woman told me that there was another one about a mile up the road. (These miles certainly start to get discouraging when you are walking, and especially when your feet are sore). I followed her directions and when I finally got to the house, I was greeted by a squarely-built, slightly overweight woman.

"I was expecting you," she announced in a deep, smoky voice.

Seemingly the woman in the other bed and breakfast had telephoned to tell her I was on my way. Reciprocity is the name of the game in the bed and breakfast trade. The woman in the first house told me she had sent four other people to yet another establishment: reciprocity has its own pecking order. Networks as we increasingly see are at the centre of civilisation.

I took a taxi into town to drop off a small package to a friend of mine. He wasn't in when I called, so I strolled around the town for a while. Down by the Garavogue River, a tastefully redeveloped shopping area in the town full of restaurants, bars and bookshops, I looked at a heron as he flew lazily over the water and landed casually in the fast flowing stream on one leg. There he perched partially under the bridge, more or less oblivious to the commotion above and around him. Farther on down the riverbank there was a large stone with a plaque commemorating Ambrosio and Bernardo O'Higgins, which was unveiled here by the Chilean consul.

Ambrose O'Higgins was born near here in a small village called Ballinary in the year 1720. He was born in poverty to a large family but went on to become the Viceroy of Chile. Like many large families of the time there was an expectation that at least one of the children would join the Church. If families did not have much money to donate to the Church they usually had a child or two who was surplus to requirements. These were 'donated' to the Church and if the other children were expected to contribute to the material welfare of the family, they would be expected to enhance the religious 'capital' of their family. Ambrose had an uncle in the Jesuit Order working in Cadiz in Spain, so it was decided that Ambrose would study for the Church with his uncle in Spain. When in Spain he changed his name to Ambrosio. He received his education from the Jesuits and then to show his gratitude he decided not to join the Church but headed off instead on a life of adventure to Argentina. He initially led the life of an itinerant trader and moved between Argentina, Bolivia and Peru. Later he worked as an engineer/draughtsman in the Argentinian army. It was here that he met another Irishman called John Garland who was the Governor of a city (Valdivia) in southern Chile. He went to Chile as Garland's personal assistant. In Valdivia he prospered, spread his wings and became an influential figure in Chilean life. He established a year-round postal route between Argentina and Chile and worked his way through the system until he eventually became Viceroy of Chile. As Viceroy he carried out many reforms as well as building new cities and roads. He abolished the Encomienda system, which forced natives to work on the land for the benefit of the Crown. I am sure his experience of growing up in an equally dispossessed Irish peasant culture, and living in poverty strongly influenced this decision. Later in life he even found time for love, fathering a son with Isabel, daughter of one of the most notable families in Chile. The fact that Isabel was forty years his junior did not deter him one little bit! Ambrosio and Isabel did not marry and Isabel raised their son, Bernardo. Ambrosio paid for his son's education, but that was nearly the sum total of his involvement.

Bernardo O'Higgins was hidden away from the rest of society, because he was born out of wedlock. However he went on to become more famous than his father. He became known as the founder of the Chilean navy and leader of their army. He went on to liberate Chile from the Spanish and for a while held supreme power in Chile. He is still known as 'The Liberator of Chile'. In this way I think he got his revenge on his father – he deposed the power that his father had previously spearheaded.

The story of the O'Higgins family in Chile is truly a remarkable story. If one had looked into the cot at Ambrose's birth one would have had great difficulty predicting that one day he would become Viceroy in Chile, and that his son would lead a war of independence there. When we look into any child's cot we do not know what mark they might leave on the life force of the world.

Crossing a pedestrian bridge on the river I met a local activist and teacher. He was taking photographs of the bank of the river. I wondered to myself why he bothered taking photographs of a rather barren riverbank. Could he see something there that was invisible to me? Intrigued, I passed a rather inane comment after he finished taking his photographs.

"Your creativity is flowing today?"

He regarded me with a very earnest look on his face. He told me that he was going around Sligo town, taking photographs not of wild flowers but the lack of them. He wanted to be able to show the authorities that there were no environments and landscapes being created which would allow native wild flowers to flourish. He vigorously brought to my attention all the hanging baskets on the buildings beside the river, and with disgust said that they were all filled with imported flowers.

"That's where all the money is going!" he exclaimed in an annoyed manner.

He pointed out a purple flower in one of the hanging baskets.

"That flower is native to Turkey. It suits the horticultural industry to import those flowers; we have no regard for our natural environment."

He told me that he was a teacher in one of the schools, and he had developed a wild flower garden on local authority property as part of a school project. The next thing he heard was that the local authority had covered the garden in concrete as part of an 'environmental enhancement project'!

He went on to say that he had lived in Westport for a while, and he asserted that this was another town spoiled by too much development. He said however there was a greater community spirit in Westport than in Sligo. This he attributed to the fact that Sligo was traditionally a garrison town (of the British army when they were in control of Ireland). He told me that at the time of Partition in 1922 the British wanted to keep Sligo instead of Derry. When he was young he said Catholics could not get jobs in the Protestant businesses in Sligo, and that this had changed only relatively recently. The outcome of this was that people in Sligo town had no history of working and cooperating together in a civic sense. I have usually found that this is a common complaint, encountered in every town and village along the way. Every locality has its own reason as to why people find it hard to work together.

I took a taxi back out to Yeats' Tavern, which was near my bed and breakfast. I thought it would be handy to have a pint there and something to eat before I went to bed. Nothing like coming out of the pub and staggering back up the road to the bed without having to think about how to get home. No car or taxi to think of – pure bliss. The pub was fairly full when I went in so I sat at the bar and ordered a pint and fish and chips. In Irish bars if you are on your own the best way of meeting people is to sit at the bar – you are bound to get in somebody's way.

The most memorable person I met there was a heavy-set, muscular, overweight, red-faced cattle dealer who was out touring with a group of his relatives from Scotland. I hope you get the picture, otherwise I will have to think up a few more adjectives. The reason I got to know him fairly well was because he was up and down to the bar so often. The first time he was up he ordered a round for everyone and a whiskey for himself.

"Do you like whiskey?" he asked me.

"I am more of a Guinness man."

"Wise man. I like the Guinness too, every so often."

When his whiskey came he added red lemonade to it. I was distracted for a second and when I looked back the whiskey had been downed.

"Put on a pint of Guinness for me, and while I am waiting I will have another whiskey," he said to the barman.

He lifted the glass in a salute to me and downed the whiskey in one gulp.

"Sure drink is no harm! If I am driving I never drink," he elaborated.

I think he was trying to convince himself more than he was trying to convince me, and let me tell you now he succeeded in that. His bright red face however was pointing to potential trouble for him if he did not take care. To emphasise the point he repeated this statement in a comradely way several times.

"There is no harm in a drink and a man enjoying himself when he can."

The question mark was in his voice but not his head.

His Guinness came and he left to sit down with his friends. No sooner was he sitting down than he was back up again the empty pint glass in his hand. He ordered a whiskey for himself. As he stood there talking to me, two of his companions came up and put in another order for the whole group. They promptly sat down again, leaving my friend to pay for all.

"I hate being used," my friend muttered darkly.

I gathered that all was not sweetness and light in this gathering. Yet he paid for the whole lot again, his feelings subservient to a need to show generosity to visitors. He had a further two whiskeys and a pint of Guinness. We talked about politics and football before he sat down. I thought this would be the last I would see of him but no; he was up again a while afterwards. The same procedure was repeated. He was followed up to the bar by a few of his 'friends' who put in the same order as previously. Again he paid for the lot.

"It's not often that I see them," he said.

"Aren't you lucky," I thought to myself.

"You would like to see them more often?" I asked slightly mischievously.

He didn't comment. This time he only ordered a Guinness for himself as we talked a bit about the state of farming. "The best days are behind us" was his observation on agriculture in Ireland. He then informed me that some nights within his own home he drank a whole bottle of whiskey and washed it down with cans of stout. I believed him. He rejoined his circle and a short time later I observed the cattleman shepherding his Scottish relatives into the restaurant.

Behind the bar there were seven or eight staff, who took care of the bar trade and the bar food being served. They were all young and full of energy. They needed all their energy, as the place was packed full of people. However there was some dissension in the ranks, as some of the staff were giving out that they had got nothing to eat for a long time.

"We are supposed to have a break and food after every three hours," commented one barman in an exasperated voice.

As he was saying this he was shaking a cocktail which then didn't pour for him.

"Shit, Shit!" he exclaimed.

He finally gave up on that cocktail and started the whole process all over again. The hungry staff held a hurried meeting, and an informal deputation was organised to approach management. Shortly afterwards a few bowls of chips arrived which they all dipped into as they hurried by. The revolution was thus quelled.

There were four posters on the wall beside me. The first one was:

*ROSSES POINT MACKEREL FESTIVAL*
*FEATURES*
*INTER-PUB TUG OF WAR*
*GENTS' COMPETITION (No Studs)*
*1ST PRIZE – ½ CASE OF WHISKEY*
*FEMALE COMPETITION (No Studettes)!*
*1ST PRIZE – ½ CASE OF WHISKEY*

The second poster featured yet another inter-pub competition. It was a fancy dress raft race on a local river. It sounded like good craic. The poster displayed a picture of one of the rafts that took part in a previous year, featuring a motley crew of brigands some half in and some half out of the water. Of course one of the contestants had a pint in his hands – I think he was the navigator. It is interesting to note that two of the four posters featured inter-pub competitions. It certainly points to the central role that pubs are playing in many aspects of Irish life. They are the social centres where people congregate, and a focal point for many community activities.

The third poster featured a fun day out in a local village. It was a fairly typical sports day that would be organised in many villages once a year. The main event of the day was a barbecue, which was being organised by the local youth club. Given that most of these young people have been raised in the fast food culture it is certainly a leap of faith by the community in their culinary skills. The last poster featured an advertisement of a comic drama to be performed in a local hall. It was a one-man play on Joyce's *Ulysses*. My experience of one-person comedy dramas is, no matter how good the actor the comedy is never sustained. It's OK in brief snippets but that's it. As for a take-off of *Ulysses*, well, who has read it in the first instance?

On leaving the pub, whom did I meet but my cattle dealer friend from the bar. He shook my hand.

"The next time we meet," he said, "I will buy you a drink."

## Sligo to Manorhamilton

The next day, after a hurried breakfast I made haste to the famous Drumcliffe church nearby, as my intention was to get there early before the invasion of tour buses and consequent throngs of people. This church is named after Colmcille and is the burial place of the poet William Butler Yeats. On arrival I wandered into the churchyard to look at Yeats' grave, which is located near to the front door of the church. I stopped to read the well-known lines on his gravestone:

*Cast a cold eye,*
*On Life, On Death.*
*Horseman pass by.*

William Butler Yeats was seventy-four years old when he died and his legacy now is to draw tourists in their multitudes to the church at Drumcliffe and to numerous local festivals associated with his name.

Drumcliffe church itself is the site of one of the monasteries founded by Colmcille and the church here is dedicated to him. It was also near here on the plains between Ben Bulben and the sea that the famous 'battle of the books' at Cúil Dreimhne was fought. This was the first dispute in human history about copyright.

Colmcille on one of his early travels went to stay with Finnen of Druim Finn. I am not sure whether this is the same Finnen that dreamt about Colmcille's birth; if it were I am sure he would have liked to change his dream! When Colmcille arrived he asked Finnen for the loan of a valuable book. Every evening after Mass Colmcille went to his room to copy the book without the knowledge of Finnen. He worked at this diligently for the duration of his stay. On the last night of his visit Finnen sent a young man to ask that Colmcille return the book before he left.

Colmcille was at this stage just finishing copying the book. As he wrote a great light filled the room. As the young man approached he was astounded and filled with curiosity when he saw this bright light shining from Colmcille's room. Instead of knocking at the door he decided to look through the keyhole. Colmcille sensed his presence.

"Thou hast leave of me, if thou hast leave of God," he said to his pet crane, "to pluck out the eye of that youth that cometh to spy upon me without my knowledge."

This was hardly the most Christian act of Colmcille's life; you certainly crossed him at your peril! The crane rose from his perch and poked out the youth's eye through the keyhole, leaving it dangling on his cheek. The youth ran to Finnen in great distress and told him what was going on. Finnen being a holy man himself cured the youth's eye and then went to accuse Colmcille of stealing his work. Colmcille stated that he had not harmed the book and that no one owned God's words. He demanded that no one other than Diarmaid the High King of Ireland should make judgement on the issue. Finnen agreed to this.

Diarmaid gave due consideration to the arguments and handed down the following famous judgement:

*To every cow her calf, and to every book its transcript.*
*And therefore to Finnen belongeth the book thou hast written, O Colmcille.*

The principle of copyright was thus established. Colmcille was not at all happy with this judgement so in reply he pronounced that he had been unjustly treated, and that Diarmaid would be punished for it. He said that he would go to his kinsmen and declare war on Diarmaid. Colmcille headed home and put his case before his own clan. They of course agreed with him that it was an unjust judgement, and that war should be declared. The two armies faced each other near to the spot where I stood. The night before the battle Colmcille prayed to God to give him victory, and to ensure that no one of his clan was killed. During the night none other than Michael the Archangel came to visit him. The Archangel told him that the favour he requested had been granted, even though it was displeasing to God. Michael told him that if he wanted to gain favour with God again he would have to go into exile and never return to Ireland's shores. He then warned him that no one from his army should cross the river during the battle; they would be safe if they stayed on their own side. In the battle the next day Diarmaid's forces were routed and three thousand of his men killed. Only one man from Colmcille's army was killed, and that was because he crossed the river against orders. The result of the battle was that Diarmaid's power was severely weakened, and it led to eventual transfer of the Kingship to the Cineal Conaill, Colmcille's own clan. The book that Colmcille copied is called the *Cathach*. It became in time the battle standard of the O'Donnell clan and every time they fought the book was carried into battle. The *Cathach* is now in the library of the Royal Academy of Ireland.

After the battle the saints of Ireland confirmed the judgement of the Archangel and Colmcille was forced to leave his country as penance for his arrogance. His exile was probably left more political, to do with bolstering the rule of Irish clans in Scotland. Thus started a new adventure for Colmcille – establishing a monastery on the island of Iona and bringing the word of God to the people of Scotland and the north of England. Colmcille had been exiled, but that did not mean he went alone. On the journey with him were twenty bishops, forty priests, thirty deacons and forty students. It seems they also had to pay for Colmcille's folly! This group provided the basis for the monastery on Iona and an important source of learning and power in these islands.

I went into the church in Drumcliffe and sat at the back. This is a Church of Ireland building, which like most churches had a very relaxing feel to it. There is also an intimacy about this church in that you are near to the altar wherever you sit. Many traditional Catholic churches are long and rectangular which means that one could be a long way from the centre of action.

I walked around the church looking at the plaques on the wall. The benefactors were from the local gentry, all having a military and British background. In a Catholic church it would be local business people or benefactors from the Diaspora in England or the States. The most common names on the walls here were Jones and Parke who were associated with the big landlord houses in the area; Dunally House and Cregg House. All of them either held positions in the British army like Sir William Parke from Dunally House who was a Lieutenant Colonel of the 66th Regiment or were clergy like Reverend Christopher Jones whom the plaque said was held in high esteem by the gentry. It is interesting to note that the present Roman Catholic bishop of this area is also called Christopher Jones. I wondered at the time were they related and does religion run in the genes?

These plaques were interesting reflections on a way of life now gone; the influence of the Anglo-Irish class has seeped away over the years. Its main testament now is the ruins of old houses and the glorious literature spawned by such a small population. At the altar of the church there was a beautiful lectern, carved in walnut, in the image of an eagle. This lectern spoke of a connection to Nature and whoever crafted it did it lovingly. Its job now is to hold the bible: a Bible held in the cradle of Nature – how apt.

I walked outside in the early sunshine to make a phone call home, and stood beside an art gallery with a line of etchings and small paintings arranged on the wall. As I finished the phone call I became aware of a persistent snipping sound behind me. I turned to see a man on his knees, energetically at work on the garden behind me – all I could see through the flying shrubbery was a bald head and an enthusiastic pair of shears. I shouted out 'hello' and a slight, energetic man hopped to his feet and came over with a cheerful greeting. A piece of shrubbery fell from his shoulder as he rose. His dog, which was tied with a long chain, now also aroused by the new activity, got up and let out one *woof*, then duty done, lay back down again. I asked the man what breed he was. He told me he was a Shi Tzu, but he added that nobody recognised him as being of that breed because he was so fat. He blamed the dog's corpulent appearance on the fact that he had the 'snip job' done, and that he had to keep him tied up in case he frightened some of the visitors to his gallery. He advised me that he was always amused when Yanks commented on how fat he was, because invariably the people making the comment were obese themselves. It seemed that he was a bit sensitive about his dog's appearance! To change the subject and before I made some inappropriate comment about his dog I complimented him on the garden.

"I don't really like gardening work," he replied, "but you have to keep it tidy to entice the visitors."

He was taking the chance to tidy up his garden before the tourist buses arrived. He then told me that he produced the majority of his work in the wintertime in a studio in town. When he opens the gallery here in the summer months he is unable to complete much work, because there is always a flow of visitors coming in to have a look at the art.

"And you have to be available to talk to people," he added.

As art was his first love, he had taken early retirement when an opportunity presented itself and now he classified himself as a full-time artist. He was fortunate to own this small house beside the church, as it served as an ideal selling location during the tourist season. The paintings and etchings that were placed on the wall were all geared to the tourist market, as they were either portraits of Yeats or a landscape featuring Ben Bulben. There were none of Colmcille – it seemed that he was not in fashion any more.

I went back into the church; the first thing I noticed was the box into which you could place your written intentions. These are later taken to a prayer service and are offered up to God's will. I decided that whilst in Rome I should do what the Romans do so I took up the pen and wrote, asking that my family would lead contented and fulfilled lives. I reckoned it was as good a prayer as I could come up with, or maybe 'visualisation' is the more modern word.

As I left the church the first tour buses were arriving, the restaurant was opening and people were starting to wander around the site.

I found the back road to Glencar lake. The hedgerows and the verges were uncut and full of wild flowers. Aubretia was standing up proudly amongst the delicious smelling meadowsweet. Various varieties of blackberries were flowering encased in their thorny home. Straggly woodbine with languorous scent climbed through hawthorn hedge and foliant banks. Herb robin was spreading its spriggly tendrils across the grassy verge. Hogweed to my eye spoiled a delicate balance as its monstrous stem and spreading crown bossed the hedgerow. This highly invasive foreign ornamental plant and lover of wet damp places can only but thrive in a climate like ours: it has found a home from home. Like everything else the roadside foliage is in constant flux, forever changing, adapting, moving on, following its own inexorable logic.

I passed a line of very expensive houses. This was obviously one of the exclusive areas around Sligo. I saw a man pulling a lawnmower behind him, cutting an awkward strip of grass. It would seem that to push it forward would be too easy a task for him to carry out! Pulling, indeed, would be too gentle a word for what he was doing, horsing would be a better word. He was a big strapping man of about forty-five with a slightly bulging stomach spreading over the top of his jeans. He stopped to talk to me.

As both Co. Donegal (my county) and Co. Sligo (his county) were playing fixtures in the All Ireland football championship that weekend, we had an immediate source of conversation. No chatting about the weather here, we went straight into discussing matters of the utmost seriousness. He looked at me with zeal in his eyes and enthused.

"Both Sligo and Donegal will win," he enthused, "if their fullbacks attack the ball, and the corner men stay back and sweep in behind them."

I took it from this show of animation that he once played in the fullback line himself, and he had strong opinions on how fullbacks should play the game. For anyone who knows Gaelic football it takes a special breed of hard man to play in this position as they are expected to let no one pass, and hard hitting is a matter of honour. Nothing stirs Gaelic football spectators so much as the sight of a fullback battling for the ball, gathering it and bursting out through the forwards to clear his line. The crowd's roar rises in the bottom of their stomach then gathers in the chest and explodes out through the skull. This is a distinctly west of Ireland cheer that echoes the noise of the Atlantic Ocean which stirs in the depths of the sea, gathers in a powerful swell and then explodes in a cascade of noise on the shore. If you listened closely you would be able to hear the cheer ebbing away, leaving an energising and tingling sensation in the air. The fullback told me that he could not go to the game as he was going away on holidays the next day, much to his regret. He asked me, if I was going to the Donegal game? I told him jokingly that I was waiting for the final and that I couldn't be bothered going to these 'unimportant' matches. You have got to understand that this was the first time in a long time that Sligo had got as far in the Championship, whereas Donegal had won the All Ireland title ten years previously. There had been tremendous hype about the game in Sligo in the weeks leading up to this quarterfinal. We in Donegal could afford to be a 'wee bit superior' to all that. He laughed and told me that he would see me at the final then. About 100 metres up the road a reserved elderly couple were out working in a lovely wooded garden with a stream at the bottom. They both were heading to the match in Dublin, and they were leaving a day early to savour the atmosphere. On this weekend there was football in the air.

There were blisters under both feet now and I spent a few miles cursing the decision to just take a pair of sandals and not my walking shoes. I had thought it better to travel lightly upon the earth but the tarmac road is unforgiving on feet and joints. As the feet got sorer I endeavoured to transform my heavy-footed thump with a flat-footed padding action. However the damage had been done the previous day as I had walked too far. I remembered how my father taught me to walk lightly over marshy ground, but that only works over short distances, so there was no help there.

I then decided I would have to blame somebody for my predicament. Who better to blame than my parents? My mother had small, high-arched feet that I of course inherited. However the prognosis on my father's side was no better, as a cousin of mine gave me the ominous news one time that I was a descendant of the seven Sweeney sisters. It seemed that in the nineteenth century those seven Sweeney sisters came to my area and married seven men in our parish. They all had large families, thus ensuring their influence lived on over the years. My cousin informed me that the result of this 'invasion' was that now most people living in the parish are related in some way to each other.

"The legacy they left to the parish was bad eyes and bad feet," she added in a dramatic manner.

When talking to my kids though, I tell them to make sure and don't blame me in any way, but to be sure and blame some distant relative like the Sweeney sisters – may God rest them! On the basis of this recollection I muttered darkly to myself.

"So that's why I am limping now, and furthermore that's why the sweat is steaming up my glasses. On top of all that that's why our football team kept losing over all those years – people of the parish could neither see nor walk properly! Those Sweeney sisters have a lot to answer for."

The mist was playing around on the mountain tops, seeping up and down the slopes, mingling and merging, expanding and contracting. I thought for one brief moment that those tenacious tendrils were going to let go of the mountain tops and let the sun seep through. Ahh it was just a brief moment, one fleeting glimpse. Having given me a sight of what was possible, the mist crept down the mountainside again and enshrouded me in a curtain of misty, wetting rain. A steady stream of gulching traffic passed me as I headed to Glencar Lake and waterfall, splashing me with disregard as they went by. The road was narrow and the overgrown verges made it an uncomfortable walk as one had to be constantly on the lookout for oncoming traffic.

I was not the only mad person on this wet and miserable day. Coming towards me out of the mist there emerged two other walkers, a man and a woman, who turned out to be German hikers. They told me that they hoped to climb Ben Bulben the next day, after camping at the base of the mountain overnight. I showed them my map and pointed out the best route to take. Like the other German tourist I had met on the previous days these hikers had researched their journey and were prepared to take the road less travelled. As I had nothing better to do I told them the story of how Fionn Mac Cuamhaill the legendary hero let his friend Diarmaid die on this mountain because of jealousy concerning a woman. This is a tale of how resentment can corrupt the most noble of people and friendships if it is allowed to lie in the heart.

I came to Glencar Lake. The mist was now clinging to the lake, blurring the banks on the far side. Grasses and reeds poked their heads eerily up through the mist at the edge of the lake. The mist now transformed itself into saturating drizzle which caused me to put down my head and march on. There were two small caravans parked at the edge of the lake, owned by two traveller families. Both caravans were packed full, with adults and children taking shelter out of the rain. The door of one of the caravans was open, and I could see the adults drinking tea. A girl of about ten or eleven was feeding a baby with a bottle, and the other children were looking at television. What a great spot to camp. It definitely is one of the benefits of a nomadic culture if one can choose to park in beautiful spots such as this. However this nomadic culture is increasingly coming into conflict with the settled community, and there are numerous instances of differences of opinion throughout the country in relation to 'illegal parking'. This is particularly prevalent in the summer months, when many otherwise settled travellers move around the country in large family groups. Most of these summer travellers are traders in anything from fireplaces to antiques to tarmacadam. Obviously one part of the community wants to get rid of them but another part obviously keeps buying from them. However it is indictment on our society that many traveller families who are not traders do not have decent living conditions and are forced to live on the side of the road summer and winter. The local authorities are obliged to provide suitable accommodation for them but progress is slow because of objections from the settled community.

During the walk I met many people who told me that they would love to do what I was doing, which was basically 'fecking off', travelling around the countryside with no perceived ties to anything. When you think of it we as a species have only adopted a settled lifestyle relatively late in our history. Before that people lived transient lifestyles. All the hunter-gatherers and even early agricultural peoples moved from place to place. There is a great sense of shared excitement and community in the notion of heading off as a group together. There is something within us still that yearns for that wandering lifestyle and leads to restless feelings. If circumstances prevent you from giving expression to this feeling, the only option is to repress it with whatever force is necessary. In some ways I think that some of the animosity between the traveller and settled community is born out of a resentment of the perceived 'freedom' of the traveller lifestyle.

As I left Glencar lake the mist lifted, the rain cleared and I chose the smallest road I could find to walk on. I had enough of traffic. What a contrast; the back roads now were deathly quiet and took on a slightly oppressive atmosphere. The mist was rising and falling on the surrounding hill and mountains. The air was still and heavy with a hint of thunder in it. Everything was quiet – even Nature seemed to have retreated into a shell or at a least a watchful silence. The eerie thing was that during the next ten miles' walking, I never saw another person. There were houses old and new on the side of the road, but there was not a glimpse of a person to be seen anywhere. I came to a two-storey house that had all its windows and doors open. Outside the front door of the house there was a car with its doors and boot open and mats lying on the ground. There was music blaring from inside the house. I stood there for a few moments hoping to talk to someone but no one appeared. It was like one of those films in which a stranger appears and finds no human life left. All the trappings of recent human life are still there, dinners on the table, clothes in the washing machine, fire in the hearth as well as the music on the radio. Everything seems normal, but of course it is not. For some mysterious reason everyone had disappeared. They probably had been abducted by aliens or obliterated by some weapon or other.

I went up the road a short distance until I came to a deserted house with a small wall outside it. I sat down on the ground with my back to the wall, took off my shoes and socks and started to eat my lunch. I could still see the house with the car and open doors from where I sat. Suddenly there was a movement at the house.

'Maybe it was only my imagination that everyone had disappeared!'

Then an old fat sheepdog walked out onto the road. Obviously, whatever had obliterated the humans did not affect dogs. The dog saw me, I looked at him, he looked back and barked and he started waddling towards me.

'Oh, oh,' I thought. 'I am on his territory and he is coming to sort me out. I am probably near one of his marking posts, maybe even sitting on his favourite look out spot'.

I need not have worried though for after walking a few yards towards me on this thundery day, he promptly lay down in the middle of the road and ignored me totally. The effort was just too much bother. We remained like that for a while in peaceful coexistence and tolerance each giving in to the mood of the day listening to the whirr of insects. Peace settled again, though I could still faintly hear the music in the background. I sat there for at least twenty minutes and nothing else stirred. I sat back and let the place seep into me.

When I finally got up and walked on the dog did not even look up.

Further on I came to an old abandoned two-storey house surrounded by old stone barns and a variety of trees. At one time it had an extensive garden to the front but the shrubs had all grown wild. A flowering cherry tree lay uprooted on the ground, surrounded by clumps of daffodil stalks and cow manure. Structurally from the outside this house looked to have potential, though there were a few holes in the slate roof. All the windows in the house were broken but the blue front door was shut tight against the elements. Suddenly there was furious barking and a young sharp-eyed sheepdog appeared in a second floor window full of rage at my transgression of his supposed territory. I stopped and looked at him as well. He did not stop barking; instead he became more voluble and aggressive but I am pleased to inform you that he did not jump! Perhaps now that the humans had disappeared he felt that he was the 'head bottle-washer' around these parts.

For miles I walked along this road, and the feeling of being in a disaster movie still had not left me. I passed a stunted oak tree growing out of the hedgerow, an old disused corn mill on a stream at the roadside and two black and white ponies in a field busily chomping the grasses. I came to an ivy-covered ruin of a castle that looked out over a valley below and onto mist-covered hills in the distance. Sheep were spread around like confetti in the field beside the castle, some idly grazing, some simply lazing. There was the sound of larks in the air. Some dark clouds gathered.

In disaster films a survivor or two usually appear. In this instance it was a car with two occupants, a woman and small child. The car stopped at a house and the woman got out. The woman was a lithe, fit-looking brunette in her late twenties. I approached her and asked how far it was to Manorhamilton, which was my goal for the day. She said she did not know how far it was, but she could tell me that it would take me one and a half-hours to walk there, as she walked the road to Manorhamilton regularly.

'Just my luck,' I thought to myself, 'the survivor was a power walker.'

It would take me more like three hours, I rather pessimistically thought to myself.

Did she not realise that I had blisters on my feet and a big pack on my back? She told me that she loved to walk and spent a lot of time in the surrounding hills. She thought what I was doing was a great idea, one that she would love to do herself. Luckily for me she decided that she had better go into the house with the child and did not give any further thought to coming with me. In the movies, particularly of the disaster type, she would have come with me and we would have rounded up a few more strays along the way, before confronting the evil force of destruction. All I can say is that she would have had to carry the child herself!

Two hours later I entered Manorhamilton. By then the day had taken a turn for the worse. In other words it had started to pelt rain. My immediate priority was to find accommodation. I walked around the town and was only able to find two houses providing bed and breakfast. Both of them were full, as luck would have it, or maybe they just told me that when they saw the sight of me dripping at their front doors. They also informed me that there was not a bed to be got in the area, because it was a holiday weekend. In desperation I tried the hotel, as I thought they were bound to have some room. I got a friendly reception here but was informed by the young receptionist-come-bar tender that they too were full.

"Is there not even one wee spot in this big hotel where one could lay down one's weary head?" I entreated.

The receptionist gave a regretful shake of the head – but they might be able to find a place here for me tomorrow night. She strove to be helpful. On reflection it is the height of incompetence to arrive in a place in the middle of summer, on the busiest weekend of the year, and expect to get a place to stay. However the receptionist, determined to do her best for me, found a phone book and suggested that I look through the list of bed and breakfasts there. She then offered me the opportunity of using the hotel phone for free. I thanked her for her helpfulness but declined the offer as I had my own mobile with me. This interaction had not gone unnoticed, and the five men who were in the bar decided to try and help as well. One of them was nearly sure that he knew a house that did bed and breakfast. He told me it was hardly two miles away and I would be there "in two shakes of a lamb's tail". I looked at him in mock horror.

"Aye, and two miles back again! Are you trying to kill me all together?"

He couldn't remember the name of the owner either so there was no prospect of phoning. The fact that nobody else in the bar was sure of whom he was talking hardly inspired confidence in this suggestion. An old man with cloth cap attached who was sitting at the bar shook his head.

"You should have booked ahead," he said, "given the weekend that was in it."

He said it in such a helpful manner that all I could do was laugh.

After spending some time ringing any bed and breakfast within shouting distance of the town and getting the same story, I gave up and booked a place in a town about twenty miles away. I then rang a taxi to take me there. The taxi driver was a youngish lean woman with long hair. She told me that she had come to live here after marrying a local man. I could not believe it when she told me that she was a grandmother. Whatever she was on was certainly doing her no harm; probably plenty of fresh air and exercise. I told her about my walk and she said that she would love to go on holidays, but her husband had no interest in going anywhere different.

"Maybe one day," she said.

Holidays are such a consumer product nowadays that it is interesting to note that not everyone has succumbed to their charms. Some people are happy and contented to stay in the same spot, why should they want to go anywhere different? Why complicate things when one can live simply? There are many rural people who share this value and who could not be dragged on a holiday for hell or high water. What interests them deeply is their day-to-day work and their daily routines. Many of these people would find going to new places of little interest, because the place has no context or meaning for them. It is like you should have a relationship with the place in which you live. As tourists we often skim the surface of any locality we visit, and we then leave it with no greater insight or understanding. For many, holidays are escapes from a meaningless and bleak reality. Life outside the holiday holds no passion, involvement or connection.

## Manorhamilton to Drumshanbo

It was a misty, dampish morning as I left Manorhamilton – in other words it was a rainy day, without any of the usual wind! Just outside the town I took a small road to the left. On the mountains above me the mist was playing a game of peek-a-boo, which sometimes yielded a tantalising view of the mountain ridge. Not sure of the way, I called into a house to ask directions. An elderly man with a friendly engaging face answered the door and started a conversation. After a few minutes a rather stern woman (whom I took to be his wife) walked behind him from one room into another and then directly back again. The man turned to her.

"This man is from Donegal," he said.

She seemed distinctly unimpressed by this information and continued about her business without comment. I got the feeling that I had not called at the most opportune moment, as the atmosphere could be cut with a knife. The man turned back to speak to me. In a rather apologetic manner tinged with embarrassment, he gave me some information and bade me a safe journey.

Farther up the road I come to a signpost, which grabbed my attention:

*CARRAIG UÍ DHÓNAILL*
*O'DONNELL'S ROCK*
*BRANCH OF THE DONEGAL*
*O'DONNELLS SETTLED HERE*

I presumed that this 'settling' took place prior to the seventeenth century, when the O'Donnell Clan were chieftains of Donegal. Right beside this sign there was another, which read: *'No hill walkers. No horse trekking.'* Obviously my Donegal ancestors hadn't integrated too well with the local community, and more to the point still don't. I can't see the purpose of a sign pointing to O'Donnell's Rock when one can't go to see it! The local authority probably erected the sign in a blaze of publicity in the local press with the picture of some local politician unveiling it. You can visualise the speech he might have given, which would include words about how this development would play an essential part in enhancing tourism in the area and would help bring prosperity to all.

If my theory that the O'Donnells didn't amalgamate too well in the local community holds, then they would not be the last immigrants to do so. In a small nearby village called Dowra, tension between newer immigrants and locals has arisen. This was outlined to me in a pub one night, by a man who said that a German family had aroused the animosity of local people there by objecting to planning permission for a house, which was going to be built near to them. This had a caused a heated debate on the national airwaves about the rights and wrongs of the case from various perspectives. One of the results of this was that the German family was ostracised by some sections of the local community. This mirrors debates ongoing around the country where local people perceive that foreign people move in and want to prevent any further development and building near to them. There is a suspicion that environmental groups such as 'An Taisce' which has power in the planning process is taken over by people such as this. The perception would be that they are all from privileged positions. Some 'foreigners' on the other hand perceive local people as having no regard at all for their environment, and that they will build higgledy-piggledy anywhere. There is a mutual incomprehension of each other's positions. Perhaps the best of both worlds will emerge eventually?

I stopped for a drink beside a recently abandoned house, which was still eminently habitable. A concrete path ran up to the front door in a straight line from a small entrance gate. Obviously the people who originally built this house had no need for a large entrance for either a car or indeed a donkey and cart. A raggle-taggle fuchsia bush with its vibrant red flowers was draped across the front pillar like a beacon for the traveller and the scent of meadowsweet filled the air. The house occupied a large site and was surrounded by green fields, framed by mist-covered hills in the background. One would think that this was prime real estate and that lots of people would like to live in a location such as this. The irony of course is that people in the cities cannot find decent places to live, and there are not enough people in the more remote rural areas to fill the houses that are already there.

After a time I came on to the main road to Drumkeeran, as there was no obvious route via a back road. The road was relatively quiet until a small car passed close to me going very quickly. It put the heart sideways in me, and for the first time I realised how accurate a description that saying is. I could actually feel the heart jumping sideways in my body with the fright. If I had an unhealthy heart I think it would have continued jumping – causing me to partake in the ultimate high jump.

Drumkeeran is a small but nicely located village and as it was still mizzling with rain I thought I would go to a café for tea and a sandwich to savour the atmosphere. The only problem was that there was nowhere in the village serving food. One man told me to go down to the pub and the woman there might make me a cup of tea. I decided that I could spend all day talking people into doing that, so instead I settled for my own sandwich and a bottle of water at a picnic bench at the top of the town. I placed a plastic bag on the seat below me to keep my rear end dry. A dry rear end is a great comfort when you are walking, as any toddler will tell you. For entertainment I looked down on a cemetery and a fairly large church below me. I could not see much beyond the church, as the mist was thick. I thought to myself that this view was better than I would have got in the pub.

Outside Drumkeeran I decide to take the miners' hiking route to Drumshanbo. By this time of day the mist had risen higher into the hills. This route was supposedly developed to encourage walkers into the area. I turned right and headed up a small steep road into the hills overlooking Lough Arrow, the first significant lake on the Shannon. Two young men who were walking in front of me climbed over a gate into a field and disappeared around a small hill. An old slightly dilapidated two-storey house was visible in the distance near to the top of the hill. It was located on a remote hillside tucked in beside a conifer plantation and shrouded in mist. It was the perfect setting for a ghost story. The house had a definite eerie dimension to it. I guessed that the house was my target, as usually where there is a house there is a road of some sort beside it. Before I got that far I passed a beautiful two-storey stone house which was festooned with hanging baskets full of red and yellow flowers. Beside the blue doorway were two large pots with ornamental shrubs. On the door itself was a heart-shaped sign with the name of the house on it. To the front of the house was a large patio area, which had seats and tables made from natural stone and wood. From here there were beautiful views over Lough Arrow, now glinting mercury silver below me. I envied the people who lived here in this beautiful spot.

The road after this was totally empty, though this was a walking route in midsummer: there was not another person to be seen – I was the only walker. I sat for a while on a recently cut log pile of recently cut forestry and took in the view below me. A peaceful grey-themed setting spread out before me consisting of grey sky, light grey transparent mist, dark grey mountains, which appeared here and there through the mist and the mercury water of the lake that had different seams of grey within it. I never thought that the colour grey could be so interesting and diverse. On the hillside below and between the lake and me, a new conifer forest had been planted. 'Typical,' I thought to myself. 'We must be one of the most short-sighted races on Earth. In a few years time this view will be totally obscured, and we will be gazing at a monoculture of a plantation. There is something in our psyche which means that as a people we cannot and do not cooperate together. Everyone always looks to their own individual interest. This is not only evident in us as individuals, but the same plague affects all our institutions of State, as is evidenced here.

Heavy thoughts: I made a conscious effort to leave them to one side. I sat on the logs, looked out over the lake and thought what bliss it was to having nothing in your head, no stray thoughts, no deadlines and no necessity for amusing oneself with thinking. An energetic, buzzing fly landed on my forehead. With an idle swipe I brushed him away with no more thought than the swish of a bullock's tail.

The nurturing balm of stillness infused the soul. All was quiet. The earth hummed its song; its vibrations entered my body like small electric charges, energising, repairing and connecting. A relaxed heaviness descended, and my body sank into its depths. I did not want to stir. My breathing slowed, becoming barely noticeable. The hum of the earth got louder. Then nagging voices arose from the depths of my being and emerged onto the surface of my mind. 'Time to go.' 'Must get up.' 'You will be late.'

The body twitched and the moment of silence passed. Reluctant legs rose and ploughed on up the road.

One of the reasons that I had come in this direction was that this route contained a number of collieries that were marked on the map. As a child I remembered my father talking about the coal mining in Co. Leitrim so I thought 'Hey, I should go and see a colliery, and put a face on the memory."

Coal mining had once been a thriving industry in Co. Leitrim, now sadly no more. The coal produced here was by all accounts fairly low-grade stuff. During the Second World War this coal was used on the railways. It is said that every time the train came to a hill, all the passengers had to get out and walk, as the power the coal produced was insufficient to take the load up the incline. Well at least I suppose it helped to keep the nation fit. After a period of time walking I realised that I had not yet seen a colliery, so I took out the map and peered closely at it. From studying the map I saw that I had passed one earlier, but I must have had my head down watching my toes, because I definitely had not seen it.

All was not lost however, because there was another one marked on the map. The only trouble was that it was on a track in the completely wrong direction. It was difficult to determine how far it was away because the mark for it on the map was a large round circle, and not a dot. It might only be a half a mile away or then again it might be two miles. Anyway, I decided I would dander on up the road and see if I could spot it. A few hundred yards farther along a horrible thought hit me. Did I know what a colliery looked like? I had visions in my head of a large, rusting machine, with lots of moving parts and spreading tentacles that reached into the earth through a cave and pulled that black gold to the surface. There should be some rusting, disintegrating outhouses as well. But what if it were only a hole in the ground that is by now long overgrown? Sure I could be walking all day and see nothing or worse still fall into the hole! Maybe that was the reason that I had not seen the colliery earlier – there was nothing to be seen! I looked up the road as far as the corner in the distance. Perhaps if I walked up that far I would be able to see something from there. Did you ever climb a mountain and after ages of climbing you think the summit is over the next ridge, only to find when you reach the top of that ridge there is yet another ridge in front of you and so on and so on? I had the same feeling about that corner. I am sure that Columbus had similar thoughts when he set out to discover the Americas. The mission of any intrepid traveller is to search out the unknown and to overcome all hardships and obstacles. I decided, all things considered, I should turn and go back the way I had come. After all – Columbus did not have to walk!

Later on I met a couple out for a walk with their dog. We expressed surprise at seeing each other. This gave an idea of how well known and used the place was. They told me they came here most days and they rarely see a soul. I descended from the hillside onto the main road that led into Drumshanbo. After the quietness of the hills the not-so-frequent traffic was uncomfortable and jarring. I put my head down and ploughed on impatiently towards the town, oblivious to all that was around.

On finally reaching Drumshanbo, I tried Berry's Tavern for bed and breakfast. A young woman answered the door and took me into a small narrow kitchen where I met Nessa, the owner of the premises. Nessa was a small, thin middle-aged woman with a youthful voice, sitting beside a table in the rather cluttered kitchen. On the gas stove a number of saucepans were belching steam into the atmosphere. 'From one misty location to another,' I thought.

Nessa looked at me with penetrating quizzical eyes.

"I have a bad hip and I need this stick to get around," she told me.

Taking the stick she leant heavily on it and the table, to enable her to rise. She went over to turn down the heat on one of the saucepans, and as she came back she asked me if I would like a cup of tea. I nodded and said that I would love one, warming to her straight away. I know I am easily influenced, and people have sold their soul for less! However my hope were thwarted in the short term as at that moment a delivery man came in to the kitchen, carrying two big boxes of groceries.

Immediately there was intense and concentrated activity. The deliveryman handed over the receipt and was dispatched out to the bar to await payment. Nessa and the young woman started to take groceries out of the boxes, checking them for accuracy with the receipt. Much confusion reigned as prices and goods were checked and rechecked, but finally order seemed to reign and the younger woman packed the groceries away in fridges and presses. Then Nessa smelt a rat; there was something not right. All the food had to be taken out again and rechecked. There did not seem to be any great degree of logic in how this process was conducted, but finally Nessa put down the pencil and declared in a self-justified manner that she had been charged for some items that had not been delivered.

"You need to keep an eye on these boys," she said to me with a glint in her eye, which told me of her satisfaction of having caught the shop out.

The deliveryman was called back in. He came in with a glass of Guinness in his hand and a slightly downbeat demeanour. I take it he had been called to account before this tribunal on other occasions. He was informed of the mistakes, which he accepted without demurral. This process took about twenty minutes.

I was still not sure of whether Nessa had a bed available for the night, and on top of that there was no sign of the cup of tea. Nessa's sharp eyes must have read my thoughts.

"Oh you didn't get your cup of tea yet?" she asked.

She then directed me to the kettle and told it to make it for myself.

"We don't stand on ceremony here," she chuckled.

Nessa and the other girl then started talking about how they could arrange a bed for me. Seemingly they had a lot of rooms, but most of them were full of holidaying English fishermen. A lot of discussion took place about moving named people from one room into another, in order to make space for me. I had visions of being stuck in a room amidst burly fishermen, fishing rods, wellingtons, buckets of maggots etc. However it would be better than sleeping on the street, so I sat back and drank my tea, as the two women plotted and schemed. Finally they sorted it out to their own satisfaction. After a while the younger woman took me up and showed me a room, which – surprise, surprise – I had all to myself. I wondered what poor unfortunate was lying on the floor in some other room. Well, having said that I didn't wonder too much about it.

After a shower I decided to go out around the town and look for somewhere to eat. As I was leaving the tavern I met a whole group of the fishermen, who happened to be from Yorkshire, and were sitting down to dinner that was being provided by Nessa. People from Yorkshire are stereotyped as being blunt and gruff, but with hearts of gold.

"Grub is great here," a small bald man in his sixties said his distinctive Yorkshire accent. He nodded approvingly at the spread around the table. There was vigorous agreement to this statement. I asked them if they knew "Jackie Charlton"? For those of you who do not know, he was a former manager of the Irish soccer team who hailed from Yorkshire.

"Miserable beggar," one of them said.

The rest laughed knowingly, as if that attribute was a badge of honour.

I took it from this statement that Yorkshire people were as parochial as the Irish were. 'Maybe that's why he got on so well in the job,' I mused to myself. He also was an avid fisherman. I wondered aloud to all of them, whether fishing was in Yorkshiremen's blood? They told me that they (about twenty of them) had been going on fishing holidays together for about twenty years. For most of that time they had been coming to this spot. One of them said that they were in Mullingar a few years previously but they had not liked it there. The man who mentioned food previously, came in on cue.

"The grub was downright poor," he said.

Again everyone nodded in agreement. Good grub certainly seemed to be an essential criterion for a good holiday for this group. I left them all in a great mood as they tucked into potatoes, vegetables and lashings of meat.

I went to another pub down the street, sat at the counter and ordered food for myself along with a good heady pint of Guinness. A man came in and sat close to me at the bar counter. He was a construction worker who specialised in building boundary walls on new housing and industrial developments. He told me that he was going to Naas to work on a building project there. He was a fairly fit looking man in his fifties who had spent all his life working on construction sites in various parts of the world. He told me that he started working in London and then went to Glasgow, Birmingham, to the States and then off to the Gulf. He finally came back to Ireland in the last few years because of the building boom here. He was from Leitrim originally, and he was now trying to base himself near to his original home, even though there was no one known to him there now. When he heard I was from Donegal he said that he hoped to get building work in Killybegs because of the developments of oil and gas off the coast. He told me that he had been "wandering for too long" and that he wanted to work near his original home now.

A few weeks previously on a bus from Dublin to Donegal I met another construction worker who told me virtually the same story. He was originally from Dungloe, on the very west coast of Donegal. He had followed nearly the same geographical route as my friend at the bar, pursuing the flow of concrete across the globe. He went full circle around the world, arriving back in Dublin in the mid-1990s. For all his work he had saved no money, and had no family or lasting relationships, just the passing camaraderie of other transient migrant workers. He had no house or car, no possessions bar what he carried in a small suitcase. He had spent his life moving and his only social outlet had been the pub. He said that every weekend he went on a six-hour bus journey to Dungloe in order to re-establish some connection in his life. However all his family were gone, either dead or emigrated, and nobody remembered him there now. He looked at me.

"Where else is there for me to go?" he asked.

As a youth he had been cast adrift upon the sea. He bobbed and weaved like a loose buoy upon its surface, and was bashed around by the elements until the current washed him up along with many others on shores of its choosing. They stayed for a while on the shoreline until the next high tide swept them off again. I am sure there were moments of ecstasy on this journey, amidst the pounding waves. However no new roots or connections were developed or nourished. All these men had headed off on an adventure; little did they know that life would turn out the way it did; sad and lonely. Life has a trick of passing people by. All one has to do is get into an unthinking routine, and suddenly nearing the end, you wonder where all the time went. But then again there probably was no choice to be made – there was no safety net offered. Still a slim cord kept dragging at them; its persistent pull nagged them to come back home, to connect. Was it too late?

I think of these two men sometimes and hope they found meaning and connection. They left this country because it was not able to sustain them. In a sense they sacrificed themselves so that we could eventually prosper. Of all those who left Ireland in the 40s, 50s and 60s, we usually only hear about the people who have the sweet scent of success about them. These are the small minority who overcame adversity and the pounding sea. The majority did not reach the dreamed of shores.

After the dinner I thought I would get an early night. However my plans were scuppered as I passed through Nessa's bar.

"Where are you from?" A slightly high-pitched, inebriated voice assailed me from the bar counter. It was one of those moments where you had a choice. If you kept going and pretended you never heard the salutation, the likelihood is that you would reach your goal. However countless generations of civility took their toll and I turned around to answer. There were two men at the bar. The one who spoke was a thin man dressed in a sports jacket who looked like an archetypal college professor. He was standing with an all-embracing smile, widened by drink. His arms moved eloquently as he spoke, though his feet were a bit tottery. The other man was quieter and heavyset; he sat on a stool at the counter, holding his own counsel whilst the other man talked. This was the type of man who did not become eloquent or loquacious with drink, but was the type who could drink all night and you would never know it on him. His eyes were wary and alert. He was wearing a cap so maybe that helped keep it all together.

Of course I replied "Donegal" to the first man's enquiry. His smile then got wider and wider, a gleam came into his eyes and he addressed me in Irish. Everyone assumes that if you are from Donegal that you can speak Irish fluently, so not to let the side down I replied in a rather curtailed way to try and cover up how limited my repertoire of spoken Irish was. I must not have been up to the required standard, or else his own grasp of Irish was limited, for he transferred into English and asked the precise details of where I lived, down to the lane that led up to my house.

"You will have a drink?" he asked.

Despite my protestations he shouted over to Nessa.

"Nessa, get this friend of mine a drink, because any man from Donegal is a friend of mine."

Nessa had been serving in the lounge. She came around the corner of the bar, leaning heavily on her stick as she walked. She looked rather amused by the scene. You could see by her expression that she was wondering how I was going to handle the situation.

"No thanks, I don't really want anything to drink," I said.

"Nessa, take that man's order."

I thought the best way of getting out of taking a drink was to make a joke of it and of course being smart about it.

"All right," I said. "I will have a bottle of brandy then."

"Nessa, get that man a bottle of brandy straight away."

Recognising that I was snookered and totally defeated I changed my order to "a half pint of Guinness".

"Nessa, get that man a pint of Guinness," said he rubbing in his advantage.

Despite my further protestations a pint of Guinness duly arrived, for Nessa was definitely no fool. It was certainly more in her interest to keep my friend happy rather than me. When the pint came I gave up any pretensions of going to bed, so I climbed on to a stool at the bar. We introduced ourselves. My 'lecturer' friend was named "Michael" and my quieter friend was called 'Packie'. Michael did all the introductions for Packie as well, calling him his "financial advisor".

Packie smiled and said that if he was employed as his financial advisor he didn't see much of his money. Michael then with extravagant gestures searched his own pockets, finally locating a battered wallet, which he waved above his head.

"There isn't much in this," he declared loudly, "and it is all because of the bad financial advice I got."

They both then started to talk about their relatives in Donegal. It seems that between the pair of them they had connections in a lot of places in south Donegal. Michael reminisced a little bit about staying in Carrick. He remembered going to school there for a few weeks. Michael then got poetic as he described the landscape of heather and mountain. During this epic if he got stuck for something to say, he would reach for his drink whilst he was thinking, saying over and over: "Sound as a pound. Sound as a pound."

Michael then turned to me.

"Have you got anywhere to stay tonight?" he asked.

Seeing Nessa behind the bar, I said I had a lovely room right here in the pub. This didn't seem to deter him in the least, for he went on to loudly announce that he had a spare room and that I would be welcome to it.

"It won't cost you anything," he said.

Nessa was standing at the counter. She didn't react in the slightest to this potential loss of business, as I presumed she was used to such generous offers by Michael to her customers. I again told him I was all right but that the next time I was in the area I would be sure and look him up.

"It would be a shame if a traveller was stuck for a bed," Michael said. "I have plenty of room, sure you may as well stay with me?"

I shook my head but thought to myself that if I had met him earlier it would have been an interesting experience. I can just imagine him waking up the next morning and wondering who is that stranger wandering around my house?

He put up his two hands placatingly in the air and said: "Sound as a pound." However a few minutes later he was again urging me to accept his offer. I was saved by the fact that two women now entered the bar to see if there was any chance of bed and breakfast. Michael's eyes perked up immediately, and he tried his darnedest to engage them in conversation. He was firmly put in his box by Nessa, as any matter concerning bed and breakfast was Nessa's domain, and Michael was barred from the conversation. Nessa explained to them that she was full but that she would phone another bed and breakfast for them. When Nessa left to phone, Michael sensed his opportunity and went in for the kill. Using all of his considerable charms he made eloquent verbal approaches to the two women. However he got no response as the two women ignored him, and went to sit in the lounge. They were obviously well used to dealing with flattering attention. Disappointed, Michael passed comment.

"Two nice cailíns there," said Michael with a wink.

I sort of cringed inside in case the 'two nice cailíns' could hear us. I was decidedly non-committal.

At this stage Michael was starting to teeter on his feet. Up to this stage Packie had been mostly contenting himself with an amused smile at Michael's goings on. He now suggested to Michael that it might be time that he went home to his bed, as he had enough to drink. Michael accepted this readily enough, but absolutely refused any help from Packie in getting him home. After another offer of a bed for the night and a short speech on his relatives in Donegal, Michael head high and feet slightly askew, wandered out the door.

Packie turned to me.

"It doesn't take too much drink to get him drunk," he said.

It was my guess that it would take quite a bit more drink for Packie to show any signs of drink.

Packie then went on to tell me some of Michael's story. It seems he inherited property in the town and as a consequence was never stuck for money. However after a time he went to New York, where he stayed for a long time and according to Packie, made a lot more money. However a bit like the construction workers mentioned earlier he returned home a few years ago, to live in his own house in his own town. That same thin cord had obviously pulled him home again. Packie then told me something in a confidential manner.

"He never spent a penny until recently," Packie said, with his head coming closer to mine.

I sensed that we were now getting to the crux of the story. He then told me that Michael had been diagnosed with cancer. With his head even closer to mine he whispered.

"He won't make it to Christmas."

There was no reason for Packie to whisper because there was nobody else within shouting distance in the bar as even Nessa was off somewhere else.

"He hasn't stopped spending money since," added Packie.

Packie then told me that Michael had tried to tell him once about his illness, but that he had given him no encouragement to do so.

"That's his own business," said Packie.

I asked Packie how long they had been friends.

"All our lives," he said.

Packie then told me about his connections in Donegal, and how they used to take turf with them to school for the fire, and how they used to drink buttermilk with the dinner when he was there. He told me he never really liked the stuff.

"But you had to drink it."

As I got up to leave he said that there was an old Donegal saying that he remembered.

'Don't you tell him
That I told you
That he told me
Not to tell you.'

"Did you ever hear that?" he asked.

He seemed disappointed when I shook my head. However it pleased him that I repeated it a few times.

## Drumshanbo to Strokestown

The alarm clock went off early in the morning thus spoiling a delicious dream – that is the price to be paid for wanting an early start! A feeling of weariness swept over me; it was as if I were stuck to the bed. I lay on whilst at the same time berating myself to get up and get on with the day. An hour went by in this manner, though it only felt like five minutes. Where does time rush to in the morning? That is what I want to know! And why is time so contrary? When you want it to slow down it speeds up, and when you want it to pass quickly it does the opposite. The internal voices finally got the better of me and I dragged myself out of the bed. I decided to pack my rucksack to enable a quick getaway after breakfast. This was a mistake because as I was sleepily searching for a missing pair of socks under the bed, I heard an avalanche of footsteps on the corridor outside. I deferred the packing and hurried out the door, only to find that I was following sixteen fishermen down the stairs to breakfast. The reason for the rush wasn't apparent to me at the time, but became obvious when the queue came to a full stop. This wasn't the type of establishment where you sat down and an array of waiters and waitresses rushed out to take your order for breakfast, returning seconds later with a microwaved fry for your delectation. No, this was a self-service, queue job. Nessa was ensconced in the kitchen beside the cooking stoves, surrounded by an array of frying pans all sizzling away. The smell of bacon and sausage blended with cheap aftershave and carbolic soap filled the atmosphere.

Nessa was managing on her own this morning, and had all the food she would need laid out for ease of access on a table beside her. Her walking stick was propped against the chair beside her. This meant that she could cook away and not move from the one spot, whilst at the same time directing traffic with the stick. The procedure was 'wait for your breakfast to be cooked, take your plate over and get loaded up with nice greasy food'. Nessa ordered one of the first arrivals to make the tea, the next person was delegated to make the toast, another to cut the brown bread and so on. It was all hands to the pump. She jokingly threatened one of the men with her stick if he did not get a move on. The fishermen seemed to love this informal arrangement, and some of them took the initiative and started to make sandwiches for their fishing trip. I am sure their wives would have been proud of them – maybe Nessa could pass on some tips and hints on to them!

"So much for an early start then. Why did I not leave the packing until after breakfast?" I muttered to myself.

Being at the back of the queue and of course fearing that I too might get a job like scrubbing frying pans, I decided to escape from this maelstrom of activity. The public bar adjoined the dining room, so I went in and sat down on one of the plastic sofas. The light was dim in here as the heavy dark curtains were still drawn against the day. The air was musky and heavy with the lingering smell of the previous night's stale beer, cigarette smoke and body odour, all mingling together awaiting the dreaded onslaught of fresh air, hoovers, cleaning agents and disinfectant. The two men who were in the queue before me decided to abandon ship as well and sat down beside me. These were big men in either their late fifties or early sixties who were bedecked in gold necklaces and rings, and had an air of prosperity about them. They were the only other people staying here who were not fishermen. They were friends from childhood who were touring the area for a few days and had decided to base themselves here with Nessa. Both spoke with English accents but were from Co. Waterford originally. Their story unfolded during the wait for breakfast.

Like many similar young people of their era they had emigrated together in their teens and had worked in construction in England, finally setting up their own company in Cheshire. They both got married and had families and lived near to each other. Every so often the two friends would return to Ireland for a visit, especially to Co. Waterford. They enjoyed these visits but they adamantly insisted that their home was now in Cheshire. I could not help but contrast these two men's lives with the two men I had mentioned earlier. They were also involved in construction, but had led nomadic existences and were now rootless in their later years. These Waterford men had strong connections and a sense of rootedness. They described their lives in terms of family outings, football matches, greyhound racing, holidays, and carrying out activities with their wives and children. There was a contentedness here, a feeling that life had more blessings than sorrows.

They had left the country as young men. In all probability, their expectations were similar to those other two young men. Why did their lives turn out so differently? What role did their friendship play in all of this? I never thought to ask them at the time, but my guess is that it would have been a significant factor. Wherever we go in life we need a network of significant others to refer to, not people who you meet in bars, not acquaintances at work who want to use you for what advantage it brings them. It should be ordinary connections, which allow people to be themselves first and foremost, and which are supportive through times of change. It was great to see an enduring friendship.

One hour later and it was my turn for breakfast. Nessa was semi-surprised at my late arrival, with expectant plate at the ready.

"I nearly forgot about you," she said.

'Thanks very much, perhaps I should have left without paying?' I thought to myself.

You can see that my mood was not too good. These thoughts were transitory; it is not easy standing in front of a frying pan for a couple of hours, slapping up fries for big grown men, and let me tell you some of them were fairly grown all right.

"Just throw on the rest of what you have there for me," I joked.

The pan was half full of grease at this stage and my food had a great opportunity to soak it all up, especially the fried egg that went on last. I thought again to myself that this would give me some fuel for the day. The aroma of grease and sizzling sausages once again filled the air. When all was finished, Nessa shook the grease off them and slapped the food on to my plate. I can honestly say that it was as tasty a fry as I ever had.

As I was the last to be fed it provided an opportunity for Nessa and I to talk. Nessa asked me where I worked. I told her the North Western Health Board. A flicker of concern came into her eye.

"Look at the state of my kitchen!" she exclaimed.

She turned a sharp accusatory eye towards me, as if I had been surreptitiously spying on her all along.

"I knew that there was something about you," she said.

I have no idea what she meant by this, though I presume it was not entirely complimentary. Perhaps she meant I had big biceps, or perhaps she meant that I had a big head. More probably she thought I might be a fifth columnist for those dreaded Environmental Health Officers, or the 'conformity enforcers of the European Union' as I prefer to call them. After a few moments (sometimes I like to be cruel), I assured Nessa that the state of her kitchen was the least of my concerns, and told her that I would only take a case against her if I keeled over and died. This lame attempt at a joke lightened things between us. Nessa started telling me that her youngest daughter was leaving home this autumn, and she didn't know how she was going to manage without her. She then told me that her husband had died recently and this left the weight of the business on her shoulders. Her daughter wanted her to go for an operation on her arthritic hips.

"But if I go how will this place work?" she exclaimed, leaving the question in the air for a few moments.

"It's so hard to go on," she concluded with pain in her eyes.

I felt a strong sympathy for her, this small woman with a tough exterior, obviously in daily pain, trying to manage this enterprise on her own. Everything seemed to be leaving her at once: her partner; her family; her mobility and possibly her business. She felt she had to keep the show on the road. It's strange how at times changes all seems to come together in a flurry, after a time of stasis.

Finally, hours after I had planned to be on my way, I got my rucksack and 'hit the road'. Just outside of town a red car stopped beside me. It was Packie, who gave me a cheery 'hello' and a positive weather forecast for the day ahead. He also conjured a link with the night before, by reciting his Donegal saying with full emphasis and meaning. With a final wave and an expression of good luck he was on his way.

The road out of Drumshanbo was hilly. A few miles from the town I looked over a fence at two brown horses that had a big field of long grass and wildflowers all to themselves. A varied hedgerow that included full-grown ash and sycamore trees formed the boundary of the field. It was the picture of a rural idyll. It amazed me all through my journey; the number of horses that were to be seen even in Counties not traditionally known for horse ownership. There is definitely a link between people and horses that is not economic in nature.

The day started to cloud over and there were light showers of rain. So much for Packie's positive forecast! After climbing the next hill I was confronted by a prominent hill with a cross on top of it. This particular hill dominated the landscape in some strange way, although it was not that large. From the map I could see it was called Sheemore and that it had a number of megalithic tombs marked on its slopes. No wonder it looked strange.

'It has something to do with the fairies,' I thought.

The Irish word for fairies is *Sí*, its anglicised spelling 'Shee'. The hill seemed to draw one's eye to it, but then maybe that was because there was a large cross on top of it. Curious about the hill and the cross at its height, I looked for someone to ask about it. As usual there was no one around when you really needed them. Not to be deterred I knocked on the door of a nearby house, to see if there might be someone there from whom I could find out details about this hill. This house was the only one with smoke coming out of the chimney, so I judged that there was a good possibility that there was somebody at home. As I waited on a possible reply, I saw a cat with newly born kittens perched on top of straw bales in a shed beside the house. Another shed was full of turf; these people certainly intended to be cosy during the coming winter. There was no reply at the door, but as I was about to leave the skies opened and it literally hammered down with rain, so I took the softy's option and decided to shelter under the arch at the front door. I heard a car coming and to allay suspicion I turned around and pretended to knock at the door. I was sure that they would be wondering what I was up to if I was just standing, with no seeming purpose at the front of somebody's house. This procedure was repeated every time a car approached.

When the rain eased somewhat I abandoned my shelter and headed down to the bottom of the hill. I saw a large dwelling, and debated to myself whether it was a house or a small hotel. I saw a man sitting in a jeep beside the house, so I went up to him and asked him about the hill. He was a large man with a friendly smile. He told me that the hill was called 'fairy hill', but that in 1933 the Roman Catholic Church put the cross on top of it as part of the celebration of the Marian year. The hope was that it would be used afterwards as a place of Christian worship.

'Typical imperialistic behaviour,' I thought. Colmcille in his time superimposed symbols of Christianity on top of pagan sites and the Church was still at it 1,500 years later. The symbol of a cross on top of a fairy hill is symbolic of our top-down approach to religion; suppress people's views by telling them the proper way to think. No matter how hard formal religion tries to suppress something, the repressed energy (in this case the fairies) are bubbling underneath waiting for their time to come again. The old belief system still lurks there, if only as a trace in people's consciousness awaiting the conditions within which it will be able to flourish. I wondered what type of fairies were supposed to have lived there and indeed more importantly, were they still living there? Was there any strange music to be heard on a clear moonlit night that lured humans to live in fairyland? When we were young, older people always warned us that the fairy music and the music from the Beatles were equally dangerous, and both were to be avoided at all costs! The man pointed up to the cross and told me that lights were put up on the cross when it was erected, and that these lights used to come on nightly until relatively recently. He laughed softly when struck by a memory. He said that the house was at one time a guesthouse. American visitors would be told that if they could see lights on the hill at night, it was a sign of the fairies, and that it would bring good luck to them. When the lights came on the Americans would point to them, but he would pretend he could not see them. Whether this fooled people is anybody's guess.

He went on to tell me that he had now turned the guesthouse into a nursing home for older people because of our ageing population.

"It is a guaranteed growth business," he said.

This is one of many such homes that have sprung up all over the country especially during the 90s boom times. It certainly seems we have less time for older people now; they don't fit in with the frantic modern lifestyle. However we do not have to worry, as consumer products such as residential homes will cater for all older peoples needs; physical, emotional and social, far from the consciousness of the rest of society. Indeed extra packages of caring services are provided if you can afford them. Older people can be taken on outings etc. and every extra 'package' of care will help salve our conscience. There are indeed many types of death.

I walked on another bit and looked back up at the hill. In the foreground there was a field with long grass and some wildflowers. The river flowed by in grey, blue and black, with ripples slipping sensuously across its surface, aroused by the caress of a slight wind. A swan glided equally lusciously beside reeds and bushes at the opposite side of the river, occasionally tilting upside down in the water, feet in the air, feeding below. After a few moments the swan would swing back upright and glide on, carving a new design into the water. A fly landed on my cheek, I blew him away with a stream of air directed by my lower lip. On the slopes of the 'fairy hill' stood a scattering of small, stunted hawthorn trees, which had survived the ravages of wind and sheep. It was a place to remember.

I wandered up to the bridge to get a closer look at a cruiser, which was coming down the canal with two people on board, a man and a seven- or eight-year-old boy. The boy was wearing a bright yellow life jacket. The man however was not; he probably felt that he had done his bit for safety by ensuring that his son was wearing one. Like all young boys he was watching his father very closely indeed. The cruiser pulled into a lock. That's the part of cruising down a river I would hate, pulling into all those locks and waiting whilst they filled or emptied. The water flowed over the edge of the lock in ribbons of black and silvery gold, churning into foam when it hit the water below. I sat down where I had a good view of the canal and ate a banana.

Looking at the canal, I thought that the actions of water are a real symbol for us in our day-to-day lives. Water is soft, pliable and persistent and leaves its mark on the landscape at all stages of its journey. In the beginning the river is full of energy, in an awful hurry to get where it is going. It bubbles out of the earth and pushes itself into the landscape; it tumbles around rocks, splashes into pools, takes shortcuts and forms waterfalls. Its waters are clear and fresh and smell like the first flush of spring. Its sounds are insistent, infectious, gregarious and sometimes overpowering. The young river flows onto a flat plateau where it pauses for a while in a restless lake until it spills out the other side with eager enthusiasm. Later on having bounced through the landscape it decides, 'hold on a minute, we will get where we are going soon enough and for long enough. Let's slow down and savour the journey.' It now more assiduously joins forces with other collections of water. Its power is dependent on the level of connectivity it makes. An accommodation is made with the landscape. It nourishes life on its way: fish spring from its waters; it sates animal thirst; it helps vegetation to grow and insects to breed. It occasionally exhibits a burst of energy and enthusiasm, bursts its banks and for a while nourishes the surrounding land. After wandering a while the river retreats to its established route and continues on its journey. At the end it starts to lose speed and direction. It develops a lived-in smell and meanders into the sea where it mingles with all the other waters, indistinguishable now as an entity to the human eye.

After fairy hill, the small quiet road meandered through several small hills. The fuchsia was in full flower and the only noise was the sound of birds chirruping in the dense hedgerows. I was lost in a world of my own and walking in the middle of the road when I was jolted out of my reverie by the beep of a car. Startled, I jumped on to the ditch out of the way of an English-registered car that was being driven by two Asian men wearing turbans. 'They are probably from Pakistan,' I thought and then wondered what the heck they were doing here on this innocuous back road in the middle of Ireland. To be on this road, they had to know the roads intimately, or else they had gone totally astray. They could have been English tourists!

At the next crossroads I saw a man in a field walking through a herd of cattle. On seeing me he came over to the small wall beside the road, leant against it with one leg and settled in for a chat. He was a man in his thirties with a round ruddy face, a happy demeanour and a loud friendly voice. We passed the usual pleasantries about weather, football and important things like that. He also had seen the two Asian gentlemen. They had stopped momentarily at the crossroads before turning right, heading in the direction of the nearest village. It just shows you that you do not need satellites to track people in the countryside!

My new acquaintance had a predicament in that he had a cow that had lost a calf, and he also had a calf whose mother had died. He was now trying to establish a relationship between the orphan calf and the recently bereaved cow. The calf recognised that any port would do in a storm especially if it had milk in it. The cow, with the benefit of considerable experience no doubt, was slightly more circumspect about taking on a ready-made family. The farmer, with great passion, explained how he was trying to establish this bond. He had put the cow and calf together in the one field. Obviously the calf smelling milk was hot on the trail of the cow. However there was a problem; every time the calf went to suckle the cow, she walked away, off again about some important business or other, leaving a frustrated calf in her wake. My farmer friend found that if he shouted at the walking cow she stopped, giving the calf an opportunity for a short suckle. When the cow had enough of this and proceeded to walk on he shouted again, once more she would stop and the calf would suckle, and so and so on. In this way he hoped to establish a bond between the calf the new foster mother.

"Perseverance is the answer," he said.

He told me that after he was finished shouting at the cow he was off to visit a 101-year-old man who was still living on his own, even though he was in a wheelchair. He said that a few neighbours helped him out and that they all loved going in to see him, as he was such a happy and positive man. What a great achievement, I thought, both for the old man and for the community. A well-functioning community is as natural as breathing; concepts such as cost, duty, effectiveness, effort don't come in to it. People just get on with living together in the best way they can. For the old man it was an achievement to come through the travails of life and hold on to his positivity. I left my friend still shouting at the cow. I think she had a choice: either become a foster mother or go deaf.

This episode brought back the memory of a shorthorn cow giving birth on our own small farm when I was a child. At an early stage of delivery my father recognised that she was having difficulties. The vet was called and a few neighbours arrived, as they must have sensed that there something dramatic. The cow was lying flat out on the floor of the shed and I recall a hoof appearing. Everyone pitched in to help the cow first by manually pulling on the hooves. This however did not produce any results and consequently a rope was tied around the hooves, which was pulled by a number of men still with no effect. The vet arrived and he immediately declared that it was critical – both cow and calf would be lost if something didn't happen soon. After some more fruitless pulling on the rope he ordered a neighbour to go quickly and get his tractor. The rope was tied to the tractor and the driver was told to inch forward very slowly. Success! A creamy slimy ball fell onto the floor of the shed.

"The calf was too big for her!" exclaimed the vet.

The calf being born was a Charolais calf, a bigger breed than the shorthorn. Despite her ordeal and near total exhaustion, the cow struggled to her feet with the aid of a few neighbours. She then went over to the calf and with her grainy tongue started to lick him with sufficient force that he was moved across the floor of the shed. Finally a scrubbed calf emerged, and it is safe to say that he would probably never be as clean again. He had the look of young boys of my youth after their mothers scrubbed them before going to Mass. It was as if they had a different skin on them altogether. The calf eventually tottered to his feet on shaky legs. With a collective sigh of relief all the men came into the house for a drink. There was a sense that they all had participated in something important. My father took a special interest in the calf after this. It was more or less reared as a pet, which resulted in it often coming to the back of the house for extra feeding from the bucket.

One day a cousin of mine was walking out at the back of our house when there was no one else around. The Charolais, who at this stage had grown into a very large bullock, spotted him and naturally thought that there might be the prospect of a bucket of nuts in the offing. Off he went in the direction of the cousin, with a lively and expectant gait. My cousin misinterpreted the intentions of the bullock. He raced in a panic to the nearest tree, up which he scrambled, in the nick of time, as he thought. It was there some time later that my father, to his great amusement, found him when he came home from a neighbour's house. The pet Charolais bullock still waited companionably near the bottom of the tree. The story went around the neighbourhood for weeks afterwards. Even many years later the story is occasionally told, much to my cousin's still-acute embarrassment. This bullock went on to win prizes for best bullock at local shows. All of this, from such tenuous beginnings.

At the next crossroads I came across a sign erected in a field:

*Site of Pearse – Connolly*
*Memorial Hall*
*In memory of Jimmy Gralton, Leitrim Socialist*
*Deported for his political beliefs in August 1933*

'Hey, I must find out more about that,' I thought. Why would anyone be deported from Leitrim in 1933 for political beliefs? At that stage we were an independent, sovereign nation. What had he done? Where could he be deported? How could we deport someone just because he was a socialist? Who would take him?

I noticed that the sign was rotting and as there was no indication of any building I thought, that this gave testimony to another good intention, never fulfilled. My immediate feeling was that perhaps a green field is a better symbol of the socialist ideal than a rectangular monstrosity of a hall. The hall might be a reminder of some of the worst aspects of socialism in Eastern Europe, a big featureless, rectangular building with basic facilities and no aesthetics. We have enough of such buildings in the Irish landscape, I smugly thought.

After I finished the walk I decided to find out what information I could about Jimmy Gralton and the enigma of his deportation and the missing hall. One day when I was in Keoghane's bookshop in Sligo I asked the owner there if he knew anything about the man in question. This man, who is also named Michael, has always struck me as knowledgeable about literary and historical events, and sure enough I was not to be disappointed. He thought for a moment and then told me that some years ago there had been a commemorative event held on the life and times of Jimmy Gralton. He told me that Ken Livingstone the eminent London Labour Member of Parliament had spoken at the event.

"Declan Bree," he continued, "would be the best man to fill you in on Jimmy Gralton."

Declan Bree is the local Labour T.D. for the Sligo/Leitrim constituency. Michael then asked one of the staff in the shop to ring Declan Bree. When the call came through I introduced myself, telling him how I had been on a walk and I had come across the sign, which had sparked my curiosity. I also mentioned that I knew Manus Brennan fairly well, the Labour candidate for Government in my own constituency. This strategy is always a risk, because in politics there is often greater enmity *within* political parties than *between* political parties. The following short account of the life and times of Jimmy Gralton is based on that conversation and on a document written by Declan Bree himself.

Jimmy Gralton was born at Effernagh near Gowel in Co. Leitrim in 1886. Like many of his generation he was forced to emigrate, first to Britain and then to the United States. In the States he became involved in trade union issues and joined the Connolly Club there. This club also had other eminent Irish members such as Jim Larkin, Nora Connolly and Liam Mellows. He also joined the United States Army for a short period.

Jimmy returned to Ireland in 1922 as the War of Independence from Britain was coming to a close. The British paramilitary force called the 'Black and Tans' had burned down the local community hall in Gowel. In response one of Gralton's first activities was to build a large hall on his parent's lands, which he called 'The Pearse–Connolly Hall' after the 1916 revolutionary leaders. This information answered the second part of my question. The hall referred to on the sign was not a proposed building, but an historic building, now destroyed. This hall then became a focus for social and political activities in the area. Using the hall as a base Gralton organised social events and political study classes for the local people. From this activity there emerged a 'Direct Action Committee' which was established in order to enable tenant farmers to regain the land from which the landlords had evicted them. Cattle were driven on to the large estates and former tenants were settled on the land.

You interfere with local power structures at your peril, however. The Catholic Church frowned on his activities and there now began a period of sustained attack on his character, and on the people who attended his hall. The powerless people in society were being radicalised. This not only upset the wealthy but also the middle classes and small farmers, who felt that the agitation would impact negatively on their future prospects and power. This was not a liberation theology Church but a Church that supported the *status quo*. Maintaining control and power over the populace was its prime concern. As a result of the Church's agitation, troops from the newly formed Irish Nation came to arrest Jimmy Gralton. Before they could catch him he fled back to the United States.

Gralton was certainly a man of action. He organised the building of a hall, the organisation of courses and the formation of a direct action political group, all within one year. The fact that he alienated the Catholic Church during that time was also an accomplishment. There are many committees up and down the country who could learn from his example, as some have spent up to forty years trying to build community centres in various communities throughout Ireland. The impression of Gralton was that he was always a man in a hurry.

In the United States he again became involved in workers' issues and was a co-founder of the Transport Workers' Union. However his connection to Ireland was not broken and in 1932 he returned to Leitrim because his parents had become frail and were finding it increasingly difficult to manage.

He re-opened the hall and again became involved in local political education and action, much to the disapproval and annoyance of the local politicians and clergy. Declan Bree tells the story that one of clergy at that time:

"...denounced the hall as a den of iniquity and said that he would put horns on Gralton and on anyone else who attended it. Some days later Gralton presented himself at the priest's doorstep – to have his horns fitted!"

The local campaign against Gralton organised by the Church and the local political establishment aroused local passions. This was further fuelled by the 'Red Scare' that was part of the political scene of the day. This resulted in shots being fired into the hall when a meeting was in progress in November 1932, and on Christmas Eve 1932 the hall was burned down in an arson attack.

The new Fianna Fáil government then issued a deportation order against Gralton, calling him 'an undesirable alien'. So Gralton had to go on the run from the authorities once again. The Government was able to justify the proposed deportation of Gralton, a person who was born and bred in Co. Leitrim on the basis that he once served in the U.S. Army. In order to join the U.S. Army it seems one has to take American citizenship. Despite the efforts of local and national organisations, Gralton was captured in August 1933 and the 'alien' was deported. His mother asked if she could see him before he went but was refused permission. She never saw her son again.

Gralton took up his former activities, working on behalf of the Labour movement in the States and was involved in many campaigns and actions. His adopted country never made any attempt to deport him. If they had, who would have taken him? Certainly it would not have been the narrow-minded country that was Ireland in the 1930s. Are we any different today? Maybe we are just narrow-minded about different things. I still think we take a perverse pleasure in kicking someone when they are down and excluding people who are not on the politically correct side today. Our public pronouncements about such people are delivered in condemnatory, moralistic tones. It is certainly true to say that for the majority of the twentieth century we forced our bravest and brightest people to leave these shores for one reason or another.

Jimmy Gralton died in 1945. John Mullaly at the graveside gave the following short oration.

*"Stone monuments were built in memory of men in the past. This is not the kind of monument that Jim Gralton wanted, but a world in which human beings can have security, free from hunger and misery, with sufficient leisure time to study art and music; a world wherein there will be no wars, famine or depression in the midst of plenty."*

In an appropriate addendum to this story, Packie Gralton, a cousin of Jimmy Gralton played a considerable part in the campaign of Declan Bree who was the first ever Labour T.D. elected to the Dáil for the constituency of Sligo/Leitrim. One action always influences another in the web of history.

A little bit up the road from the Jimmy Gralton site I came to a country pub. It was a two-storey, grey building incorporating a pub, shop and dwelling area with an array of signs for Guinness, Smithwick's and bottled gas hanging on the walls. Gas bottles were stacked beside the shop door. A large horse chestnut tree grew in the street directly in front of the pub; its foliage cast a dark shadow across the front of the building. This tree was architecturally part of the house and of the road, both had been accommodated around it. On the opposite side of the road to the pub a Donegal flag was waving high, attached to a stripling of an ash tree. Intrigued as to why a Donegal flag would be flying here and also wishing to find out more about Jimmy Gralton, I decided I would try to find someone to talk to. The shop door sign on read: 'open 10.00 am to 10.00 pm'.

I looked at my watch; the hands pointed to 12.50 pm. However the door was locked tight and there was no one to be seen anywhere. I then tried all the other doors in the pub and the house with the same result. I resigned myself to the fact that the mystery of the Donegal flag and Jimmy Gralton would have to wait a while longer. I sat down opposite the pub to have a sandwich, partly to alleviate my hunger and partly in the hope that someone would come along to answer my questions. The road remained empty, the pub and shop remained still. Quietness descended. I examined the horse chestnut tree that was in front of the pub in detail. Most of the tree was in shadow but a shaft of light illuminated one side of it. As I sat there the shadows from the tree crept across the light of the road. One of the shadows touched my foot like a tentative explorer from a foreign land. I think it decided it wouldn't invade when it was confronted by the reality of my feet, which in their condition at that time provided a formidable obstacle to anything with a bit of sense, including a shadow. A shadow is a wee bit like a ghost, a presence without substance that has the power to cool the surrounding atmosphere. I looked across at the building and wondered what tales were contained within its four walls; did the shadows extend into the house as well? Feeling this draught of coolness on my skin and sensing that there would be no opportunity for a cool draught of Guinness either any time soon, I arose and walked on up the road.

Sheltered and shadowed by tall trees on either side of the road, ghost stories from my youth filled my head. I can still see my uncle's earnest eyes as he told me about the time that he had been out fishing on a moonless night in a small punt. He described the calm dark waters and the slight ripple of the sea on the boat, when out of the darkness a silent hand appeared over the edge of the boat. My uncle, thinking that it might be someone from one of the other small craft out fishing, went to grasp it. To his horror and surprise his hand went right through the hand. Suddenly his being was filled with an intense fear. With serious eyes he told me how he felt drawn to jump overboard, how he got up and stood on the edge and prepared to jump in. He said that only for the intervention of his friend on the boat he would now be in a watery grave. Or the story of the woman in our locality who every night runs up the road to a ruined house with two buckets of water in her hands; seemingly she is still trying to put out the fire that killed her children. It is said that if you see her that there will be a fire in your own house.

Accompanied by these ghosts I arrived in Drumsna and in the process had arrived back at the Shannon River. Drumsna is a pretty riverside village, except for one thing it does not exist on any maps. Perhaps there is the making of another ghost story here featuring the wanderer who arrives in a town that does not exist. However the explanation is a bit more mundane and uninteresting. It seems that when the new road bypassed Drumsna the mapmakers decided to consign the existence of the village to history. This of course has caused much consternation locally. People of the village complain that a little place with two houses, a little bit out the road, is on the map but yet the powers that be have decided to omit Drumsna. They say that the other place should be omitted from the map and not Drumsna, which in comparative terms is a large village.

People always tend to define grievance by comparing themselves with the fortunes of other people or locations close to them. They state the reason that they should get something is because they are more deserving than others in similar circumstances. At one time I used to work with traveller families, and at one time a number of these families applied for housing in a new local authority housing estate. When the houses were allocated only one of the families was housed. This led to much anger towards the family who got the house, as all the other families said that they were the more deserving. It was interesting that the anger was directed towards the family rather than towards the local authority that was obviously implementing a discriminatory housing policy. The other families all said that they were more deserving because they had more children, were living in worse conditions, had a sick relative etc., etc. They also said that one member of the accommodated family had got the ear of one of the local politicians and had therefore wiped their eye so to speak. Probably the people of Drumsna should be campaigning for both areas to be on the map, in the same way the travelling families should have been working together.

Seeing that I was in Drumsna I decided I would go into a pub for a sandwich. There was a fit looking middle-aged man serving behind the bar and a less fit, more sedentary member of the species ensconced at the bar. I ordered tea and sandwiches and got talking to the barman who turned out to be the owner. It seemed that he was the activist in the local community and he told me that it was his aim to develop walking paths and canoeing facilities in the area. He talked passionately about canoeing and told me that the new road had not only isolated Drumsna but had ruined the experience of canoeing on the river. The road runs alongside the river for long stretches so when you are gliding along in a canoe the constant din of traffic assails you. He then said that he had been out canoeing the previous night and for a period there was very little traffic on the road.

"It felt like Heaven on Earth," he said with a satisfied smile.

As we modernise, the pristine places that we once took for granted are becoming more and more scarce and difficult to get to. We will not realise their value until they are gone. At the moment though money is the god to be worshipped. If something does not have immediate financial benefit it is considered to be of no value. Even the aesthetic is a commodity to be marketed and sold. Flashy art galleries, craft shops with over priced commodities are supposed to satisfy our aesthetic sense. A few Nature reserves and big houses, which we naturally have to pay to get into, are supposed to satisfy our need for communing with Nature and appreciating our heritage. Our traditional music is increasingly consigned to pubs. Our vision of ourselves as a nation is completely at odds with the image that we try to present to the world. The image of a wild beautiful landscape that regenerates soul and spirit is useful in the modern value system only if it brings in revenue.

He asked me about where I had been walking, so I told him where I had been to date, emphasising in particular the beautiful views over Lough Arrow, soon to be obscured by conifer plantations. He told me that a local hotelier had wanted to build a hotel there, but had been refused because the local authority believed that it would be too much of an intrusion into the landscape. The bar owner outlined the dilemma. A hotel would bring in jobs and revenue into a depressed area of the country and would enable the tourist infrastructure to be developed. It would impact somewhat on the local landscape but surely not as much as the conifer plantation? What is the right balance in all of this? In one instance we have under-regulation and in another instance we have possible over-regulation. When things go wrong the rules then become so stringent and nonsensical that it makes life a misery for everyone.

A good-looking girl of about eighteen entered the bar and asked the owner if she could have a word. She was tall with long fair hair and was wearing jeans and a short top. She was obviously a part-time employee in the pub and she had come in to let the bar owner know what days she would be available for work: not available might be a more accurate description. She told the owner in confident tones that she would not be able to work on the day the Leaving Certificate results were out, and she could not work the following day because she would be recovering from the celebrations (optimistic girl). She then informed him about other days when she was meeting friends and would not be available. Her parting shot was that she would not be able to work that very evening because she had to go out socialising. The bar owner barely restrained his exasperation and threw his eyes to the ceiling. Bar staff must be in short supply because he agreed to all of her wishes and demands. The girl then breezed out as quickly as she had entered.

"Staff now want to suit themselves all of the time," the owner said to no one in particular.

There were now a few new faces in the pub. One was a man in his forties with a long angular face and a lean body and twinkling eyes.

"What happened to you in the raft race then?" he shouted across to the bar owner.

The bar owner put on a mock-severe expression and ignored the question for a moment. However everyone knew there was no getting away from a question like this as the questioner and everyone else in the bar would not be denied an answer. The bar owner now realised that he had a captive audience. He told us all about the raft race. It seemed that all the pubs in the area had entered a raft in a race on the river. There were no rules other than all the sailors, navigators and crew on the raft had to come in fancy dress and all money collected at the event was given to local charities. There was great rivalry between the pubs and our host assured us that a lot of effort had gone into making his raft in particular.

"Is that why it broke up in the river?" joked the questioner again.

"It did not break up, in fact the raft is still available for inspection in the yard."

"He will be telling us next that he won the race," insisted his tormentor.

Our intrepid bar owner then cited a number of excuses as to why his craft did not fare better in the race. He first of all blamed the bad organisation of the event, which meant that his raft was late getting on to the river and he had no time to set up the raft properly. This was of course accompanied by the sceptical noises of all present.

"The race was started when my raft was facing in the wrong direction," he stated. "It would not happen in the Grand National," he insisted to more guffaws.

"Anyway, the raft that won the race was not really a raft at all, it was a catamaran. The race was won by a pack of cheats," he concluded triumphantly.

To prove his point he brought us out to see his raft, which was in pride of place in the back yard. All I can say is that it was a feat for this assemblage of pieces to finish the race at all. It was either that or there were mighty rapids on the river that had inflicted severe punishment on the vessel. Having satisfied our curiosity we all crowded back inside again and the talk turned to the new call centre that was opening in the area. The barman once again posed the question whether there should be ethical objections to the opening of such a centre because of the low levels of pay.

"It's a way of impoverishing the people," he said.

It was a pity to leave such a cauldron of argument and debate. A pub that exercises the mind as well as the stomach has much to recommend it. So if you somehow find this village, which is not on the map, but which I assure you does exist, then look for a pub with a raft in the back yard. If you find it, go in and join in the argument. But I warn you, don't mention the raft race! I crossed the bridge over the river Shannon and headed towards Strokestown.

On this tranquil road I sat down on a small wall, outside an old barn. The wall had old flowers straggling over it. Bees were busy all around me, each bustling in and out of flowers collecting food for the winter months. There was a whole beautiful system and collective brain at work there. These were not a few random bees that happened opportunistically upon a source of food. These bees were precisely organised entities working for the good of the whole.

Of course human beings in their history have operated in a similar manner for a similar purpose. What are explorers and adventurers but the equivalent of the scouts in the bee world? What happens when these adventurers and divergent thinkers make a new discovery? When explorers find new lands the powerful hierarchy of State, industry and Church inevitably follow them and organise the harvesting of their discovery. The explorer (whatever their individual motivation) is the precursor to harvesting behaviour.

I came into Strokestown and headed towards Strokestown Park House, home of the Pakenham-Mahon family from 1660 until 1979.

Thirty thousand acres of land were confiscated from the local chieftains and given to the Pakenham-Mahon family as reward for participating in colonial wars. On this vast estate they constructed Strokestown House, one of the finest Palladian houses in Ireland. The family continuously occupied this house until 1979 when shortly before her death, the last of the family sold all to a local garage owner. He decided to open the house to the public, and turned part of it into a museum commemorating the Irish Famine of the 1840s.

I walked along the big main street that was constructed by one of the original owners of Strokestown House. His objective was to make the main street in the village of Strokestown wider than the Ringstrasse in Vienna. That is why ever since people can talk about Strokestown and Vienna in the same breath! The street was impressive and lined with lime trees. At the end of the street I passed through a Gothic arch and entered the grounds of the house. The main part of the house before me was three stories high with a variety of outbuildings. I walked up the drive to the house and then moved on to a narrow gravel path for a while. Did you ever try to walk quietly on gravel? No matter how stealthily you creep, there is always a slight crunch as one piece of gravel rubs on another. I tried practising my ninja warrior, noiseless walk but I gave up when I saw someone looking rather strangely at me.

When I arrived at the ticket office I was informed that the last house tour of the day was just about to begin, so I decided to join it. This tour was being led by an enthusiastic, sturdy twenty-year-old male whom truth to be told gave a bit of life to the tour of the house. Even though he did not know as much as he might have about the history of the house and times, he always gave an educated guess and did it in an entertaining way. I have visited a number of these types of houses over the years and I can never empathise with the lifestyle contained within these walls. To be honest they symbolise for me the effective colonisation of the Irish people and represent how the landlord and aristocratic class presented themselves as superior to ordinary people. During the war of Independence, at the beginning of the twentieth century, many houses like this were burned down in a gluttony of stored up vengeance. The reaction was totally emotional. The logical reaction of course would have been to turn them into hotels or training colleges.

The entrance halls of these houses invariably have pictures and portraits of long lost relatives cluttering the walls. The men are usually in military dress and display medals of different sizes and shapes. The women are bound up and squeezed into wads of tight clothing and it looks like their bodies are screaming: 'Let me out of here! Let me out of here!' That is, of course, provided the bodies have not already been forced into submission. The furniture in the rooms is generally dark brown mahogany or walnut. The library has tomes of British law that I am sure were avidly read at the time! The dining rooms, drawing rooms and sitting rooms in the house are very formal and unappealing to my eye. Usually the only room that captures my imagination in these houses is the breakfast room, which is light and airy, situated to capture the early morning rays of the sun. It represents some degree of optimism before the heaviness and rigidity of the day again dominates the scene. Strokestown House fitted this mould.

From a window in the breakfast room of Strokestown House our guide pointed out the store where the guns were kept and handed out for a day's 'sport' after breakfast. We were then brought to the bedrooms, which were interesting, to the extent that husband and wife slept in different bedrooms. Maybe it is beneficial to keep a little bit of mystery alive! The men took extra precautions, in that they kept their favourite dog in the room with them in a dog basket under the window. This was probably to ensure that the master was not disturbed during the night! Beside the woman's bedroom there was a toy room, which was full of hand-made wooden toys, that would enchant children even today.

During the tour our guide gleefully imparted two other pieces of information, which highlighted the extreme formality of the nineteenth century, when this house was in its heyday. The first slice of information was the guide's *pièce de résistance*. He seemed to grow at least two inches as he spread out to tell his story. It seemed that after dinner, men and women went their separate ways to engage in social chit-chat. The women went to a special drawing room where they sat around the fire. Fire screens prevented their makeup from melting. The men however remained sitting around the table in the dining room discussing matters of mutual advantage. Our guide informed us that the manners of the time dictated that no one should leave the table until the appointed time. Having eaten and more pertinently drunk their fill, this created what might be called a pressing problem. This was solved by the ever-dependable butler, who would appear at a certain stage in the proceedings with a chamber pot that would be passed discreetly around under the table. It boggles the mind a bit as to how people could keep a straight face when listening to the sweet melody being played on a tin pot, and still talk about important matters of local governance. I am sure the butler had a great time running around the table catering for and disposing of emerging needs.

The second interesting part of Strokestown House for me was the impressive kitchen, which had a variety of cookers and ranges. When the house was inhabited all were going at the same time. There was even a special stove for cooking pheasant. We were told that this meant the kitchen was a real sweat house of activity with intolerable temperatures. Every consideration was given to planning the cooking needs of the kitchen, but none was given to the people who worked within it. Above the kitchen there was a balcony with a door that opened into the main house. When the lady of the house decided on the menu for the day she would write it down, walk out onto the balcony and drop it down to the people working in the kitchen below. Our guide told us that this was because it would not be seemly to make any physical contact with the staff. This seemed like a good explanation to me, until I talked it over with my wife Terry, who offered an alternative explanation. She said that it was probably due to the fact that she did not want to get the smell of the kitchen on to her hair and clothes, and perhaps the heat would smear the makeup. I suppose saying that they did not want servants to touch them is a bit strong, as they did not object to help with getting dressed in the morning etc.

Part of Strokestown House is now a memorial centre to the Famine in Ireland. The trauma of the Great Famine, which occurred principally in the years 1845-48 has shaped Irish life up to the present day in all aspects of our relationships. Before the Famine one-third of all agricultural land was used to grow potatoes, the staple diet for more than half the population.

The black putrefaction of the Potato Blight was first seen in America in the 1840s. It then spread through Europe to Ireland with devastating consequences in 1845. At least half of the potato crop was destroyed. For a people who depended mainly on the humble spud for food, disaster was inevitable. The economist Amartya Sen said that 'in no other famine in the world was the proportion of people killed as large as the Irish famines of the 1840s'. When you consider all the famines that we have witnessed around the world this claim is startling. The figures associated with the Great Famine are horrendous. In the early 1840s there were eight million people living in Ireland. By the end of the following decade the figure was down to four million.

It is estimated that during those years landlords evicted some 600,000 families from their farms and homes, as it was more profitable for them to switch from labour intensive tillage to the not-so-intensive beef industry. These evictions were assisted further by a law which was sponsored by Sir William Gregory. His wife Lady Gregory rather ironically became renowned as a collector of Irish folk tales that spread her fame in the literary world. The new law stipulated that alms should only be given to those tenant farmers who renounced their right to the land that they worked. Families were put into the position of choosing destitution as a way of life for their families; it was either that or starve to death. Indeed some families chose death over destitution; there are stories of families boarding up the windows and doors of their small houses to wait for slow death to arrive. Such a picture of despair and hopelessness is hard to imagine.

With the arrival of the Famine the British authorities were faced with a dilemma of how to deal with the situation. They encouraged 'good works', but decided not to redistribute the food of the country to feed the populace at affordable prices. Decisions were made not to interfere with the free trade of goods, as the Famine was seen as an opportunity to reform the Irish agricultural system by clearing people off the land.

The Famine was seen to be the fault of the people themselves and of the way that they chose to live their lives. This reflected the prevalent view of the times that the Irish were a feckless race not to be trusted. They were also considered to be incapable of any fruitful enterprise. *The Times* in London stated the following in one of its editorials:

'*The Irish are a people born and bred from time immemorial, in inveterate indolence, improvidence, disorder and consequent destitution.*'

Charles Trevelyan, Secretary to the Treasury in London asserted:

*'Unless we are much deceived, posterity will trace up to that famine the commencement of a salutary revolution in the habits of a nation long singularly unfortunate, and will acknowledge that on this, as many other occasions, Supreme Wisdom has educed permanent good out of transient evil.'*

Some of these attitudes are still knocking around in relation to other poor areas in the world, especially Africa. We have short memories. The voices of reason in British public life and the media were not listened to. Some local landlords impoverished themselves in efforts to allay the effects of famine on their tenants. Groups like the Quakers came and gave of themselves totally. In the end however these were but weak candles in the indifferent winds of the times.

The Famine left a most profound mark on all aspects of Irish life, from agriculture to trade, from politics to social life, to sex, to the decline of the language and the shaping of a new style puritanical religion. The puritanical religion inevitably grew out of the social conditions existing after the Famine. Before that people could afford to subdivide land amongst their children, confident that there would be enough food to maintain life. However the Famine changed all this. Instead of subdividing the farm amongst the children the farm was now left to one child usually the oldest boy. The rest had to fend for themselves, usually by taking the emigrant boat. The farm however was not handed over to the eldest until death or infirmity struck. This meant that the son who was to inherit the farm had to postpone marriage because he had not the means to support a family. Very often the opportunity for marriage passed these people by altogether. This indeed was a new, stark, joyless reality. A philosophy of living had to be developed, that justified people's celibate realities. It was because of this that the puritanical aspect of Catholic philosophy came to the fore and celibacy became the ideal and the highest expression of human worth. It is indeed interesting that the worship of the Virgin Mary became a really strong feature of Catholic worship at this time. The philosophy grew to fit the people's living reality. Sex rose up the pantheon of sins to become the greatest sin, a legacy that has reverberations into our own times. All this allowed zealots to take control of the Roman Catholic Church and to become the enforcers of these norms on a relatively compliant population.

'Control', of course was the operative word. There was to be no room for self-expression, just 'do as you are told'. Self-expression and sex were dangerous licences that had got the people into all types of trouble in the past. In the new regime these people would be duly punished. Social living would be blighted by this contamination for nearly 150 years afterwards. Only now is that particular house of cards beginning to crumble. We are now graphically exposed to the revelations of sexual and physical abuse of children by clerics over the years. It could be argued that their own philosophy and their denial of the joys and fulfilment contained in Nature warped them, so they became twisted by the pain of living a sterile existence.

Our puritanism is still with us though; it just takes different forms and wears different skins. If you exist and perform within politically correct definitions you are fine, but stray outside these and you are fair game. If a weakness or a fault is exposed in a person we show little understanding or forgiveness – we immediately want to expose it to the harsh light of publicity, and demand retributive justice. No account is taken of a person's other contributions. They are isolated from society and no forgiveness is proffered. The concept of forgiveness as an idea seems to have disappeared from our consciousness.

The spectre of the Famine still walks the land.

The story of Strokestown House is intimately linked to the Famine. Denis Mahon, owner of the estate at the time, decided that he would 'assist' his 2,400 tenants to emigrate to Canada. This was because they would only be able to produce one-third of the food they needed. His agent John Ross Mahon estimated that the cost of maintaining these people for one year on the land would be greater than the cost involved in helping them to emigrate. The owner's bonus was that the land would be freed up for cattle farming. It appeared to be a win-win situation for Denis Mahon: it was not. One-quarter of his tenants died at sea on their journey to Grosse-Île off Quebec, and the medical officer said that the survivors were the worst he had ever seen, as they suffered both starvation and disease.

Denis Mahon also instructed his agent to evict thousands of people from their lands and homes on the estate; this was in addition to the assisted emigration scheme. He was murdered a short while after this by relatives of the people who emigrated and who were dispossessed, in direct reprisal. *The Nation Newspaper* (Dublin, 6th November 1847) recorded the event thus:

*'As Major Mahon, a gentleman holding large estates in Roscommon was returning home about twenty minutes past six o'clock on the evening of Monday, from a meeting of the board of guardians of the Roscommon union, he was shot dead by an assassin, about four miles from Strokestown. There were two persons engaged in the murder, according to our informant. Both fired; one piece missed, but the other proved fatal, lodging a heavily loaded discharge in the breast. The victim exclaimed, "Oh, God!" and spoke no more. Major Mahon was formerly in the 95th Dragoons, now Lancers.'*

That night I stayed in a bed and breakfast just at the gates of Strokestown House. In days of yore I would have been able to watch the comings and goings from 'the big house'. Maybe I just imagined that I heard the noise of horses and carriages rumbling past, through the night?

# Strokestown to Kiltoom

On waking the next morning I heard the rain *tink ta tink dink, tink ta tink tink dink*, pattering down the waterspout outside my window. I got up and pulled the bright floral curtains apart to be greeted by torrents of water, falling from a low-lying leaden sky.

"The rain is down for the day," I murmured to myself pessimistically.

This pessimism was justified on the basis of close encounters with Irish weather over many years.

I stared out at the grey weather, mesmerised like a spectator at a snake charming festival. Raindrops were streaming down the window pane in front of me, racing as fast as they could go, to get to the bottom. As a boy I had spent many similar dreary days watching raindrops race down windowpanes, and like many other boys I always tried to make a competition out of it. I would select two or three drops that would appear at roughly the same time at the top of the window. I would then select my favourite, which was of course the one I judged most likely to get to the bottom first. This decision was usually based on size, or some other judgement that would allow my selection to get the drop on the field at the start. Invariably my selection would be in the lead at the beginning and things would be looking very promising indeed. Then disaster (and I do not use the word lightly) would usually strike, because one of the drops that was far behind would suddenly shoot past and win the race. They did this by cheating of course; usually taking the cleared route of a drop that had made the journey in a previous race. Even worse was the drop that would combine forces with others, form into a giant drop and with the (illegal) help of gravity would disappear into the distance leaving my (honest) drop toiling forlornly in its wake. It was then that I discovered if one was to make a profit in this type of racing then one had to join the band, and cheat. To do this effectively one had to choose a racecourse which could be manipulated in some underhand way. This was best done on windows with heavy condensation. This enabled me to intervene by creating an easier path for my drop or by blocking the other drops in some nefarious way. In this way a good profit could be made and in the process my choice would be declared champion.

I went down to breakfast where I met a French couple who were touring the country with a car and bicycles. Their plan was to cycle a circular route nearly every day and then drive to the next base. However when they looked out the window they concluded with a resigned shrug that this was a day for driving, with the bikes safely stowed in the boot of the car: *cowards*. I looked at them with envy; a cold shiver ran up my spine at the thought of going out in the pounding rain. However the only other option available to me was to sit in and look out at it all day and that was less appealing. I wished the French couple 'good luck' for the rest of their stay, and I talked the landlady into making me some sandwiches, wrapped in tinfoil, to protect against the elements.

As I left the town, I passed by the Percy French Hotel on the main street in Strokestown. The name Percy French holds a certain resonance for me, since my mother and her sister loved his music, and I often had to put up with them extolling his virtues. I liked one of his songs 'Are ye right there, Michael?' for the sole reason that it contained my name. Upon undertaking this walk I never knew anything about him; he was just the name of another songwriter and a fairly ancient one at that. It seemed therefore apt that I should find out a little bit more about him. Percy French was by all accounts a loveable genius, who spent his life expressing the creative muse as an actor, a painter, a writer of songs, a singer, a playwright – and a performer. He was Mark Twain-like in appearance, had dishevelled hair and disorganised clothing, and additionally had little regard for money. He had a quick wit and a way of engaging with everyone, including British royalty and Irish small farmers. His songs were like himself, full of the simplicity of childhood and a humour arising out of intense, playful observation. He had a strong urge to wander this earth demonstrating his God-given talent.

French was of the landed Anglo-Irish gentry, one of nine children born in Cloonyquin House in Co. Roscommon just a few miles from the present location. He was educated by private tutor before he went to university at Trinity College, Dublin. He always had an artistic view of life but believe it or not, after graduation, he worked in Cavan as 'an Inspector of drains'. There was never a more unsuitable appointment, and it was not long before he had abandoned this promising Civil Service career in order to follow the creative path. In other words his employers felt that he should look for work elsewhere! He married twice, his first wife tragically dying in childbirth. He had three further children with his second wife. The creative path brought him all over the English-speaking world, to great critical acclaim and much personal popularity.

There must have been a shadow side to all of this engaging spirit and creative energy. The only example of it that I could find was when he sued the West Clare Railway for arriving at its destination late, causing him to miss his engagements. He won this claim partly because the judge had been similarly delayed a few days earlier. It seems that the West Clare Railway was really a total community service. As it chugged merrily along it would suddenly come to a stop and the driver would get out to deliver a parcel to somebody who lived near the railway line. Of course if you were delivering a parcel, you could not leave the house without having at the very minimum a chat, and maybe even a cup of tea as well. It would be poor form indeed to act in an ill-mannered way. Passengers were a very understanding lot in those times! It was also common for the train to wait on regular passengers who may not have made the train station on time. It would tarry for 'a reasonable time' to see if they would turn up. Even if it had pulled out of the station and someone was spotted arriving late, it would stop and reverse to pick the grateful sleepaholic up. Now that is what is called a personal service.

Brendan O'Dowda in his book *The World of Percy French* tells the story of Michael Talty, who worked a long time for the West Clare Railway and was partially responsible for making this the most famous railway in Irish history. The Percy French wrote 'Are ye right there, Michael?' was based on the life and times of this man. One of the stories told about him by went as follows:

One tranquil day as the train was speeding through the countryside, it came to an abrupt halt. When there was no immediate progression the passengers became restless. Eventually somebody shouted out the window at the intrepid driver.

"What's up Michael?"

"There's an ould cow on the line," came the reply.

A little while later the train took off again at full speed for about a half an hour or so, and then suddenly the train once more came to a juddering stop. The same passenger shouted out the window.

"What's up Michael? Is there another cow on the line?" he asked, rather cheekily.

"No," came the reply. "It's the same one."

The first verse of the song gives an idea of the reputation of the West Clare railway.

*Ye may talk of Columbus's sailing across the Atlantical Sea*
*But he never tried to go railing from Ennis as far as Kilkee.*
*You run for the train in the morning, the excursion is starting at eight,*
*You're there when the clock gives the warning, and there for an hour you will wait.*
*And as you are waiting in the train, you will hear the guard singing this refrain:*
*'Are ye right there, Michael, are ye right?'*
*Do ye think that ye'll be there before the night?*
*Oh ye've been so long in starting that ye couldn't say for sartin,*
*So ye might now, Michael, so ye might!'*

The song continues in this vein. Percy French produced more famous songs such as 'The Mountains of Mourne', 'Slattery's Mounted Fut', 'Come back Paddy Reilly' and 'Abdul Abulbul Amir'. Incidentally he sold 'Abdul Abulbul Amir' for five shillings, and he never got a penny royalty when it became a bestseller all over the world. However it was 'Are ye right there, Michael?' which was my favourite.

I walked for a mile on a busy road out of Strokestown in order to get on to my back roads for the day. Heavy lorries and other traffic passed continuously, spraying water and mist over me. They were all heading for one of the crossings over the Shannon. When I reached the back road I gave a huge sigh of relief – not only that, but I gave out a shout of joy at the sight of the quiet road. This shout scared a group of cattle that were sheltering under a ditch by the roadside. It must have been a real scary shout, because they all stampeded over to the other side of the field. This brought back memories of other experiences I had with animals as I was growing up.

Weapons always seem important to small boys and I was no exception. I remembered making a catapult with an appropriate Y-shaped stick and an old bicycle tube. When I finished with it I was very proud of myself.

Of course I then had to get something to shoot at. Having mastered the ability to hit large trees I then decided to raise the difficulty level and go for moving targets. Our back yard at that stage was full of hens and ducks that roamed freely, like all other small farms around. They became my prey. I crept up on them and started shooting, and of course kept on missing. All I succeeded in doing was to create a squabble of squawking noises as hens moved out of my way before continuing the important job of feeding and scratching. They should not have scorned my efforts however, because with one of my next shots I hit my favourite black hen on the foot. I was filled with shock, as I had never expected to hit anything, especially my favourite hen. I had always insisted in fact on eating the egg that this hen laid – and now I had shot her. I ran in to tell my mother, who laughed and told me that the hen would get over it – but I was to stop annoying them, as it would affect them laying their eggs. For weeks afterwards I was filled with guilt every time I saw the black hen limping around the yard. In fact I think she did it on purpose every time I saw her. Afterwards I took to shooting at songbirds but I soon gave up on that as I usually even missed the tree they were perched on. I went back to shooting at the byre door, which I was moderately successful in hitting until my father told me to stop shooting at it and go and do something useful.

I always suspected the black hen of being in some way involved in a disagreement I had some time later with a goat. This happened at a neighbour's house, when the hay was being taken in from the meadows and built into a stack. All the neighbours were helping out and my father brought me as well (after much nagging). Whilst everyone else was helping I went off exploring around the yard. I was bent over looking under a piece of tin when I got this terrific bang on the backside, which landed me face down on the ground. The old billy goat had hit me a wallop with his horns, much to the amusement of everyone working at the haystack. I can still hear the laughter.

I crossed a bridge under which flowed a small river. The banks of the river were covered in dense foliage. The colour of the water there moved on a spectrum from black to dark green. This was alleviated by a bright line of white-grey, which went down the centre of the river, where the light had succeeded in cutting through the foliage. Ripples of rain spread across the nearly stagnant surface. A wooden pallet was fixed to one bank by a complicated looking series of ropes tied to trees. Between the pallet and the other bank there stretched a long log. This was either the brainchild of a group of children or some impossible task being set for a group of executives on a leadership development adventure course. I walked on head down into the rain.

"You are in a world of your own there," said a voice.

I nearly jumped with the surprise. I looked up hastily, thinking that I had been found out. A lean man in his late thirties or early forties was leaning on a gate into a field. He had a big friendly grin on his face.

"It's the best place to be this day," I replied.

"You are right there. I wouldn't be out unless I had to come and check up on the cattle."

I stopped, and we talked about where I was from and a little bit about farming. He introduced himself as Seamus, and he walked up the road with me as he was heading home to his house, which was in the same direction. Seamus was extremely friendly and talkative. He looked a bit like Errol Flynn in his prime, or Johnny Depp if one was to give a more modern day example. You are probably thinking that these two characters are in no way alike, but this is my book.

"Come on in now for a cup of tea," he said, when we reached the house.

"No," I said. "Sure look at the state of me. I am all wet."

"We don't pass any remarks on that. We are well used to it; anyway it will help you on your way."

He walked on ahead of me into the yard, leaving me no option but to follow him. He ushered me ahead of him into the house. We went into the dining room, where stood a big table in front of a range. Sitting at the top of the table reading a paper was an elderly man. He looked up and showed no surprise at this invasion of his privacy. In fact he had the same engaging grin as Seamus.

"This is my father," said Seamus rather unnecessarily, as the resemblance was obvious. "This man has walked from Donegal," said Seamus, as if it were something remarkable.

"Sit down there and have the cup of tea," said the father, pointing to a wooden chair at the end of the table. The tea was already brewed on the range, so all Seamus had to do was get the cups. He also brought out brown bread and apple tart. Let me tell you, we had a right feed. Our main topics of conversation were football and politics. This was a politically astute family, as they could name all the T.D.s in Co. Donegal. I to my shame could name only one in Co. Roscommon, and I only knew him because he had been quite a chancer in the past. We talked about the coming general election and all the promises that would be made by the politicians to get power. Seamus's father then told us about an election campaign that was held in Cavan when he was a young boy.

It seemed that all the politicians would try to speak after as many Masses on a Sunday as was possible to fit in. A platform was erected for this purpose outside the gates of the church and all the people would congregate there after Mass. On this particular Sunday three politicians arrived to speak, one from Fianna Fáil; one from Fine Gael; and one from Clann na Poblachta, which were all political parties of the time. The Fianna Fáil candidate got up and talked for a long time, making loads of promises about what he would do for them if they voted for him.

Next up was the Fine Gael candidate who talked longer still and made even more promises than the Fianna Fáil candidate.

'Just vote for me and I will work tirelessly for you all,' he pronounced.

The Clann na Poblachta candidate saw that the crowd were getting restless at this stage and wanted to go home. He got up on the platform, tore up his speech and said that he would keep in short. He said that he had listened to what all the candidates had promised to do for the people of Cavan.

'If you don't vote for me, I don't know what I will do,' was his plea for election.

He left the platform to tumultuous applause and was later elected. Seamus's father recounted this story with real amusement in his voice.

A door opened and a sleepy eyed teenage girl appeared. She nodded hello, and went to get her breakfast. This was Seamus's daughter who was just rising to face the day. I supposed her clock was somehow synchronised with my teenager's clock at home.

I thanked Seamus and his father and continued on my way. Farther on I stopped and watched ducks flying low over marshy land, their wings beating rapidly as they seared through the mist. This land was the Callows, a mixture of marsh, farmland and bog renowned for its bird life. This is especially true in wintertime, when migratory wildfowl and waders stop here to feed on the way to their eventual destination.

It was definitely one of those days when the rain tried to invade every crevice of your being, incessant, unremitting, sweeping in grey torrents across the flat lands. It seduced you at times by massaging and stroking your face with its tapping tendrils. And then it would trickle into your eyes and ears, creep down your neck and up your sleeves, and drip into your socks. It would invade your underwear and any other dry garment, cling to it until saturation had been achieved. As you walked you could feel the cold heavy weight of it pressing into you. Rain was not just picking on *me*; it treated me the same as the rest of Nature. All around everything was sopping, glistening and dripping. Puddles appeared in every available hole and crack, crevice and gap. Water flowed into channels, which swept by in search of more water. In the fields it softened the soil into pliable dough that was moulded by unthinking footsteps. This created yet more holes for the rain to fill, inhabit and possess. Animals stood with their rear ends to the wind and, their feet ensconced in the muck that clothed and warmed their feet like thick socks. Every footstep was a *splash*, every car was a wash, but then it didn't matter any more, for what is wetter than wet? The mind accommodated to the rain and was suddenly free from it. There was exhilaration in every step; it was just the rain and you, together, in a world of your own and the sheer sensation of it all.

My mind drifted into other memories of childhood. I remembered the time I was playing high jump at my friend's house. A rope was attached to a tree and one of us held the other end. My friend reached impressive heights before finally failing to get over. It was then my turn. At the time I was rather fat, and couldn't get off the ground too well. I took a run up, tripped over the rope and landed flat on my face. I got mad, went back and took a longer run up, and again landed flat on my face. My friend lowered the rope with much fanfare, again to my dismay with the same result. No matter how low my friend put the high jump I tripped over it. There was a young girl sitting at the front door of a neighbouring house looking at us. Every time I fell flat on my face she burst her sides laughing. I got madder and madder, and the madder I got the more I tripped over the rope. I still remember the shame of it. Thinking back on it now, it I believe I was the victim of a devious trick perpetrated by my friend. He must have raised the rope every time I tried to jump over it. All I can say is that there is still time to get my own back on him; after all, his figure isn't so svelte now!

I was playing football with this same friend of mine some time later. He was two years older than me and was a good footballer. His mother came out and told us to be sure and not hit the windows with the ball. At this stage I was lining up to take a penalty. He said to his mother not to worry, as I would not be able to kick it that far. I took a big run up to the ball, connected with it perfectly and to the consternation of all it sailed into the air and right through the window at the front of the house. We all stared in horror at the gaping hole in the window. My friend's mother was livid with the both of us, but she decided on our punishment by declaring that my father would have to come and fix the window. Despite my concerned and apologetic public face, I secretly felt very pleased with myself because I had demonstrated a new-found expertise and strength. I can still recall the puff of pride in my feat. My father though was not too pleased that I had broken the window, because he had to go to Donegal for glass in order to repair it, which he duly did. However it was not done to the satisfaction of my friend's mother – every time I visited the house she gave out that the window rattled in the wind and that my father would have to come back and fix it properly. I don't know if he ever did, though I suspect not. My father was such a friendly person, people hated to fall out with him. I think my friend's mother was hoping that I would act as the messenger, but such ploys were lost on me at the time. I had more important things to be doing than relaying messages to my father, like playing football or seeing which of us cowboys had the fastest draw.

With these thoughts and more I came to a main road, which was buzzing with traffic. I crossed it and took the back road towards Kilteevan. I was now feeling peckish with hunger, so I was relieved when I saw the spire of the church at Kilteevan poking its head through the swirling greyness.

'Good,' I thought. 'There must be a pub here where I can get a sandwich.'

I stopped at the crossroads, looked left and right. There were no tell tale signs for Guinness or Smithwick's to be seen. I spotted a small shop, so I headed up to it. When I opened the door of the shop, one of those annoying tinny bells rang. There was no one to be seen. I poked around the shop and lifted a bar of chocolate and a bottle of water. A man in his early seventies then appeared with two bright-eyed young children in tow, a girl of about five and a boy about three. This man was the children's grandfather. I figured this out because one of the children called him 'Grandda': bright aren't I?

The man was lean and fit looking with calm contented grey eyes. I paid for the few bits and pieces, and asked him if there was any pub or café where one could get a sandwich.

"Oh sure come on in I will make you a sandwich," he said.

"That would be too much trouble."

"Don't be silly, come on in."

With that he opened a hatch in the shop counter and ushered me into the living quarters of the shop/house. This was a comfortable kitchen in the old style with a range, table and comfortable chairs. He told me to sit down beside the fire. Immediately the little girl took control, her face full of excitement and determination. She went over to the fridge and announced loudly that she had found ham and tomatoes, which she put on the table. She then raced into the shop and came back moments later with a fresh loaf of bread. Whilst she was doing this I was making small talk with the man and boy. The young boy with earnest wide eyes told me what he had been doing at playgroup that day. He showed me a painting, and he told me all about it. Communication was bursting out of him. The grandfather and I talked about Donegal, tourism, farming and politics, all whilst he wet the tea from the kettle on the range. A car pulled up in front of the house and moments later the front door opened by a homely woman who was the man's wife. She exuded friendliness and competence, and showed no sign of surprise that a strange man was sitting beside the fire in her house. After greeting me she looked at me quizzically, as if I was a wee bit mad in the head. She had been told that I was walking on my holidays. With a laugh she took over the coordination of food and sent the little girl to get other items from the shop.

Finally a large plate of sandwiches appeared, topped as in most restaurants now with crisps, accompanied by a side salad of lettuce, tomatoes, peppers, onions and cheese. A fruitcake from the shop was opened and cut. All of this was placed in front of me along, of course, with a big pot of tea. I protested at the large amount of food, as I was embarrassed that people would go to such trouble. The woman laughed.

"I am sure you will need it after all that walking," she said.

The little girl, her work then finished, stood beside me as I ate and told me what she had been doing in infant's class in National School that day. She had the same earnest eyes as her brother, full of life and interest. Soon, both children were standing beside me asking me a barrage of questions that I did my best to answer. After a while the grandmother told the children to go and play somewhere else and "to let the man have a bit of peace". This was immediately backed up by the grandfather, who reiterated his wife's instructions. One sensed that this strategy would probably have worked with the couple's own children, and probably indeed would have been insisted upon. However one of the great things about the relationship between grandparents and grandchildren is that the rules are soft and pliable. The main emphasis is that first and foremost they enjoy each other's company. These children had learned that they could ignore such instructions from their grandparents, who obviously doted on their every move.

The children moved back from the table a bit and started playing a game with me. They hid behind doors and chairs and, using their fingers as mock guns, pretended to shoot me. When I held my chest and faked my death there was great laughter. The grandparents realised that I was as a big a child as the children. They gave up and laughed too.

"They are awful," said the grandfather, nodding his head in amusement.

At this stage the grandmother said she had to go and pick up her daughter from work in Athlone, so I said goodbye to these people who had shown me such spontaneous hospitality. At one time Irish families used to set an extra place at the dinner table just in case somebody called. It is good to see that the remnants of that tradition still remain.

I walked along this road until I came to Knockcroghery. There I entered onto the main Roscommon–Athlone road. There was no prospect of any back road bringing me in the appropriate direction so I had to endure a ten-mile hike along this main road. This was probably the most tedious part of the whole journey. The rain was falling and the traffic was incessant. This time there was no meditative trance as I walked, just a feeling of wanting to get there and get it over with. I tried bed and breakfasts along the way but they were all full, because of weddings in the area. I came into Kiltoom sore, wet and bedraggled and not fit to go any further and still having no luck with the bed and breakfasts.

I finally came to one, which had a room available, but the woman said she would not let it to me. She informed me that it was a double room, which she would have no problem in letting later on. I decided to take it (even though my principles bristled at paying double the odds) because I had no energy to go any farther. I have made worse investments. The woman took all my wet clothes and put them into a hot press for drying. I had a long hot shower and after I came out – believe it or not – the rain had stopped.

That evening I found myself in the Hudson Bay Hotel, as it was the only place I could get something to eat. The place was full to the rafters with people, mainly a mixture of a wedding and a conference. I finally weaselled myself onto a stool at the bar where I ordered my evening meal, a pint of Guinness and a sandwich. It was there that I met Pat Porter, who had been at the wedding and was now buying a round of drink. He was a tall, robust elderly man who spoke to me in an American accent. I got a potted life history from him as he waited for his drinks. He told me that he was originally from Roscommon but had emigrated to New Jersey fifty years previously, where he met his wife and got married. They decided to come home to Roscommon when the children were born, because they thought it would be a better environment for raising children. That was all right of course, until the children grew up and decided for themselves to emigrate back to the States. Despite all their planning they were here in Ireland and all their children were back in the States. After some consideration they decided that what they wanted most in life was to be near their children, so they sold up and went back to live in New Jersey.

"Guess what happened then?" he asked.

He told me his children all got married, and two of them made the same decision their parents had made years ago. They came back to Ireland in turn to raise their children. The circle of living had come round again. I asked him would he consider coming back to live in Ireland again.

"No," he replied. "We have done enough moving. We will just come regularly on holidays."

With that, a little girl of about seven came over to him. He looked at me with pride in his eyes.

"This is my granddaughter."

She gave him a spontaneous hug.

"This is a great girl," he said.

She just smiled and put her small hand in his. He asked the barman if he would take the drink over to the table for him and then grandfather and granddaughter went back hand-in-hand to rejoin the wedding group. A couple of minutes later the barman brought over a pint of Guinness and put it in front of me. He told me it was "with the compliments of the American man".

A pint of Guinness from Pat Porter, it sounded apt. I lifted the pint and drank to his good fortune and good health. Here was a man who had put family first during his life and was now reaping the benefits of it. A spontaneous hug is such a small thing, but with a different turning on the road it might not exist. I reflected that this was a day of generous gestures from people in Co. Roscommon; from Seamus in the morning, to the grandparents and grandchildren in Kilteevan through to Pat Porter at the hotel.

Robert Lloyd Praeger in his travel book *The Way That I Went* advises people to avoid the Roscommon side of the Shannon as he says there is not much to see there. I however am thankful that I met such nice, genuine people there.

My mobile rang; it was my friend Martin. He told me that he would come and give me a lift home, after I reached Clonmacnoise the next evening. We then started into our usual slagging. Whilst I was talking to Martin a man in his late sixties sat down on the stool beside me. When I finished on the phone I turned to say 'hello' to him.

"You had my head annoyed, listening to you on that phone," he said.

I suddenly realised that I had been shouting above the loud din in the hotel when I was talking to Martin. I thought to myself 'I have turned into my worst nightmare, one of those people who spend their time going around talking loudly on the mobile to show that they are the centre of the universe'. I laughed at the thought.

"I have to exercise the voice now and again," I said.

He asked me what I was doing in this part of the world, so naturally I told him, adding a few embellishments along the way.

"I'll forgive you all that shouting," he said, "seeing that you are on your way to Clonmacnoise."

He looked at me again.

"Are you some sort of eccentric?" he asked.

I had never thought of myself in such terms. On reflection, how would you know if you were? What standards would you use to judge the matter?

Rather than dispute the matter I said, "I hope so."

"It's great to be free," he said.

He then went on to tell me that his wife and himself were leading completely separate lives. He told that they had not had sex for over twenty years.

"But I still respect her," he said.

I thought to myself that this was fairly intimate information to be giving to a stranger. Maybe it wasn't me who was the eccentric after all?

"Do you know what my favourite song is?" he enquired.

"There are lots of possibilities!" I laughed.

"It was written by Phil Coulter, about his son," he said.

"Nah, I can't think."

"'Scorn Not His Simplicity'," he replied. "That song says it all, about what is important in life."

'I should have known that,' I thought to myself. This song was written by Phil Coulter, about his eldest child who had Down's syndrome. I judged to myself that this guy had one good perspective on life anyway. I had no more time to dwell on this when the next question was launched.

"Guess what I do for a living?"

"A salesman?" I guessed.

"How did you know that?" he asked quizzically.

I think a fleeting thought crossed his mind that I might have seen him somewhere before. I just laughed, keeping him guessing about how I might have known.

"What do you think I sell then?"

"I have no idea," I said. "Maybe drink," I offered tentatively.

"No, I sell anti-fatigue mats!" he replied triumphantly.

He must have seen the perplexed look on my face for he went on to tell me that anti-fatigue mats were the greatest thing since sliced pan. He asked me to imagine all the people who were standing on their feet all day like hairdressers, shopkeepers, barmen etc., which meant there was a good market for his product. He had been travelling all day but had not made any money, but on other days he assured me he would make "thousands".

"That's just the way this business is," he said.

It seemed that his son was now getting involved in business, and he informed me rather proudly that he was going to import a very good product from Sweden and sell it in Ireland.

"It will make him a very rich man," he assured me.

I pressed him on what the product was but no amount of asking would get the information from him. He then told me that his son wanted him to go and work for him. His son had told him that he would have to get rid of his Volkswagen Golf and get a Mercedes instead, as it was important to give the right image at the outset. I thought to myself that it would probably be better if the father stayed selling anti-fatigue mats, rather than getting involved in a business such as this. I certainly would not want to be investing money in it, if the first task of the business is to buy Mercedes cars.

He got up of his chair and said that he had better go home, as his wife would be wondering if he had forgotten the way. This seemed to stir a memory within him. He turned to me.

"What is the good thing about Alzheimer's disease?" he asked.

I shook my head, after a suitable pause, which indicated that I had thought about it seriously.

"You get to meet new people every day!" he pronounced.

With that he was off.

I left to go back to the bed and breakfast. It was a starry night and I stopped for a pee in a hidden bank along the railway line. In many similar banks on our way home from school as little boys we would have peeing competitions to see who could pee the highest. There was never any resolution to these competitions, no agreement about who had won. The only exception to this was when we would find an appropriate wall where the evidence of prowess could be assessed more easily. This trait is not confined to the human race but seems to be a common among all the animals of the world. I have a setter dog, a mixture of a Welsh and Irish setter, so he has little chance of having too much of an integrated personality. 'Mad in the head' would be a good description of him. If he is on the lead he will want to make his mark on every tall object with which he comes into contact. One day a very large dog must have been there before him because he lifted his leg so high that he fell over in a heap. Rather shocked and chastened, he got up sniffed at the object again and with a more conservative approach he left his mark. I don't think he even convinced himself that his was the dominant scent, but at least he could hold his head up in the public arena of dog intercourse. I am sure the human of the species would never act in such a manner…

## The Last Day: Kiltoom to Clonmacnoise

I woke up to sunshine, a few white clouds in the sky and a fresh breeze. What a contrast to the day before – not a grey cloud to be seen anywhere. The woman who ran the bed and breakfast left my now dry clothes and rucksack outside my door. After breakfast I asked her where I might be able to attend a Mass or a religious service, as I thought it might be interesting to see what sorts of issues were being talked of in this neck of the woods. I am a lapsed Catholic and rarely attend Mass, so in a way I don't know what I would be comparing it with – but we don't always have to be logical do we? She gave me directions to a church, which was near to Athlone.

The road which I had thought terrible yesterday in the rain did not seem so bad in the sunshine. It was still far too busy for my liking, but it was bearable. After about ten minutes walking I noticed a van parked at the side of the road. Beside the van, amidst a scattered assortment of tools, a man was attempting to attach a Bord Fáilte Bed and Breakfast sign to a pole. This sign is common throughout the country and is erected to indicate that a particular bed and breakfast is approved by the national tourist agency, Bord Fáilte. Wherever you travel throughout the country you will see these awkward three-sided triangular signs with their shamrock motifs glaring out at you. They are all beckoning to you: 'Come on into my house. Come on in'.

The man trying to attach the sign was a small thin man in his fifties. I could see that he was struggling so I offered to help. Initially he muttered that he was "all right" and that he could manage. However, as I started to move off he must have thought better of his predicament. He asked if I would hold the sign for him whilst he fixed it on to the pole. He told me that his wife ran a bed and breakfast house and had asked him to put up the sign. He said that it was impossible to get anyone else to do the job.

"Nobody is interested in taking on small jobs nowadays," he said.

He mentioned that only for the fact that he was able to make the fittings for attaching the sign to the pole, he would have been waiting a long time to get the job done.

On his instruction I duly held up the sign, which was surprisingly heavy, up over my head against the pole. He attempted to fix the sign onto the pole, but lo and behold the fittings did not seem to work. He pushed, screwed, hammered and then cajoled and cursed at the nuts and bolts in turn, all with no success. They were either a bit too short or too thick, to hold the sign securely onto the pole. More colourful words filled the air. This precipitated much agitation and searching in his large toolbox for improvised fittings. Finally he got one part secured and warning me to keep the sign steady. He went looking in the van for more bits and pieces that might be applied to the job in hand. I was now starting to feel like Moses who with arms wearily aloft in the desert could not take them down in case disaster struck.

In between all the comings and goings he told me he was a plasterer.

"I am right good at plastering and building work," he proclaimed. "But engineering isn't my strong point," he said apologetically.

After a final bit of manipulation and experimentation he was successful. He stood back to survey his work, an expression of accomplishment on his thin face. This look slowly turned to one of consternation. Wondering what was wrong I too stood back and looked. It took a moment for it to dawn on me. The sign was attached to the pole all right, but it was on upside down! A smart quip came to the edge of my tongue, but on seeing the annoyance on his face I decided to keep my own counsel and suppressed a smile. Now we had to start all over again: like it or not I was now his designated helper. I was allocated the extremely onerous task of holding the sign whilst he loosened the bolts. During this procedure he told me about his apprentice, incidentally another Donegal man.

"I have not seen him for the last week," he declared.

He had called to his apartment a number of times but there had been no reply.

'Wise man,' I thought to myself. He probably went into hiding when he saw my plasterer friend coming.

"He has woman trouble," said the plasterer.

From the way he said it I gathered that this was a calamity from which there was no coming back. He certainly would not be coming back to something as mundane as work any time soon. He told me that his apprentice had been a good worker. He wondered out loud where he might get a replacement.

"Don't look at me," I said jokingly.

We started back to work at the sign again and after more Moses-like endeavours on my part we finally got it back up.

'Whew,' I thought.

However if I thought that that was the finish of the episode, I was sadly mistaken. When he stood back from the sign and looked at it, he started to scratch his head once more. I wondered to myself what could possibly be wrong now; it looked all right to me. After ruminating for a moment he pronounced that the sign was "crooked" and that "the wife would kill me if I left it like that".

This led to another stint at adjusting the sign. When we were finished once more he stepped back and surveyed the work. I waited with bated breath, wondering to myself whether I would see Clonmacnoise anytime soon. Then to my relief he pronounced himself satisfied. He loaded his tools back into the van. As he was leaving he told me that he would have given me a lift if we had happened to be going in the same direction. I thanked him for his consideration, slightly relieved that he wasn't offering me the job as his full-time assistant. I must have failed the audition, and I got a strong feeling that the saga with the sign was entirely my fault. I can visualise him telling his wife sometime later that it took him so long because the assistant he had recruited could not hold the blasted sign straight. I headed off towards Athlone, and a little bit up the road I looked back at the sign. It looked pretty good to me now. If I ever pass that sign again I will look at it and think, 'Hey, I helped put up that sign!'

The only other sign I remember as having made any significant impression in my life was that indicating the entrance to our village. To say that it made an impression on me is slightly misleading. It would be more accurate to say it was the impression I made on the sign. One day on our way home from National School another boy and myself pelted the sign with stones, with such gusto that it left dinge marks all over it. Ever afterwards when I looked at that sign with the dinge marks still plainly visible, I felt slightly proud that those were the dents that I had partly caused. It was my contribution to the history of deviance in my village. The village has been bypassed in the past couple of years and it is with regret that I now see that the old sign has been replaced by a brand new 'characterless' sign. On the way into Athlone I passed signs for the Prince of Wales Hotel. This was the place where Terry and I had our wedding reception. Though the signs are still up the hotel has closed.

All the commotion with the sign meant that I arrived at the church slightly late, and I was surprised to see people standing outside the door. I then saw the hearse and realised that it was a funeral. I decided I would go in anyway, even though I would not hear a sermon, which I thought would be the interesting part to hear. I pushed my way past the stragglers at the door until I came into the porch where it was impossible to get through. I found myself a spot to stand like everyone else. There was a long aisle in the church and it was full of people. I could see the coffin in the aisle at the front of the church. Amongst the people standing in front of me was a man with four young girls, all probably under six years of age. He was carrying the youngest who was about a year old in his arms. One of the other young girls was holding on to his trouser leg.

Inevitably the young girl that he was carrying started to cry, that insistent cry of a tired, bored and constrained child. She started to squirm vigorously in his arms. There were two women standing directly behind the man and child. The oldest of these women, who was grey haired and matronly, lifted her hand and touched the baby's hand, which was placed on the father's shoulder. The baby reluctantly stopped crying, and looked at this intruder. With a big pout on her lower lip and a frown on her forehead, the signs were that this little girl was not going to be won over easily. The father was oblivious to this intervention; I think he was just happy the baby was suddenly quiet, and was probably congratulating himself on his prowess as a consoler. The woman chanced her arm again and touched the baby's hand, this time giving it a small rub. The baby took back her hand and looked at it closely, trying to understand the sensation. The frown subsided a little, and she put out her hand again. This time the woman, having established a connection, took the baby's hand in hers and traced more confident circles in her palm. The baby was now becoming totally engaged in this interaction, and for a while vacillated between taking back her hand, looking at it intently and putting it out again for more tickling. The baby then took back her hand, and started trying to draw circles on her own palm in imitation of the woman's actions.

The baby processed this interaction and was suddenly seized by a sudden surge of delight. Vocalising strongly she bolted upright in her father's arms and clapped his face with her hands. She then nuzzled into him head-to-head and nose-to-nose with a shiver of joy. Satisfied, she turned her attention to the wider world once more. She started vocalising to a younger woman, who was standing beside the older grey-haired woman, as if she were trying to have a conversation with her. The woman rather self-consciously mouthed back noiseless vocalisations to the child. She obviously did not want to spurn the baby's overtures and disappoint her, but at the same time she did not want to disrupt the Mass in any way. The child was obviously not interested in this watery, insipid type of communication and she turned her attention to the umbrella of another woman standing near by. Initially she caught the handle of the umbrella in a strong grip and then started to feel the material on the umbrella. The woman allowed her to play with it and pull it whilst at the same time keeping a grip on the bottom of the umbrella. This did not satisfy the child however: she wanted the whole umbrella to herself and she pulled at it in a determined manner. She wanted it all to herself. The woman then proceeded to distract her by jiggling the umbrella up and down and around in small circles. I don't know if this strategy would have worked, as suddenly there was a distracting motion in the church congregation. It was communion time, and the father of the children reckoned that he had enough penance and praying done. He decided to head off. With the youngest girl in his arms and the other small girls in tow he left the church. The little girl didn't look back to her new friends. Her gaze was forward. The circle of interaction ceased.

So this was the way I passed the time at the Mass. I heard the sermon all right. It extolled the virtues of the dead woman, how she had always been a religious person, and that she would now get the reward she deserved in Heaven. The words of Mark Twain came to mind:

*'If you take epitaphs seriously, we ought to bury the living and resurrect the dead.'*

These words of consolation from the altar were fairly standard. I wondered if people still had the same certainty about Heaven as they used to. Probably people did not worry about it too much – the meaning of the standard ritual words were glossed over, dulled by their repetitiveness. The priest at the end of Mass stood praying over the coffin, an altar boy shook the thurible, a grey smoke arose and the smell of incense filled the church. The priest and the altar boys and the coffin came down the aisle followed

## The Last Day: Kiltoom to Clonmacnoise

by a black wave of grief.

I did not go to the graveyard, so I left the church and headed towards Athlone. The Shannon is the boundary between the west of Ireland and the east of the country. Historically speaking this town was the main gateway across the Shannon River on the Galway–Dublin route, and lots of battles were fought here to maintain control of the town. This town had echoed to war down the centuries. Even to this day it is host to one of the main army barracks in the country.

As I came into view of the Shannon River, thankfully there were no echoes of war or views of opposing armies testing their mettle. All there was to be seen was a river cruiser tied to the bank and festooned with tubs of flowers. They must have known I was coming! A few small cruisers were going past up the river, navigated by tourists who flock onto the river in the summer months. I crossed the bridge over the Shannon, thus leaving the west of Ireland and heading into the east. Feeling slightly peckish I went into a large café that had a bakery attached. A young woman came up the length of the café pushing a trolley in front of her. The trolley was laden with trays of scones and an assortment of sweet buns. She rattled to a stop right beside me, took off a tray, which was filled with hot currant scones.

'Yummy,' I thought to myself, my mouth beginning to salivate.

The girl was tall and energetic with a slightly round face. It was the type of face on which it was impossible to see any kind of worry or trouble. She flashed a smile to everyone and started to unload the tray. On one of her hands she had a light transparent plastic glove, used for handling food. She held the tray with the gloved hand and proceeded to unload the scones from the tray with the ungloved hand onto baskets arranged on the counter. When she completed the transfer she then counted the scones in the baskets by touching them individually, again with her ungloved hand.

'Good on you,' I thought to myself. 'You are a rebel against conformity-enforcing environmental health officers whose job in life it seems is to ensure that we all get the same bland mass produced 'clean' food, full of additives and preservatives.'

All small producers who do not have mass production capabilities are closed down in the 'public interest'. All the interesting foods of Europe will certainly disappear if these Bureaucrats (or should I say Eurocrats!)

who are supported by big business have their say. In a show of solidarity with my new found rebel friend, I bought one of those scones with my cup of coffee. There is nothing like a nice hot currant scone with melted butter sinking into its steaming crevices to satisfy the senses. This is especially true if the scone has the potential to boost my immune system. In the meantime my rebel friend was proceeding along the counter, continuing the good work.

To get out of Athlone in the direction I wanted to go would necessitate walking along the Dublin road for a few miles. I did not fancy this prospect in the slightest as it is one of the busiest roads in the country. I decided that the best way would be to get a lift to the Limerick road. I knew if I stood thumbing on this busy road I would have little chance of getting a lift – better to take the bull by the horns in the town. I spotted a bread van at a shop, which was being driven by a short round-faced man in his fifties. I went over to him and asked if he was by any chance heading in my direction. He told me that he would be going in my direction in about five minutes, and that he would be happy to give me a short lift.

Before me now stretched a long straight road. This was still a busy road, the main Limerick road, but relief came when I reached Ballynahown and came into Co. Offaly. There I turned right off the main road on to the last stretch of ten or so miles to Clonmacnoise. This is a green rolling landscape with lots of cattle lying out in the fields. The road is dotted with bed and breakfast houses, showing that this is a popular route with tourists. If the worst comes to the worst I thought to myself, there would probably be a place to stay tonight. I came across a number of signs stating that *The land is preserved, By order of…Gun Club*. I wondered what they meant by the word 'preserved'? Well no, I know what it means – that no one can shoot the wildlife on this stretch of land, except for the local gun club. I pitied the poor birds that were given a perfect environment in which to grow up and mature, and then at a certain date they have the *bejasus* shot out of them.

I came to a small bungalow, outside of which stood a young oriental woman who had a welcoming smile. I stopped and asked her how far it was to Clonmacnoise. She laughed, saying it was a long way for someone walking. She said this in good – but not fluent – English. She then asked me if I was from Ireland. I explained to her the best way that I could where I came from.

"Are you an Offaly woman?" I asked.

At this she pealed into full-hearted laughter.

" No," she replied. "I am from the Philippines."

She went on to tell me that she had married a local man, and had come to live here in rural Co. Offaly. One got the impression that it was a bit of a culture shock to come and live here. I got the feeling she was from a more convivial culture where there were many interactions between people on a daily basis, and that she may be lonely living here in a rural culture, which is increasingly becoming more isolated in its way of living. I asked her if she had much contact with home. She told me that she had been on the phone to her father the previous night. He told her that a huge storm had hit their home area and a lot of destruction had taken place. All his mango trees were uprooted. This was his main source of income, so it meant more difficult times for the family for a period.

A little boy of about three or four years old came around the corner of the house, pushing a wheelbarrow with two footballs on board.

"Do you like football?" I asked him.

He smiled and nodded his head. The woman then told me that she had two children. A moment later another oriental girl in her late teens came around the corner, obviously in pursuit of the boy. I asked the woman if this was her daughter? I realised as soon as I had the words out that I had put my metaphoric foot in it. I knew when I was speaking that I should stop, but words have their own momentum once started. The woman looked slightly embarrassed and told me that this was her sister, who was over from the Philippines for a holiday. I unconvincingly tried to cover up my faux pas by making a joke of it but it fooled no one. The smiles continued but they had a different flavour.

I waved good-bye and walked on. The smiles of the people from the Philippines and my own smiles brought back to me a memory of smiles in a different context. One day when I was driving to work I listened to a chat show on the radio. An American expert on mental health was being interviewed, probably promoting a book she had written. She recommended that it would make a great difference to our mental health if we smiled at people. She said it not only helps the individual smiling but also helps the observer, the beneficiary of the smile. I think she explained in scientific terms that smiling releases some chemical in the brain that produces a beneficial effect. She concluded the interview by exhorting us to smile at people during the day, and to see for ourselves the difference it would make. She must have made an impression on me because I decided to myself that I would make a conscious effort to enlarge the level of my smiling during the day. As it happens my office is opposite a hairdresser, which has a glass door. As I left my office I made eye contact with a middle-aged woman who was looking in my direction, and who was getting her hair done at the time. Her hair was gathered in a massive bun on top of her head and was held in place by curlers and a mass of pins and other accoutrements. I thought to myself that this was my opportunity to make a difference and to dispense mental health around the place, so I gave her my biggest and best smile. The reaction was not what I expected. Instead of a returned smile and increased good will all I got was an eyeful of anger, resentment and embarrassment.

"That didn't work too well," I muttered to myself.

At this stage I remembered what one of my teachers always said: "It was the exception that always proved the rule."

It was good to know that something of his teaching had stuck in my head. Undaunted, I pressed ahead with my mission.

My next stop was the butcher's shop. The butcher who served me was a slightly overweight, broad-shouldered man in his late thirties. He had a jowl and a reddish complexion, which gave the impression that he enjoyed a good steak himself, and that he might also have a slightly elevated blood pressure. He had a stern manner and large lips, which turned downwards at the edges. A good candidate for a piece of mental health I thought, so I gave him my best smile as I ordered. Suddenly the atmosphere got frostier and a steely, annoyed look came into his eyes. A dangerous looking redness spread from the base of his neck to the crown of his head. I was glad that I was on the other side of the counter as his cleaver created lamb chops with each energetic swipe. The meat was then slapped onto the counter with no further eye contact. Well, so much for the mental health guru's advice, I thought, 'I don't think I will be buying her book.' Perhaps dogs have it right after all – they regard a smile as a snarl because the teeth are bared in both.

After a while I saw a medium-sized oak tree nearby on an adjoining smaller road. I sat down under the canopy of the tree that spread across to the far side of this narrow road. One of my blisters had become infected, making walking painful. I had got used to the feeling of blisters, which is like walking with gravel in your shoe, but this was in a different league altogether. I took off my shoes and socks and paraded my feet to the world. The only witness to this spectacle was a young man who nodded as he passed by on a large tractor. There were light puffy clouds in the sky so I sat back under the tree and enjoyed a banana and a bottle of water.

As this was the last day of my walk I started thinking about Colmcille again and whether there were any symbolic connections with him on this last stage of the walk. I came across two appropriate symbols; this oak tree and horses.

The oak tree is often associated with Colmcille but this is not unusual in that the oak tree has special relevance to the spiritual life of the Irish. There are many place names associated with it. It usually features as the prefix 'Doire' which means oak grove or oak wood. Examples of this are Derry (Doire) itself which was Colmcille's main base in Ireland; Derrybeg is 'little oak wood'; Derrybane is 'white oak wood'; Durrow (formerly known as Daurmagh) is 'the plain of the oak'; Kildare is 'church of the oak'; Derrygarriff is 'rough oak wood' etc. The oak has had a special place in Irish folklore from the very earliest times; connected to the 'otherworld', it was a source of food, music, wisdom and spirituality. The oak in turn became the most sacred tree of the druids, and the oak grove became the centre for their rituals. One can see why the oak became a sacred tree, as its endurance and strength were powerful symbols of earthly power. The fact that it is the tree most often struck by lightning probably did its status no harm at all, as it symbolised the connection between the heavens and the Earth. I am sure I checked out if there were any storm clouds in the sky before I sat down under that oak on the way to Clonmacnoise.

The sacred status of the oak continued into the Christian age. When Colmcille founded his monasteries in Derry and Durrow he did so in oak groves. For a long time Derry was known as 'Doire Colmcille', the oak grove of Colmcille. In *Betha Colmcille* it states that the town at Derry at that time belonged to a man called Aedh mac Ainmirech, who offered it to Colmcille for his use and to build a monastery. When preparing to build his church, Colmcille burned down the town and the fort in order to erase the works of worldly men, and sanctify the site for his church.

Aedh protested at this, stating that the people would lack food and shelter. Colmcille admonished him saying that everyone would have from God what he or she required. However it is not specified what Colmcille meant by the word 'required'! The fire was so intense that it soon blazed out of control (there must have been a lot of badness there!) and threatened to burn the grove of oak trees where he intended to build his monastery. Colmcille had to take immediate action to save the oak grove by making up a hymn to save them. The fire subsided immediately. Ever since then, that hymn is used to protect against fire and thunder. It is also claimed that no house in Derry has been set on fire by lightning from that day to this and that if a person says the hymn on lying and rising, it will protect any nine people he chooses from fire and lightning.

The oak grove where Colmcille built his monastery was an ancient druidic site. Not only the land was being handed over, but also the old religion as well. For most people this was probably a fairly seamless transfer. The only difference was that instead of having a multiplicity of gods with varying powers, they had now one main God with full control. However this one God had a lot of assistants (called saints) who had powers on fertility, health, weather etc. very much like the old gods. This was a pattern that Colmcille repeated where possible in his other monasteries in Durrow, Drumcliffe and Swords.

The oak tree is (after the yew) the slowest-growing hardwood tree in Ireland. Having planted a lot of oak trees on poorish soil, I have found that if planted small they will put on a lot of growth over the first couple of years. This was a surprise to me, as I expected growth to be very slow. In conversations with a friend we came to the conclusion that this was an adaptive mechanism, enabling the young oak tree to get above competing vegetation. Once it had achieved that it could afford to take its time, as it will not reach its full splendour for another two hundred years at least. Nature certainly has its own intelligence, or should I call it 'magic'?

The other part of this last section of the walk that had a meaning for me in relation to Colmcille was meeting a horse that was looking over a fence. In fact one of the features of the walk as a whole was the number of horses still to be seen in fields. This fellow looking over the fence was a chestnut brown with a black mane and tail.

Before Colmcille died on the island of Iona there were a number of signs that foretold his death. It is obvious from the texts that Colmcille knew when he would die himself. He not only knew when he was going to die – he had a measure of control over the timing! It seems that God came to him in a vision and told him that he would like him to join him in Heaven at Easter time in the year 597. Colmcille went out to the fields to see the monks of his community and told them that God had invited him to join Him in Heaven at Easter time. He told the monks however that he had decided to postpone the event so that the feast day should not be spoiled for the members of the community. After telling the monks about this he then blessed the island, so that from that day on snakes could not harm man or beast on the island. This was to emulate the achievements of St Patrick. In being able to postpone death and banish snakes he proved himself to be equally if not more powerful than Patrick, who was renowned for having banished snakes from Ireland. This is especially significant when you consider there were never any snakes in either spot in the first place! It just shows you that people will claim credit for anything. Observe how times have changed over the centuries!

On 9th June 597 Colmcille went for a small walk with his assistant Diarmaid to bless the barn full of grain. On this day he announced to his monks that he was going to die. On his way back from the barn to the monastery Colmcille got tired and sat down to rest on a rock. As he sat there an old white horse that used to carry the milk pails between the fields and the monastery came up to him, and put his head on Colmcille's lap. Knowing his master was going to die he shed 'a shower of tears' upon his lap and he foamed as he wept. This grieving went on for a long time. It seemed to provide a comfort for Colmcille because he would not let his assistant Diarmaid drive the horse away. The rest of his dying was taken up with comforting the monks, having visions and performing miracles, so that there was little space for real, shared, comforting grief. It was here with this horse that Colmcille could grieve for his own death in a meaningful way and gain some level of comfort from pure emotion that is truly shared.

After this encounter the old horse regained its youth, and worked on the island for many years afterwards. In fact recent archaeological digs have unearthed the bones of a horse near this site. Is it the same horse? After some more wondrous signs on that day Colmcille went to the church at midnight, and there in the company of his friends a bright light filled the church. As he blessed the people, he died.

At the same time at home in Donegal people saw in the eastern sky pillars of light ascending from the Earth to the heavens; other people saw a golden ladder. In fact like the death of Christ 'there came a trembling and great quaking and an intolerable tremor upon the land of Erin and of Alba and all the Western world at the death of Colmcille'. It was even felt in India according to the texts.

The real moment of sharing in this story is the interlude with the horse. For some people in this world of ours the only real connection they experience is with a dog, a cat or a horse. It is the same for many people in our society today who find it difficult to share feelings with people because of the fear of judgement. One can share anything with an animal without it affecting the feedback. In a sense this story also illustrated the connection between the early Church and Nature. The teaching of the Roman Church which stated that only humans had souls and that the rest of Nature was put here for man's sole benefit had not yet taken hold in the Celtic fringes. Nature may take many forms, all with their own purpose, however at the end of the day all souls within Nature were linked together. In this tradition we were a part of Nature not apart from it.

Back in Co. Offaly the pony put his head over the fence. I stroked his muzzle, but retreated hastily when I thought he was going to nuzzle me. I didn't want him crying on my shoulder!

As I walked along the road now I was searching for any sight of Clonmacnoise, as I had had my fill of walking that day. The surrounding fields were grassy and green, though one could see that these fields were not too far removed from bog. Wetland plants and rushes were persistently trying to re-establish themselves on the weak soil. Grasses are a wonderful plant. When you think about it, if they decided to up and leave this planet it would spell doom for us all within a short time. It is estimated that we might survive for a number of weeks but that would be about all. All of these grasses thrive though they are stood on, rolled on and continually pruned by ferocious teeth. This is the type of treatment that would kill any other plant or animal. Grasses grow from the base of the stalk and not from the tip of the shoot like most other plants. Of course they also love our wet, temperate climate and once the woodland is cleared the grasses have the ideal growing conditions. Grass is one of the things that gives our nation its identity: the colour green is embedded in our psyche.

The cattle here were lying out contentedly on the grass in these fields, seemingly content with the bed that Nature bestowed to them. Of course cattle and grass go hand in hand, one is made for the other. If one observes any herd of cattle, you will nearly always see the majority of them clustered together in a group, with one or two mavericks/outcasts/adventurers far away on the periphery. 'Is it just by chance?' I wondered. Is it because they have found a tasty morsel of grass and they are keeping it to themselves? Or does it reflect a recurring pattern in Nature that is indeed shared with humankind? The vast majority of a group/hive/herd are happy staying within the crowd but Nature and the process of evolution demands that a few individuals that stand separate from the crowd continuously test the boundaries. Cows are probably no different; there is always one looking to get across the fence.

I finally saw above the top of a hedgerow the top of a round tower and then a second one.

"At last, this must be it," I said to myself. "I am so relieved to have arrived."

There was no sense of achievement just relief. This is something I have noticed at other times – that when one reaches the goal, one does not get a buzz from achieving it. However in the long term there is usually a deep sense of satisfaction at what one has accomplished. There is no journey without an arrival.

On the path to the main entrance I passed a wooden sculpture. It featured a man dressed in a cloak, his head bowed seemingly in pain. He had one hand raised covering his eyes and the other holding a staff. His demeanour was of reverential suffering. The sculpture is known as 'The Pilgrim'. The inscription below the sculpture read:

*Aedh, son of the chief of Oriel*
*Died on pilgrimage. 606 A.D.*

'Things are not looking good,' I thought to myself. Perhaps all this walking meant my fate was sealed in the same way as Aedh's. This gives you some idea of how sorry I felt for myself. On another day I might have said: 'Your man there is a lot worse off than I am!'

In this mood of deflation and self-pity I had no interest in looking at the sights of Clonmacnoise. All I wanted to do was get a coffee and some comfort food. Before going into the restaurant I took off my shoes and socks and put on a pair of light sandals. The pure pleasure of this was indescribable. One probably has to endure pain in order to experience pleasure. Thoughts turned to the past and to how women in China endured having their feet bound. Did they live out their lives with this feeling of mental and physical entrapment? Did they ever experience any release from bondage? They probably lived out their lives uncomplaining, though they had just cause to give out and rebel. How self-absorbed it was of me, to feel so self-pitying about a transitory discomfort, and one that had been freely chosen at that.

I stayed in the restaurant until Martin arrived to give me the promised lift home. He arrived with his usual humour and banter, and we then went to have a look around the site. There was a group of French people in wheelchairs being wheeled around the site by young people who had come with them. 'Wheeled' is far too sedate a word to describe what was going on. The 'wacky wheelchair races' would be a better description. The wheelchairs were being raced around the paths at the highest possible speeds, some taking short cuts across the grass. All this was accompanied by the sounds of great fun and laughter. One girl gently tumbled out of her wheelchair on a grassy hump, the assistant got her back in as quickly as possible, and they merrily gave chase. Again those of us who have everything complain of, and those of us who face great adversity do it with great cheerfulness.

Clonmacnoise is a site containing at least seven stone churches, varying in date from the tenth to the seventeenth centuries. The earlier churches were made of wood, all traces of which have now disappeared. There is also a large cathedral, two round towers, a castle, the Pope's lectern and a museum containing three stone crosses. My priority was to see Teampall Ciarán, where St Ciarán is reputedly buried. This is the smallest church by far on the site, measuring approximately 11 feet by 8 feet. In addition the church is roofless and the walls are tilted due to subsidence. I went inside it and thought about the type of man that would establish such a place.

Ciarán was born in Co. Roscommon in 512 A.D., and was fostered by a deacon named Justus. St Ciarán's surname was Mac an Tsair, or 'Son of the Carpenter'. On finishing his studies Ciarán went to the Aran Islands to visit the holy man Enda. A strange thing happened there – on the same night they shared a vision. It was of a great oak tree laden with fruit, beside a river in the middle of Ireland. It protected the island of Ireland. The fruit of the tree spread over the seas, and the birds of the whole world came to carry off some of its fruit.

Enda explained the vision as follows:

*You are the great tree who is great in the eyes of God and will be great in the eyes of men as well. The whole island will be protected and influenced by your great deeds and your influence will spread overseas. Go and take God's word, to the bank of a river, and there establish a church.*

Ciarán obeyed this advice. On a grassy ridge called Ard Tiprait, or the 'Height of the Spring', situated on the banks of the Shannon, he founded the monastery and school of Clonmacnoise which was completed on 9th May 544. He was encouraged in this venture by Diarmaid who later became High King of Ireland. Ciarán did not live long after the opening of the monastery. He died from the plague on 9th September 544. He could not have had any idea of how important a role this monastery would play in the lives of people for countless generations. Kings were buried here such as Diarmaid, Turlough O'Connor, Guaire and the last King of Ireland, Roderick. All thought that being buried here was a shortcut to a happy afterlife, as the prayers of Ciarán were bound to get them through 'the pearly gates'. Scholars came to here from all over Europe, and many famous scribes, geographers architects, sculptors, metal workers and artists worked and were nurtured within these walls. Famous books, stone crosses, chalices and brooches were produced in abundance.

Political patronage was also central to the life of Clonmacnoise. It was situated strategically between the provinces of Meath and Connacht, who traditionally vied for the High Kingship of Ireland. This it made a centre of political intrigue as well as spiritual quest. For centuries Clonmacnoise transferred its allegiance on many occasions between the different provinces. An English garrison force in Athlone finally destroyed the site in 1552. For one thousand years this monastery played an important part in the life of the country, and for seven hundred of those years it was at the centre of spiritual, artistic and political life. From a vision on the Aran Islands all of this was born.

Walking around the site I looked up at the large round tower. Here is a symbol of troubled times, an indication that it was a centre of war as well as peace. This tower was built in the tenth century as a place of refuge from invaders. Growing up in school we had always been told that it was the dastardly Vikings who were the scourge of Irish civilisation and learning. These Danish invaders had no appreciation of the finer things in life, such as learning, art, literature, etc. They destroyed it if given half a chance. We had pictures drawn for us in our minds of these hordes coming up the River Shannon in their longboats, dressed in furs, brandishing heavy swords and ransacking all before them. The God-loving monks would clamber into the tower for safety, pull up the ladders behind them and wait for the barbarians to leave. Those who did not make it to the tower in time were slaughtered. Afterwards they would come down, survey the scene of devastation and start all over again. In truth the Danes did attack and ransack the place, but they were not the only ones. Clonmacnoise was as likely to be attacked by Irish tribes as by anyone else. I suppose this is not surprising given the political dimension to life in Clonmacnoise. Playing kingmaker is a dangerous business. They were bound to back the wrong horse, sometimes so to speak. One Irish chieftain called Phelim MacCriffon took a particular dislike to the place, and ransacked it three times. It is reputed that during his last attack he butchered the monks like sheep.

For some periods of the monastery's history the monks themselves would engage in warlike attacks on those they considered enemies. This was probably the origin of the concept of pre-emptive strikes that is so much in vogue nowadays. It means kill all those people who are potential enemies, because they just might attack you sometime in the future. The image of meek and humble monks dedicated to love, learning and prayer takes a bit of a beating here. Having said that there was a lot of love, prayer and learning here, and people still come here on pilgrimage to search out help from Ciarán in facing worldly trials. Good and bad exists in all, even the best of us.

I stood and looked at the meandering bends of the Shannon River set in this flat, rather featureless landscape. It occurred to me that Finnen was right after all; one should not look at this landscape in daylight – the magic of this place only emerges under the light of the moon. I could just imagine myself sitting here on the windowsill of one of the old churches with everything, buildings, landscape and river bathed in the light of a large silvery moon lying low in the sky. I imagined gazing across the river with the echoes and memories of the journey in my being. A slight breeze might arise and play with the reflection of the moon and the water wrinkling it with new patterns of creation. If I listened I would hear the murmur of the water as it explored the crevices of the landscape, for each droplet a new experience but for the river an old story.

Other things of course would emerge in the night, animals shuffling through the landscape with wary feet and nostrils, searching the possibility of food and danger in equal measure. They each would tread familiar if sometimes dangerous routes, preferring the not-too-bright light for their quest. In this dimmed world, the senses of hearing, smell and intuition are of equal value to that of sight. To make their journey successfully they have to hone all their senses and be aware of the signs of Nature. Occasionally a slight cloud crosses over the face of that moon, plunging things into darker shadow, and the pitter-patter of rain would dance softly across the river and play music on the leaves and grasses of the riverbank. A slight flurry of wind arises and builds the performance to a crescendo of swirling energy before it subsides and relaxes into the pattern of the night. The night descends further into its core and as the moon becomes higher and smaller in the sky, new figures might emerge. These are from the shadows of the collective memory, people who lived their lives connected to this place in some way. If they now come out and sit on the riverbank suffused with this brooding moonlight, how would they reflect on their worlds of power, learning, persecution, passion, pain and joy? What contribution did it make to the flow of existence? What traces and remnants of their lives remain in the collective stream? A dark cloud crosses the face of the moon, throwing further shadows across the landscape. A chill comes into the night air and they might then build a fire on the riverbank. Sometime later a log would be thrown onto the fire and they would all watch as sparks ascend into the sky to join the dance amongst the stars of Creation. As they look into that sky even the most cynical old soul is struck with awe at the sight. They feel connected to all of it. In some strange way they recognise it as home. The moon lingers in the sky as the first brightening of the dawn spreads across the landscape. It then fades away and a slightly different world is born with the light of the day.

I wondered again why someone should build a monastery here, if their sole aim was the promotion and veneration of God. Why not find some other more remote, less strategic, more meditative position, of which there are many. But the affairs of Church and State have always been interlinked; body and soul are one. The shining light of 1,500 years ago may have been mainly religious, with an element of the material world thrown in as a sauce. In our Western world it could be said that consumerism has become our God. It has become the shining light that illuminates the path that we walk daily. This is a path that is all body and no soul. There is no light shed by it into the void that we all must ultimately tread. There is no clue here for the direction we must take. My mind drifts back to the lakes and mountains at the start of my walk, the spot where the golden light shone in Finnen's dream. I am now standing in the silver light, and the transient thread of the walk lies in between. I came across that consumerist world on the walk, but there were other worlds present as well; worlds full of fun, generosity, friendship, hardship, curiosity and searching.

In this world of ours there is no overall 'gold-' or 'silver light' to guide the way. In a spiritual sense, we must light our own flickering torch and venture forth like the spark in the night. A flickering light in the void is preferable, because a bright light would blind us to everything else that is all around us. It would focus our attention on only one small part of our potential experience. The difficulty of course is how to keep these flickering flames alight. The only way, it seems to me, is by connecting with all those other beings who are heading with flickering lights in roughly the same direction. When a gale blows out your flame there is some place you can go to get another light. Together we can traverse the dark cavern. The gold and silver light of Finnen's dream is from another world, in another time. Perhaps even then that light was really just a dream, an earnest wish in the face of the unknowable. Part of the thrill of a journey is not knowing where you are going, of encountering new experiences which you would never have imagined or predicted.

A journey will always change your world.